D1527368

Another Self

The History of Emotions Series

EDITED BY

PETER N. STEARNS, CARNEGIE-MELLON UNIVERSITY

JAN LEWIS, RUTGERS UNIVERSITY, NEWARK

Another Self

Middle-Class American Women and Their Friends in the Twentieth Century

Linda W. Rosenzweig

NEW YORK UNIVERSITY PRESS

New York and London

NEW YORK UNIVERSITY PRESS
New York and London

Library of Congress Cataloging-in-Publication Data
Rosenzweig, Linda W.
Another self : middle-class American women and their friends in
the twentieth century / Linda W. Rosenzweig.
p. cm. — (The history of emotions series)
Includes bibliographical references and index.
ISBN 0-8147-7486-5 (cloth : alk. paper)
1. Women—Psychology. 2. Female friendship—United
States—History. 3. Middle class women—United States—History.
I. Title. II. Series: History of emotions series.
HQ1206 .R655 1999
302.3'4'0820973—dc21   99-6215
                                    CIP

10 9 8 7 6 5 4 3 2 1

For Richard
and
in memory of my father,
Arnold Weinberg

Contents

All illustrations appear as a group following p. 100.

Preface

In the process of researching and writing this book, I have been reminded many times of the frequent assertion by educators that the study of history fosters the development of a sense of personal identity and a sense of connection with a meaningful past. Because social history encompasses ordinary human activities and relationships, as well as phenomena and institutions with which most people have direct experience, it offers a particularly appropriate context for illustrating the relevance of this claim. The links between change at the national political level or the international diplomatic level and the lives of contemporary individuals may not be immediately apparent, but connections are easily discerned between historical and current experiences in areas such as work, health, family life, and interpersonal relationships. Thus, for example, while the historical study of women's friendships illuminates an important aspect of their lives in the past, it also provides a framework for understanding the nature and significance of contemporary women's friendships.

American women's letters, diaries, and autobiographic recollections document the importance of female friendship in their lives. Their words testify eloquently to the central roles that friends have played from the colonial period to the late twentieth century. While some women in the past also experienced friendship with men, as distinguished from courtship, such relationships were atypical. Throughout the eighteenth and nineteenth centuries, the support of female friends helped women cope with the routines and responsibilities of daily life, as well as with the crises and difficulties that disrupted these patterns. In the early decades of the twentieth century, the structure and style of female friendship began to reflect subtle changes in response to alterations in the American social and cultural climate. Such changes grew more pronounced after 1920, but continuities with earlier friendship models also persisted. Since 1960, a renewed emphasis on the value of female friendship has marked American culture, and many contemporary women have articulated a corresponding recognition of the importance they attach to relationships with one another.

As I started to understand women's friendship experiences historically, I saw my own experiences as a part of this larger framework. I thought about the group of friends I meet for lunch every month and how we look forward to getting together. I thought about other friends with whom I share the pleasure of summers in Wellfleet and phone calls throughout the rest of the year. I thought about a friend I've known since our children were infants. I thought about another friend who told me where to find exactly the right dress for my daughter's wedding and went with me twice to make sure that I bought it. Finally, I thought about the two friends I've known longer than any others—my "best friends."

I met Mary Jo Lazear when we were four years old. We lived in a duplex house and exchanged secret messages through a mock post office on the interior back stairway between our apartments. Her aunt was my aunt's best friend. My father drove us to elementary school in the morning, and her mother picked us up. When our high-school homeroom teacher made me cry, Mary Jo marched up to his desk and reprimanded him sternly. Once she shared a motel room with our family of four and four bicycles. When she was ill a few years ago, I felt as if the world had temporarily stopped. We exchange messages almost every day on E-mail. Occasionally people still ask, "Are you two sisters?" I think the real answer is yes. (See figures 17–20.)

I met Mari Sachs the day I started college. Her mother noticed me first and introduced us. By the time her roommate arrived, we were already inseparable. When I spent Christmas with her family, even her grandmothers bought me gifts. When she left college to marry Bill Gimbel, I felt lost. We visited occasionally, but our visits stopped for about ten years. Now it seems as if those years never happened. When my daughter and son-in-law moved to Chicago, they stayed with Mari and Bill for two weeks, and that seemed perfectly natural to all of us. (See figures 21 and 22.)

In the chapters that follow, I examine female friendship as a historical experience. Over the last three centuries, American women's relationships with one another have been constructed through a complex process of interaction between the personal preferences and characteristics of individuals and the dominant social and cultural influences of particular periods. But while friendships have changed over time, key elements link the experiences of women in the past with those of their late twentieth-century counterparts. In the course of writing this book, I have come to understand my own friendships as a part of this continuum.

Support from two institutions enabled me to complete this project. A Radcliffe Research Support Program grant provided funds for the first stage of my work. Chatham College provided important support through a Central Research Fund grant in 1994, a sabbatical in the fall of 1996, and release time in the fall of 1997. I am grateful for this aid, and I appreciate the interest of a number of gracious colleagues who consistently inquired about the progress of the project. I was fortunate as well to be able to rely on the competent and dedicated research assistance of two outstanding Chatham students, Kipp Dawson and Barbara Elardo. I also benefited from discussions with students in Chatham's First-Year Writing Seminar and in an upper-level history seminar; their questions and insights about women's friendships helped me focus and clarify my own ideas.

Several knowledgeable and caring librarians and archivists also helped me. I want to extend my appreciation to the staff of the Schlesinger Library at Radcliffe College and my special thanks to Eva Moseley, whose suggestions were particularly useful in the early stages of my research. I am grateful to Margery Sly and Amy Hague for their kind assistance with the Sophia Smith Collection and the Smith College Archives, and to Wilma Slaight and Jean Berry, who introduced me to the resources of the Wellesley College Archives.

A number of colleagues and friends offered unique and special assistance. Sally Wall suggested relevant references at an early stage of my research and discussed the project with her mother, Elsie Hagemann Noetzel, who graciously allowed me to include her experiences in the book. Janet Oppenheimer Landis shared her feelings about her lifelong friendship with my own mother and let me write about them. I'm grateful to Jennifer Hammer for her enthusiasm and editorial patience, as well as for telling me about her mother and her Aunt Marilyn. I also thank Marcia Hammer, Marilyn Klainberg, Sue Wilson, and Denise Meyer. Peter Stearns pointed out that women's friendship was my kind of subject and he was right. I thank him for this advice, for his interest in the book, and for his many helpful suggestions.

As always, I'm grateful for the support and encouragement of my family. My brother, Lee Weinberg, is always there to listen, and I thank him. I also want to thank my son-in-law, Kenneth Comess; my daughters, Amy and Jane, who are my most cherished female friends; and especially my husband, Richard Rosenzweig, to whom I dedicate the book.

Introduction

The theme of female friendship as an essential, sustaining influence in women's lives has a familiar cultural resonance. Over the past three decades, discussions ranging from the idealistic visions of "sisterhood" that emerged in the early years of contemporary feminism to the more academic, analytic examinations have asserted that female friends play a vital role in one another's survival. Frequently this discourse has also suggested that women not only have a special aptitude for making and keeping friends, but that they excel in this regard. Thus their relationships, as opposed to male friendships, are taken to embody the highest ideals of true friendship.

In a recent collection of essays on friendship, novelist Jill McCorkle pays tribute to her childhood friend, Cathy Lewis: "Once in a blue moon there's someone who knows it all, someone who knows and accepts you unconditionally, someone who's there for life," McCorkle writes. "I shudder to think how different my life would have been if I'd wound up in another homeroom." Carolyn See rejoices in the "miracle" of a similar relationship. "I know the world is better because Jackie Joseph lives in it. I'm lucky, so lucky to know her," See declares.[1]

However, the cultural affirmation of the value of female friendship is a relatively recent phenomenon. Although discussions of both the concept and the experience of friendship pervade Western cultural tradition, many, if not most, literary and cultural representations of this fundamental yet elusive form of interpersonal connection have stressed its importance in the public world of men. Traditional definitions and prescriptive images have emphasized the nobility of friendship, which is portrayed as a voluntary, spiritual attachment between equals. Numerous examples of comradeship and loyalty—from ancient heroic warriors and literary protagonists such as David and Jonathan or Hamlet and Horatio to modern soldiers in foxholes—have served as cultural models of the essence of friendship. In contrast, significantly fewer literary illustrations of female friendship appeared until the late twentieth century, and cultural images of the relationship have rarely conveyed positive messages.

According to the editors of *The Oxford Book of Friendship*, published in 1991, the anthology's chapter on women's friendships is disproportionately short due to the paucity of relevant literary examples. Moreover, portrayals of relationships between women typically present female friendship as shallow, insincere, temporary, and insignificant. The few conspicuous exceptions to this generalization include the biblical narrative of Ruth and Naomi, the poetry of Sappho in ancient Greece, and that of Katherine Philips, who wrote under the name of Orinda in seventeenth-century England. Although many eighteenth- and nineteenth-century works of fiction touch on the topic of friendship between women, it often appears as incidental, peripheral to a central marriage plot.[2] These contrasting images of male and female friends reflect the pervasive privileging of men within the patriarchal tradition, as well as the cultural importance attributed to male friendship in Western society.

The Western cultural emphasis on the significance of friendship and on speculation about its nature as construed in terms of male experiences can be traced from the ancient past. Plato distinguished between true friendships and those that represented only illusion or deception. To Aristotle, friendship was essentially a partnership, intrinsically noble and indispensable to human life. He described the highest kind of friendship as the recognition of another self, a self whose existence could make an individual more conscious of his own existence. Cicero emphasized the necessity and universality of friendship, "the one thing in human life which all men with one voice agree is worthwhile." Epicurean and Stoic philosophers also addressed the subject, as did Roman and Renaissance thinkers. For Francis Bacon, friends provided "peace in the affections and support of the judgement," while Montaigne celebrated friendship as the finest form of association. Closer to our own time, Emerson described real friendship as "the solidest thing we know," a relationship "for aid and comfort through all the relations and passages of life and death." These images of friendship span many centuries and national boundaries in the Western world, but they share a common focus on relationships between

men, primarily in the public arena and often celebrated in formal cere-
monies and declarations. Hence these approaches do not provide adequate models for the interpretation of women's experiences. Nor do they
address the broader issue of the historicity of friendship.[3]

The search for definitions of friendship continues to challenge and intrigue contemporary social scientists and psychologists. While research
on close personal relationships has proliferated over the past two
decades, more work has focused on romantic love, reflecting a cultural
preoccupation with the topic. But friendship studies comprise a growing
segment of that scholarship. Although Western culture has traditionally
dismissed female friendship as a sort of "relational also-ran," this perspective has changed. Much of the current empirical and theoretical work
addresses its distinctive character.[4] With the advent of the late twentieth-
century feminist movement and the concomitant emphasis on sisterhood,
a distinctly different perspective emerged, characterized by a new accent
on the uniqueness and value of female friendship. The concept of sisterhood clearly contradicts the traditional cultural premise that women lack
the capacity for true friendship, presenting instead a completely opposite
scenario. Yet any suggestion that the existence of feminism somehow
makes all women friends distorts and sentimentalizes the relationship
rather than proving its uniqueness. Nevertheless, the development of a revised, more positive image of the nature of women's friendships has dis-
lodged the traditional vision through two major new insights: the recognition that female friendships have been socially constructed and mediated through the lens of patriarchy, and the understanding that they have
often played significant and even central roles in women's lives.[5]

Empirical investigations imply that an increasing degree of precision
informs our understanding of friendship and its function, both generally
and with specific reference to women, but the essence of the relationship
remains difficult to capture. For both women and men in contemporary
American society, the word friendship denotes a range of interactions—
from associations with a relatively new acquaintance to the companionship of an intimate friend of long standing. Its meanings have also varied
in the past. In traditional American society, "friend" referred to an ally or
connection, usually a family member. By the middle of the eighteenth century, it denoted a peer or an equal outside the family. Hence friendship
came to provide women with an antidote to authoritarian familial relationships.[6] In a sense, then, friendship lacks structural and cultural definition, despite social-scientific efforts designed to clarify and illuminate

its meanings. Although relatives are defined by blood ties and neighbors by residence, friends do not necessarily share any particular characteristic, such as age, race, or socioeconomic status. Nor is friendship institutionalized and prescribed in the ways other relationships are in contemporary society. Yet certain norms, expectations, and other factors beyond the control of individuals—stage of life and partner status, for example—intersect with individual personalities to determine its nature.[7]

Individuals tend to define friendship in terms of specific components, such as the absence of blood kinship, a similarity in age, a compatibility of interests, a quality of interaction that is platonic as opposed to romantic, and an expectation of nurturance and support. In general it is perceived as less exclusive, less intense in emotional expression, less permanent, and less regulated by social rules and expectations than a romantic relationship; friends provide a lower level of caring, but also demand less of one another than romantic or sexual partners. Class differences play a role in the definition and experience of the relationship, and cross-cultural studies show that friendship norms and expectations vary in accordance with particular social and economic factors.[8] Some evidence even suggests that the rhetorical framework of a close relationship such as a friendship defines the critical component—that communication about the relationship actually constitutes the relationship.[9]

Despite the elusive qualities of this complicated form of human interaction, recent research has generated a range of interesting data and ideas about the distinctive characteristics and experience of contemporary American women's friendships. Current studies of relational development suggest that women develop and strengthen a sense of self through their involvement in both external social relationships and the internal experiences of relationships that are characterized by mutuality and affective connection. This development is initiated first by the mother-child relationship, in which all offspring identify early on with the mother as an active caretaker, but it follows a different course in women than in men. Cultural constraints discourage the evolution of the image of an interacting or relational self in boys in favor of one defined by autonomy and separation. For girls, however, the culture fosters the development of a self-image characterized by responsiveness to the emotional core of the mother and other significant individuals, including friends. Hence relatedness characterized by empathy and connection is more central to women's lives and development than to men's.[10] This distinction partially explains why women appear to have more friendships, as distinguished from relationships with colleagues or workmates. It may also account for evidence of gender differences in friendship styles and patterns in contemporary society, although the significance of such differences has been questioned.[11]

The distinctive nature of female friendships may also be linked to the mother-daughter relationship. Jane Flax maintains that through interactions with friends, adult women replay or relive the difficulties they experienced in separating from their mothers. Either they repeat old mother-daughter conflicts with friends or they compensate for those conflicts by being "better" friends to each other than their mothers were to them. This connection invests a woman's relationships with female friends with an intensity and a depth that distinguish them from her relationships with men; it also implies that female friends have the power to both help and hurt one another.

In a related argument, Eva Margolies suggests that female friendship choices not only replay separation difficulties, but also reflect other aspects of the mother-daughter dynamic. For example, one's relationships with other women may mirror the influence of a mother who encouraged her daughter to make bold choices, or that of a mother who urged a more traditional path. Women's friends, then, may symbolize the mothers they have chosen in contrast to their biological mothers.[12] For some women, the mother-daughter relationship can serve not only as an influence on friendship choices, but also as an obstacle to female friendship. Mothers who have been rendered powerless in patriarchal society, and even those who have managed to defy the heterosexual imperative to some degree, may convey a message of disengagement from other women in favor of the need to live for men. Recipients of this message might respond by distancing themselves from strong same-gender relationships.[13]

Finally, the special character of women's interactions with one another may also reflect connections between friendship and life stage. Friendship seems to play different roles at different points in women's lives. Because adolescent girls need to establish their own identities, it is important for them to have intense friendships with other girls. Links to the search for a husband often define the nature of single women's friendships, while married women's friendship choices and commitments depend on the nature of their relationships with their husbands and on whether they work outside the home. Divorce can also affect friendship choices. For women in late middle age and beyond, friendship can fill various needs, such as self-validation, companionship, and affective support, depending on factors such as the availability of family members and the presence or absence of a spouse.[14]

These findings explain important aspects of contemporary female friendship, but they do not analyze concrete experiences or cultural representations of the relationship in historical context, nor do they consider linkages between the two. Although historians have not studied friendship extensively, the research of Carroll Smith-Rosenberg and others documents the existence of intense, mutually supportive, and often physically demonstrative female friendships that sometimes competed in importance with heterosexual relationships. Their work contradicts ahistorical, patriarchal images that disparage women's friendship and offers evidence of the centrality and endurance of women's relationships with one another. In "the female world of love and ritual" fostered by American society and culture in the late eighteenth and nineteenth centuries, friends provided companionship, affection, and emotional support for one another. Women who formed deep and intimate friendships as adolescents often preserved those relationships throughout their lives, despite marriage and physical separation. They frequently expressed their devotion in extravagant language reminiscent of love letters between women and men, and they maintained their friendships over time and distance.

Thus a warm and loving tone pervades the correspondence of Sarah Butler Wistar and Jeannie Field Musgrove, whose fifty-year friendship was cemented when they spent two years together in boarding school. In 1864 Wistar, then a wife and mother, begged her unmarried friend to come for a visit: "I shall be entirely alone . . . I can give you no idea how desperately I shall want you," she wrote longingly. Musgrove's style was equally passionate: "Dear darling Sarah! How I love you and how happy I have been! You are the joy of my life," she declared after another visit. Wistar experienced extreme anxiety when her friend eventually married, but their relationship, including the use of secret names, endured into old age.[15] The expression of intensely romantic feelings between female friends was not unusual in the nineteenth century. The contrast between this friendship style and the more measured language of late twentieth-century women's interactions suggests that the emotional landscape of the nineteenth century specifically supported and fostered close relationships between women; it also invites further reflection on the role of historical context in shaping women's friendship experiences.

*

This study examines the history of female friendship through an analysis of white, middle-class American women's relationships between 1900 and 1960, a half-century that encompassed the coming of age of modern America. As Victorian values and traditional communities gave way to a fully mature, urban, industrial society, Americans experienced the emergence and development of a twentieth-century emotional culture and style, as well as other major social, cultural, and structural changes. At the same time, a kaleidoscope of specific changes continued the process of transition initiated in the lives of middle-class women in the late nineteenth century. Thus this volume builds on the existing historical literature through an analysis of the nature of middle-class American women's friendship experiences in an era characterized by major social and cultural transformations, a period that has not been the focus of previous historical research on friendship.

The book's theoretical framework reflects the emergence and advancement of emotions history, which offers substantial support for the idea that friendship between women is a historical experience rather than a universal, ahistorical occurrence.[16] Originally linked to social-historical examinations of family life and popular beliefs in the past, the history of emotions has matured into an independent focus of inquiry concerned with change and continuity in emotional standards and experience. A related effort to document the characteristic emotional styles of particular periods has contributed another analytic dimension to the field. Examinations of individual emotions such as love, anger, fear, jealousy, shame, guilt, sadness, grief, and disgust have generated a wide range of intriguing historical findings. A growing body of research on past emotional standards, or emotionology, and emotional experience documents substantial change over time in both the cultural expectations about emotion and the expression of various emotions. Some studies link changes in these areas with alterations in the ways people actually experienced emotions in the past.[17]

Such research points to the existence of a connection between personal experiences of friendship and cultural images of the relationship. As an affectional experience, friendship incorporates various emotions—love, anger, jealousy, guilt, sadness, and grief, for example. Hence evidence of change over time in the individual emotions that comprise the interpersonal interaction we describe as friendship raises intriguing questions about the historicity of that interaction in general, and about change and continuity in the specific context of American women's friendships. How was female friendship experienced in earlier historical periods? How did women in the past view their interactions with one another? How did society view those interactions? What were the dominant emotional standards? What connections can be discerned between the emotional culture and the nature of women's friendships at a particular time in the past? How have American women's friendships changed over time, and how have they remained the same? And finally, what causal factors account for evidence of change and continuity in female friendship experiences?

Another Self analyzes the historical production and organization of white, middle-class American women's friendships in two consecutive historical periods, the transitional years between 1900 and 1920 and the subsequent three decades. While it focuses primarily on relationships between women, the book also examines female-male friendship in an effort to present a comprehensive perspective on women's friendship experiences in the first half of the twentieth century. For the most part, the friendships of both young and mature women before 1920 resembled those of their predecessors. Intense, affectionate, lasting relationships continued to play central roles in many women's lives. Nevertheless, occasional suggestions of a transition in the centrality of female friendship appeared during the first part of the century. For example, the tone and content of Harriet Badeau's correspondence offer a strong contrast to the intensity displayed earlier by Sarah Butler Wistar and Jeannie Field Musgrove. In 1903, Badeau was pleased to receive "delightful letters" from her friends while she was on vacation, but she waited for a rainy day to write to them, because she preferred to be outdoors whenever the weather was nice. "Moreover," she reported to one correspondent in a lighthearted, untraditional manner, "I have gone crazy over golf"; she particularly enjoyed playing the game with "a 60-year-old Amherst man."[18]

As a new emotional culture took form after 1920, prescriptions and expectations for friendship changed. The legitimacy of close relationships between women was rejected, and heterosexual interactions often took precedence over female friendship, although they did not supplant it completely. This development, along with other social and cultural influences, produced one definitive change and several less drastic alterations in friendship styles. With the emergence of new priorities, female friends played a less central role in the lives of adolescents, college students, and young adults. In 1931, for example, Yvonne Blue planned a bridge party for both male and female guests because she "owe[d] everyone" and "the all-over carpet" made dancing impossible. Her comments about a forthcoming lunch date with a friend who "looks as frumpy and as much of an old maid in embryo as ever" also reflect a new, more casual attitude toward friendship with other young women.[19] At the same time, however, mature adult friendships exhibited a subtler blend of change and continuity. This pattern varied in accordance with age and life stage, but it generally defined the experiences of white, middle-class American women, at least until the advent of the late twentieth-century feminist movement and possibly beyond.

The chapters that follow trace the evolution of these changes and continuities through two lenses: the experiences of individual women and the social and cultural influences that shaped and represented those experiences. Chapter 1 provides an overview of the history of female friendship in America before 1900 as a baseline for the evaluation of change and continuity in the relationships of twentieth-century women. Chapters 2 and 3 examine the friendship experiences of young women before and after 1920, highlighting the advent of a distinctly new friendship style produced by the intersection of several powerful influences in American society. Chapter 4 documents some modifications, but also marked similarities, in the friendship experiences of adult women pre- and post-1920. Chapter 5 suggests that while romantic friendship no longer typified middle-class American women's relationships, this tradition was preserved in the strong bonds of a subset of woman-committed individuals. Chapter 6 addresses the specific issues that have defined cross-sex friendship historically, discerning more continuity than change in this category of relationship. The last chapter reviews the data on middle-class American women's friendship styles and patterns between 1900 and 1960 and briefly assesses the nature of their friendship experiences after 1960. Finally, Chapter 7 considers whether the cultural reauthorization of close female relationships that accompanied the late twentieth-century feminist movement's valorization of sisterhood ushered in a new period in the history of women's friendships.

Several major issues complicate the task of analyzing women's friendships historically. These reflect both the general nature of emotions history and the specific characteristics of the topic of friendship. Tracing and explaining change and continuity in emotional standards and experience poses a formidable historical challenge. Although evidence of changing emotional standards can be relatively accessible, transformations in the actual emotional experiences of individuals may be far less apparent.

Issues concerning the pace and timing of change, the internalization of dominant values by particular groups in society, and the nuances of language in the types of sources that document emotional experience add to the complexity. The task of explaining emotional continuities in the context of changing emotional standards can be even more problematic.[20]

In *The Past Is a Foreign Country,* David Lowenthal argues that no matter how carefully and thoroughly historians pursue their craft, to a certain degree the past must remain intrinsically strange and unknowable. This quality of strangeness is clearly evident in the history of friendship. Even in the present, it is impossible to understand any interpersonal relationship in precisely the same terms as its participants understand their interactions. Participants in past relationships viewed their experiences through lenses totally unlike that of the contemporary historian, while past societies defined and treated friendship in completely different manners from that of late twentieth-century American society. In addition, the historian cannot presume that surviving data necessarily reveal the aspects of a particular relationship that were the most significant—or even somewhat significant—to the participants. Friendships encompass different kinds of ties, and friends attach diverse meanings to their relationships as a result of individual idiosyncracies and social and cultural factors. Hence it is important not to place undue emphasis on what is presently visible with regard to a past friendship; one must interrogate silence as well as what is said.[21]

Human relationships consist of many interactions "across a spectrum of affect and responsiveness." They embody continuing themes as well as dramatic moments, characteristic modes of relating along with unique incidents. For example, evidence of an angry exchange or a dispute between friends may represent a single aberrant occurrence in an otherwise harmonious relationship and thus belie the essence of the relationship. This situation underscores the difficulty of grasping the nature or atmosphere of an ongoing friendship. The ability of friends to resume their relationship after a long separation reflects the existence of that elusive atmosphere, of what has been described as the choreography of their connection, the "invisible bonds of the space between" two people. The participants remember their relationship affectively. Because each friendship has its own language and rhythm, and because individuals become different with different friends, the scientific study of friendship is very difficult.[22]

Beyond the problem of understanding any one relationship, the task of developing historical generalizations about women's friendships poses additional challenges linked to the nature and limitations of available sources. As with any social historical study, one must ask how many and what kind of sources constitute an adequate body of data from which to draw conclusions about the multiple subjectivities that comprised the experience of female friendship. Because evidence of emotional standards for friendship can be gleaned from published documents such as periodicals and advice manuals, which are readily available for the period between 1900 and 1960, it is possible to develop a picture of cultural prescriptions for the relationship. But the historian must rely on personal documents—correspondence, journals and diaries, memoirs, and autobiographies—to develop insights into women's expressions of emotion and thus to reconstruct their experiences of friendship. As with women's history more generally, language conventions and the nuances of language— for example, what is said implicitly as well as explicitly—must be examined carefully. The identification and acknowledgment of customary modes of expression, such as the extravagantly affectionate rhetoric typical of nineteenth-century women's correspondence, must be an integral part of the effort to analyze friendships historically.

Accessible personal documents typically reflect the experiences of middle-class women, which highlights another aspect of the problem of representativeness. Because emotional standards are middle-class artifacts also, they offer the same perspective. It seems plausible to assume that, as in the case of family history, middle-class emotional standards were applied to other segments of society and may have had some impact on those groups, although those groups did not necessarily internalize such standards. At the least, then, the study of middle-class experiences can yield a basic historical perspective on women's friendships in the first half of the twentieth century and suggest relevant questions about the experiences of other groups.

Yet subtle regional and other contextual differences distinguish even the friendships of middle-class women during the period 1900–1960. For example, while evidence suggests that mutual professional concerns contributed to the development and maintenance of friendships between women writers generally, a shared sense of exclusion by male colleagues especially distinguished the relationships of Southern writers. More obvious differences reflect the influence of variables such as age and marital status as well. Although a small amount of evidence about any phenomenon cannot be presumed to illustrate what was typical in the past, such data certainly indicate at least what was possible at a particular time and provide a direction for further inquiry.[23] Given the nature of most of the available relevant sources and the middle-class character of the dominant emotional culture, this study intentionally addresses the history of female friendship experiences through a focus on white, middle-class American women in the first half of the twentieth century. At the same time, however, it explicitly acknowledges the multiplicity of other pertinent categories of experience and cites examples from those categories where feasible.

The question of diversity in female friendship experiences addresses a leading current issue in women's studies and feminist theory. Discussions of the idea of difference, embedded in two contexts, have dominated recent interdisciplinary scholarship. First, difference has been used in relation to the concept of gender as a way to characterize the male-female distinction and to counteract the traditional privileging of the male. Second, it has been employed to highlight racial, ethnic, religious, and class differences among women, in opposition to the pervasive tendency of late twentieth-century, middle-class, white feminists to universalize and homogenize the female voice and experience.[24] Both meanings of the term resonate in the context of the history of female friendship experiences. In the framework of emotions history, however, the concept of difference acquires a distinctive nuance. While "difference feminists" categorically reject the idea of a single norm, the study of emotions history appropriately proceeds from the examination of normative standards to a search for evidence of individual reactions to and internalization of those standards, along with evidence of other feelings. At the same time, because every human relationship reflects a unique context and represents a separate entity, each friendship symbolizes an instance of difference.

The history of female friendship also relates to the theoretical concerns of contemporary scholarship on women in other ways. The nature of American women's friendships, like every aspect of their lives in the past, has been influenced by the Western patriarchal cultural context in which they were situated. Thus, while male friendship has been valorized, women's friendships have been ignored or trivialized, and cross-sex friendships have usually been regarded only as incipient sexual relationships. The notion that women represent each other's worst enemies has endured, along with the image of female friendship as frivolous and insignificant. From the perspective of emotions history, it is evident that both the meaning and the experience of friendship have been socially constructed, in the past as well as in the present. From the perspective of women's history, it is also evident that women's friendships have been mediated by men's versions of them in terms of emotional standards, actual experience, and judgments of value.[25]

Despite hegemonic cultural influences, however, people function as active agents in their own lives. Historical analyses of the concept of women's culture illustrate that individuals make choices and resist oppression, even within the framework of socially prescribed norms and roles, cultural institutions, emotional standards, and internalized expectations. A person can present different identities and voices in response to circumstances. For example, despite the patriarchal constraints of middle-class marriage, nineteenth-century women exercised control over the lives of their children and over their own lives with regard to sex and reproduction. Hence the issue of individual human agency also defines an important variable in the effort to account for change and continuity in emotions history. Consequently, any examination of female friendship experiences in the past must take into account the role of women's agency, as well as the impact of patriarchal power on the shaping of those experiences.[26]

Friendship history also intersects with contemporary scholarship on women in the context of the craft of biography. Biographers of women have often discounted or ignored the role of friendship in a subject's life, particularly when they have discovered instances of intense female friendships such as those of Eleanor Roosevelt and Lorena Hickok, Helen Keller and Annie Sullivan, and Margaret Mead and Ruth Benedict. Biographies frequently stress an individual's uniqueness as opposed to her interactions as part of a social network, although contemporary research suggests that the latter play a major role in the construction of a self. Because the friendship patterns of any individual are complex, variegated, and socially and temporally located, the task of deciphering those patterns presents a difficult challenge for the biographer. Yet a biographical perspective that incorporates both a focused examination of the influence of relationships and friendship networks on the subject's life and accomplishments and a more inclusive selection of sources relevant to the study of lives can yield new insights and enhanced understandings.[27]

A final point of connection between the history of women's friendship experiences and other current research emerges in relation to the historical concept of separate spheres. Early work in women's history emphasized the notion of a secluded, self-sufficient, middle-class women's world whose inhabitants performed domestic and child-rearing roles totally apart from the public realm of men. Yet subsequent studies have revised the notion of a separate, private, female world isolated from the public male world. This research suggests that women in the past operated in many diverse capacities outside the private sphere as well as within the parameters of domesticity.[28] At first glance, female friendship might appear to have been a phenomenon of the private sphere in the past, reflecting images of confiding, nurturing, supporting, sharing, and helping. However, American women's friendships have also functioned influentially in diverse public contexts, such as nineteenth-century feminism, early twentieth-century campaigns for suffrage and Progressive reform, and New Deal politics.[29]

Throughout most of the history of Western civilization, men's relationships with one another have provided the model for friendship in Western society. But as the twentieth century ends, relationships between women have become the standard by which friendship is defined and evaluated. Traditional cultural images of the superiority of male friendship have been displaced by suggestions that heterosexual men are unable to deal with intimacy, do not seek and cultivate close friends, and either have no time or fail to make time for friendship. In contrast, women are now portrayed as uniquely skilled and accomplished at friendship. They are believed to offer more emotional support for each other, and they seem to experience affectively richer, more intimate interactions than their male counterparts.

The contradiction between traditional negative concepts of women's capacities for friendship and contemporary portrayals of their special qualifications in this area underscores the need for a systematic, historical examination of female friendship experiences in the context of changing emotional standards. This volume addresses several questions raised by conflicting cultural evaluations of female friendship: Does the discrepancy between past and current images of women as friends reflect actual experience as well as patriarchal, gender-based assumptions? Have women's relationships with one another and with male friends consistently mirrored the dominant emotional culture and other social and cultural influences in the past? Or have their friendship experiences contradicted or subverted these factors? Finally, this work documents the evolution of new friendship styles along with the endurance of more traditional patterns, and it confirms the abiding role of friendship in the lives of middle-class American women.

I

"The Sister of My Heart"

Female Friends before 1900

In 1790, the popular English novel *Euphemia* characterized female friendship as a multifaceted, influential force in women's lives. A friend, the work's author asserted, is "a witness of the conscience, a physician of secret griefs, a moderator of prosperity, and a guide in adversity."[1] This definition would have had a familiar resonance for late eighteenth-century women on both sides of the Atlantic, as well as for their foremothers and their nineteenth-century descendants. Nearly a hundred years before the publication of *Euphemia*, the early English feminist Mary Astell compared the friendship styles of men and women and concluded that the latter manifested a special quality:

> As we [women] are less concern'd in the affairs of the World, so we have less temptation from Interest to be false to our Friends. Neither are we so likely to be false thro' Fear; because our Sex are seldom engag'd in matters of any Danger. For these Reasons it is, our Sex are generally more hearty and sincere in the ordinary Friendships they make than Men, among whom they are usually clogg'd with so many Considerations of Interest, and Punctilio's of Honour.[2]

Nineteenth-century author Dinah Mulock Craik may have had similar ideas in mind when she characterized friendship as "the comfort, the inexpressible comfort of feeling safe with a person having neither to weigh thoughts nor measure words."[3]

As these comments suggest, antecedents of late twentieth-century images of the exceptionality of female friendship can be discerned in the observations of women in the past who placed a high value on their relationships with one another. Despite cultural denigration of the links between women, strong, emotionally expressive female friendships have existed in various historical periods, in Western society and in other cultures as well. Although some women managed to build friendships with men in spite of the inherent complexity of cross-sex relationships of this sort, over the centuries many more relied on one another for affective support and sustenance, and often for more tangible assistance as well. Frequently they expressed their feelings about individual female friends and about the relationship generally in strongly emotional terms. A complete analysis of the origins of this pattern of interaction remains beyond the scope of the present discussion, but it is evident that women's subordinate status and economic dependency, and their concomitant disempowerment, fostered the development of intense same-sex attachments and an emotional friendship style. And it is clear that devoted, mutually sustaining friendships provided crucial support for countless eighteenth- and nineteenth-century American women.[4]

The first English settlers in the New World brought with them a patriarchal ideology that assigned a subordinate place to women in society. The lives of colonial women centered on the household. They were excluded from positions of power and authority and were outnumbered by men in most of the colonies throughout the seventeenth century. With the exception of church membership, they had no formal affiliations outside the home. However, religious participation mitigated the effects of their subordinate status in important ways. It offered equal access to God, if not to power in the secular world, and thus it could provide comfort in the face of difficulties. Furthermore, it brought women together as peers who shared common spiritual beliefs, and those beliefs could serve as a foundation for the development of personal friendships. For example, within the egalitarian structure of the Quaker faith, circular letters linked female members of different meetings. While other denominations did not allow women to exercise the sort of autonomy permitted by the Society of Friends, church attendance itself offered a respite from domestic life, along with a regular opportunity for social interaction with female acquaintances. Although little evidence exists to document seventeenth-century female friendship experiences, early colonial women, like their English counterparts, probably turned to one another for support as they coped with the exigencies of daily existence and the rituals of life and death.

Religious affiliation continued to play a major role in women's lives and to promote their interaction with each other in the eighteenth century. In some congregations, female members comprised the majority. The religious revival of the 1740s, known as the Great Awakening, expanded women's religious involvement and eventually provided them with some access to public influence, as, for example, through participation in the selection of ministers and the admission of new church members. Evidence from the late eighteenth century documents the role of shared religious commitments and experiences as catalysts in the development of female friendship.

The rise of educational institutions for young women also promoted the development of friendships between women. By the middle of the eighteenth century, small boarding schools designed to teach drawing, writing, and needlework existed. Better-established female academies founded by men—and, eventually, more permanent seminaries founded and run by women—succeeded these early institutions. Such educational settings provided communities in which young women interacted with one another and began to develop gender consciousness. Moreover, by increasing female literacy, they facilitated the availability of evidence that documents eighteenth-century women's friendship experiences. Because society sanctioned group activities for women during the Revolutionary War years, this era strengthened gender consciousness and feelings of female connection. As many as sixty or seventy women might gather in sewing circles or spinning groups, where they worked together to support the colonial cause. Groups of women signed pledges to abstain from tea, boycotted British goods, and worked to raise money for the colonial armies. Like mutual religious beliefs, this collective patriotism helped to forge links between individuals, as well as to build a general sense of community.

Women's involvement in the religious movements that comprised the second Great Awakening, between 1798 and 1826, had a similar effect. During this period as well, they began to participate extensively in local associations, such as prayer groups, missionary societies, church benevolent groups, and mothers' clubs. Ultimately this participation expanded to encompass larger movements, such as temperance, abolition, and moral reform. In all of these contexts, women moved beyond the confines of the patriarchal family to act as autonomous individuals. Hence, for women in the late eighteenth century, friendship became a relationship with a potentially political meaning.[5]

Nancy Cott argues that the culture of the late eighteenth and early nineteenth centuries identified women with the qualities of the heart as opposed to the rational capacities that were said to characterize men, and thus that it defined them in relation to other persons. Didactic and prescriptive literature represented affiliation rather than achievement as women's appropriate motivation, and the establishment of positive affective interactions as their central goal. This view of the contrasting natures of males and females also implied that women would only find interpersonal reciprocity through their relationships with one another. The cultural climate, then, incorporated a specific emotional ethos that conditioned the development of strong friendships among early American women.[6]

This emotional environment blended with women's collective social condition and their shared educational experiences, religious sentiments, and biological moments—most frequently childbirth—to structure a pattern of devoted and lasting friendships. As the domestic sphere became increasingly separate from the public world of men, other distinctly female rituals played a similar role. Sisters provided the closest friendship many individuals experienced. Nineteenth-century women supported their sisters in times of distress and happiness, loved and cared for them, and collaborated with them on causes like temperance and abolitionism. They might disagree about an issue or find a request for help inconvenient, but they viewed sororal bonds as irrevocable and diligently preserved them by writing, visiting back and forth, and sending their daughters for regular and lengthy stays with their aunts. The author of a widely read volume on female friendship, first published in 1869, described close bonds between sisters as an "unspeakably important class of womanly friendships." If "base qualities, irritating circumstances, or cold and meagre natures" precluded the formation of such bonds, he observed, a household suffered "great misfortune and loss."[7]

The ideology of domesticity, which defined women as a class and valorized the role of motherhood, promoted close relationships between women and nourished female community beyond the family as well. Later nineteenth-century developments—including the rise of higher education for women, the emergence of an extensive women's club movement, and the feminization of clerical work, teaching, and retail sales positions—constructed additional venues for the development of friendship. Finally, geographic isolation from family members and mutual commitment to unconventional roles also encouraged the growth of strong, enduring bonds between American women.

One of the earliest American examples of female friendship appears in the journal of Esther Edwards Burr. Essentially a series of letters from Burr to her close friend, Sarah Prince, during the period 1754–1757, the journal vividly illustrates the centrality of female friendship in the lives of two intelligent, introspective, religious colonial women. Their correspondence in journal format began when Esther and her husband, Aaron Burr, moved from New England to New Jersey. Burr expressed a strong sense of connection with other women generally, a kind of sisterhood grounded in their shared condition of gender-based inequality and their common experiences of evangelical Christianity during the religious revivals of the first Great Awakening. She especially cherished her close friendship with Sarah Prince, to whom she felt "in some respects nerer [*sic*] than any Sister I have. . . . the Sister of my heart." Their correspondence touched on a broad range of issues and topics—marriage, prescriptive literature, works of fiction, events in the public sphere, and religious concerns, as well as friendship itself.[8]

Unlike many of her male contemporaries, who viewed friendship as an intellectual relationship, Esther Burr regarded it as a divinely inspired example of Christian love. Lonely and isolated by her husband's frequent absences, she eagerly anticipated the arrival of letters from her friend. Her quick replies often contained expressions of regard for Prince and stressed the latter's importance to her. "Your welfare in the least shape rejoices my heart," Burr wrote on one occasion. On another, she described her feelings even more eloquently: "Consider my friend how rare a thing tis to meet with such a friend as I have in my Fidelia—Who would not vallue [*sic*] and prize such a friend above gold, or honour, or any thing that the World can afford? You must not talk about dieing [*sic*] soon—I cant bare [*sic*] it."[9] Ironically, it was Prince who was left to mourn when Burr died an untimely death. Prince's sense of loss reveals that she had valued the friendship with a similar intensity: "With her went allmost *the All* in which I had sum'd up my Earthly Good!" Prince lamented. "My Earthly joy is gone! . . . [A] Great part of my attachment to this World is gone."[10]

As the editors of her journal point out, Burr's explicit recognition and elaboration of the significance of sisterhood contrasts distinctly with the absence of this theme in some earlier colonial sources, as in the seventeenth-century writings of Anne Bradstreet.[11] However, substantial evidence indicates that many white eighteenth- and nineteenth-century women experienced intimate friendships of the sort enjoyed by Burr and Prince in the pre-Revolutionary era. Diaries and correspondence suggest that, between 1780 and the middle of the nineteenth century, New England women developed a clearly self-conscious and idealized concept of female friendship that they pondered, discussed, and implemented concretely with one another. Such women often articulated the significance of relationships with female friends explicitly, and they frequently expressed a passionate hope that these bonds could be preserved. While their letters and diaries record heterosexual interactions and gossip about male suitors, these documents suggest that female friends functioned as the women's major outlet for emotional expression and source of security. Effusive declarations such as "I feel my love to you to be without dissimulation" and "You have . . . imprinted upon my soul your beloved image, in character so indelible that neither time nor absence can erase it" suggest the intensity of feeling involved in these relationships.[12]

The friendship of Emily Dickinson and Abiah Root offers an interesting example of a mid-nineteenth-century relationship. These young women met at Amherst Academy in 1843. Although both eventually left to attend other schools, they exchanged numerous letters until Root's marriage in 1854. Dickinson inquired about her friend's new school and teachers. She shared news about her family, mutual friends, and new acquaintances; reported on her studies and the books she read; and described the pleasure she found in nature. At the age of fifteen, she confided, "I am growing handsome very fast indeed! I expect I shall be the belle of Amherst when I reach my 17th year." Although Dickinson can hardly be viewed as a representative nineteenth-century young woman, her early letters to Root discuss many typical experiences and suggest that their friendship resembled those of their contemporaries. Even as she withdrew progressively from society into the seclusion that would encompass the rest of her life, Dickinson's regard for her friend remained apparent. "Thank you for loving me, long ago, and today, and too for all the sweetness, and all the gentleness, and all the tenderness with which you remember me—your quaint, old fashioned friend," she wrote. "You asked me to come and see you—I must speak of that. I thank you Abiah, but I don't go from home, unless emergency leads me by the hand, and then I do it obstinately, and draw back if I can." Yet, she assured her friend, "Should I ever leave home, which is improbable, I will with much delight, accept your invitation . . . but don't expect me. I'm so old fashioned, Darling, that all your friends would stare."[13]

While the bond between Dickinson and Root apparently deteriorated after the latter's marriage, most of the research on pre-twentieth-century female friendship suggests that bonds between women, solidly grounded in what Mary Ryan has described as a "feminine universe," took precedence over heterosexual ties and could even affect the quality of spousal relationships. Ryan suggests that middle-class young women may have actually experienced a psychic crisis in the face of the shift of emotional focus required by marriage. However, she maintains that female friends remained central to women's emotional lives even after they were married. One young woman anticipated the potential conflict between matrimony and female friendship far in advance: "[Marriage] is, I fear the bane of Female Friendship," she wrote to a close friend sometime during the 1780s. "Let it not be with ours, my Polly, if we should ever Marry."

Carroll Smith-Rosenberg's classic study of middle-class American women's relationships in the nineteenth century portrays powerful and enduring ties of the sort this individual hoped to maintain. Smith-Rosenberg describes a domestic world in which women provided love, companionship, and emotional intimacy for one another, totally apart from their interactions with fiancés or husbands whose concerns centered on the world outside the home.[14] More recent work has revised the concept of completely separate spheres, revealing that nineteenth-century couples actually confided many private thoughts and feelings to one another.[15] While these findings indicate that women were not as isolated from the male world as Smith-Rosenberg's research suggests, traditionally shared biological and domestic roles—as well as new and emerging social and political concerns—continued to foster close female friendships throughout the century.

Research by Karen Hansen raises the issue of class specificity in relation to the historical literature on nineteenth-century female friendship. Hansen challenges the implicit suggestion in that body of research that friendship played a uniquely important role in the lives of middle-class women; her findings highlight the significance of friends for the emotional well-being of working-class women as well. Hansen stresses the centrality of friendship as an essential component of social life and a linchpin of the culture of mutuality, neighborliness, and reciprocity that characterized antebellum New England. However, she also cites a major difference in the friendship patterns of middle- and working-class women. Smith-Rosenberg and others have described lifelong female friendships that endured despite the marriage of one or both partners; Hansen found such lasting relationships only between women who were related. While working-class women sought and established close friendships, domestic networks and partners seem to have limited their relationships. As Hansen points out, this apparent discrepancy may merely reflect fragmentary evidence, or it may actually document a difference in the duration of women's friendships in the two groups. If the latter is the case, it is possible that female friendships harmonized more comfortably with marriage and the domestic context as experienced by middle-class women than by their working-class counterparts.[16]

The late nineteenth-century diary of a white, rural Arkansas woman of limited economic means corroborates Hansen's view of the importance of female friendship to women whose economic circumstances placed them outside the middle class. It also suggests that even a husband's strong objections to her relationships with friends would not necessarily diminish a woman's reliance on them. Nannie Jackson recorded daily visits with her best friend, Fannie, who lived a half mile away, and with a network of other neighbors, both white and black. When she visited Fannie three times in one evening during the eighth month of her third pregnancy, Jackson's husband was angry. This reaction apparently did not distress her: "I just talk to Fannie and tell her my troubles because it seems to help me to bear it better when she knows about it. I shall tell her whenever I feel like it," Jackson observed defiantly.[17]

Not surprisingly, female friends played important roles in the lives of the growing number of nineteenth-century women who chose to remain unmarried. Along with kin, they provided crucial emotional and logistical support for the development of independence and the achievement of vocational aspirations. They also fostered each other's intellectual development through reading clubs that met regularly to discuss literary works and through more informal conversations about books. Some evidence suggests that, over the course of the century, relationships with friends began to replace those with sisters among middle-class single women. At the same time, such friendships manifested similar qualities to those that defined the connections between blood sisters.[18]

The pattern of strong ties between sisters, then, provided a model for sororal friendships between unrelated women, married as well as single. Like those of biological sisters, these relationships often encompassed shared burdens and obligations based on gender identity, emotional and financial commitments, and reciprocal support for social and political endeavors. For example, Lucy Stone and Antoinette Brown developed a close friendship soon after they met at Oberlin College in 1846 and maintained their relationship for forty-seven years.[19] These women shared personal concerns and provided solace and support for one another in their joint pursuit of women's rights. In the course of a prolific correspondence, they examined the common bonds of womanhood and analyzed the qualities of their relationship. Their letters reveal an explicit recognition of the parallels between friendship and biological sisterhood and a self-conscious desire to preserve the close ties they had developed at Oberlin. Brown's first letter to Stone addressed her friend as "My *own dear Sister*" and expressed a wish that "my dear sister Lucy was here, to share every thought and feeling." A subsequent communication voiced a similar desire, along with the hope that their sisterhood would endure. "Write Lucy very soon a long long long letter," Brown urged. "Tell me everything and let us be sisters forever wont [*sic*] we."[20]

This desire for enduring sisterhood was fulfilled in a literal sense when the friends married brothers, Samuel and Henry Blackwell, within a year of one another, although both women had previously professed their mutual disinterest in marrying. Stone, who had declared "Tis next to a chattel slave, to be a *legal* wife," remained ambivalent about this choice even as she planned her wedding: "The *day* is not set. . . . But when it is fixed—I will write you, so that you may think of me, and fancy if you can, what of thought and feeling goes on, under the surface. . . . I *expect* however to go to Cincinnati and have the ruin completed there," she confided to her friend. Only a few months later, however, she assured the latter, "You will write your book better dear Nettee, and do everything better when you share the personal presence and full sympathy and love of Sam—have not *I* a right to affirm, who have been nine months married?"[21]

As sisters-in-law, these women continued their close friendship, exchanging family news, reminiscing about Oberlin, gossiping about acquaintances, planning family visits, and discussing shared political concerns. The tone of their correspondence grew less intense as they matured, but the bonds between them remained strong. When Stone died, her friend eulogized her as a public figure, "a pioneer . . . she went forward confidently, wrapped in . . . sustaining conviction." She also offered a simple eloquent tribute to their personal relationship: "In the older days, to me she was close friend; in the later days, she was both friend and sister."[22]

Other nineteenth-century feminists experienced similarly powerful and enduring relationships. Shortly after they met in Seneca Falls, New York, in 1851, Susan B. Anthony and Elizabeth Cady Stanton formed a strong friendship. "Soon fastened, heart to heart, with hooks of steel in a friendship that years of confidence and affection have steadily strengthened," Stanton recalled in her memoirs, "we have labored faithfully together." Without her friend's inspiration, she noted, the responsibilities of marriage and a large family might have absorbed all of her energies and thus limited her political activities. Fortunately, Stanton observed, their efforts to achieve suffrage complemented each other, and their relationship was never threatened by any sort of discord:

While she is slow and analytical in composition, I am rapid and synthetic. I am the better writer, she the better critic. She supplied the facts and statistics, I the philosophy and rhetoric, and together, we have made arguments that have stood unshaken through the storms of long years; arguments that no one has answered. Our speeches may be considered the united products of our two brains. So entirely one are we that, in all our associations . . . not one feeling of envy or jealousy has ever shadowed our lives.

Although these reminiscences, published in 1898 near the end of Stanton's long life and career, reflect her perception of their friendship filtered through the lens of memory, they clearly document the relationship's importance to her.

Unlike those of Lucy Stone and Antoinette Brown, the personal lives of Susan B. Anthony and Elizabeth Cady Stanton followed completely different paths. Stanton was a wife and the mother of seven children, while Anthony never married. Nevertheless, their shared commitment to the cause of women's rights linked them in a strong and devoted friendship that lasted for half a century. In their final years their professional agendas diverged to some degree; eventually Stanton withdrew from active participation in the suffrage movement, while her friend continued to pursue political possibilities. Yet the personal attachment endured. When Stanton celebrated her eighty-seventh birthday, Anthony observed that her friend was "over four years ahead of me," but she told her, "in age as in all else I follow you closely." Stanton described the significance of their relationship in unambiguous terms: "So closely interwoven have been our lives, our purposes, and experiences that, separated, we have a feeling of incompleteness—united, such strength of self-assertion that no ordinary obstacles, difficulties, or dangers ever appear to us insurmountable."[23]

The relationship of Mary Cassatt and Louisine Elder, who met in Paris in 1874, offers another interesting example of a long, close friendship promoted and nurtured by mutual interests. At first more of a teacher-student association between the artist Cassatt, who was thirty, and a nineteen-year-old woman with a serious interest in collecting art, their interactions evolved into a mature and equal friendship. After Elder's marriage to Harry Havemeyer in 1883, the friends were separated for six years, but when Louisine and her husband resumed regular trips to Europe to buy art, she and Cassatt reconnected. Cassatt also enjoyed a warm relationship with Harry Havemeyer. Linked by their common dedication to art, these women shared more traditional bonds, too: Havemeyer consoled her friend when an older sister died, and later supported her emotionally through the death of her mother, even sitting with the latter for long hours during her final illness. Although sea travel made her physically ill, Cassatt forced herself to make a final transatlantic trip in 1908 to comfort Havemeyer on the first anniversary of her husband's death. From that point on, they saw one another only when Louisine visited Europe, but frequent correspondence kept them in close touch. In one letter, Cassatt, who had developed cataracts and feared that she would have to stop painting, wrote poignantly, "I never felt so isolated in my life as I do now. Your letters are the only things that made [*sic*] me feel not altogether abandoned." The relationship endured until an increasingly frail Cassatt ended it, two years before her death, after an unfortunate misunderstanding caused her to question her friend's loyalty.[24] (See figure 4.)

Virtually all of the existing historical literature on friendship between women from the late eighteenth through the nineteenth century conveys a sense of the importance they attributed to their interactions. Female friends enabled many conventional wives and mothers, unmarried women, and women who pursued untraditional vocational, political, or social goals to cope both emotionally and practically with the vicissitudes of daily life. The literature also reveals that for some women, an additional physically demonstrative dimension distinguished female friendship. Thus the emotional intimacy that pervaded the intense, long-lasting friendships experienced by many nineteenth-century women often encompassed physical intimacy as well. Explicit references to physical contact suggest that this type of intimacy between close friends was not unusual throughout most of the nineteenth century and that it continued into the early years of the next century.[25]

A phenomenon known as "smashing," the romantic wooing of one young woman by another, was prevalent at boarding schools and women's colleges. If the affection was mutual, a couple might spend their days together and share a bed at night; if not, the rejected individual experienced the misery of unrequited love. "Smashes" could produce the same problems as heterosexual romances—distracted students, neglected studies, jealousy, and hurt feelings. Occasionally a teacher became the focus of a young woman's affections. While students at coeducational colleges and universities often had what were referred to as "particular friends," "smashing" appears to have been unique to women's institutions.[26]

Historians have relied extensively on personal correspondence for evidence of friendship, but letters represent only one tangible expression of the esteem in which nineteenth-century middle-class women held their female friends. Many women recorded their affection in autograph albums, which grew very popular during the 1830s. Between 1840 and 1875, the friendship quilt provided another vehicle for the expression of similar sentiments. This fad originated in the eastern part of the country and eventually moved west across the mountains. Like autograph albums, friendship quilts served as keepsakes and reminders of treasured friendships. Quilt patterns varied; they incorporated biblical and secular verses, as well as personal information such as friends' names, significant dates, addresses, and bits of advice. Often designed as going-away presents for women moving west, friendship quilts were also exchanged by local friends and sisters. They could be created by one particularly skilled seamstress or by a group of friends who used indelible ink or embroidery to convey special messages. These gifts were carefully preserved by their recipients, displayed decoratively, or handed down through families as part of the female inheritance. One individual, lonely for the companionship of family and friends left behind in New England, wrote that reading the signatures of the women who had made each quilt square "brings sister spirits into communion with my spirit and I feel that the same cause and the same Savior, induces you all to help me bear my burden." As concrete symbols of women's regard for one another, friendship quilts offer durable evidence of nineteenth-century sisterhood; in some cases they also provide the only record of a woman's existence other than a gravestone or a notation in a family bible.[27]

Close female friendships and their tangible manifestations in the form of affectionate letters, autograph albums, and friendship quilts reflect the development of a characteristic Victorian emotional culture. Recent re-examinations of the image of Victorian restraint have revised the traditional portrayal of emotional repressiveness as a distinguishing feature of the period. Beginning around 1820, a Victorian emotional style that stressed the management and appropriate use of emotions rather than their systematic suppression emerged. Succeeding decades witnessed the further evolution of a mature Victorian approach that emphasized loving family relationships, particularly between mothers and their children, and supported a conception of intense, enduring, spiritual love between men and women.

The intensity with which Victorian culture treated love in general fostered both the development of affectionate female friendships and the use of extravagantly romantic language to express that affection. Nineteenth-century publications romanticized the idea of female friendship. Thus, for example, *Godey's Lady's Book and Magazine* published poems and verses for women to copy into friends' autograph albums and friendship quilt blocks, while William Alger's popular book, *Friendships of Women,* asserted that "the cultivation of high-toned friendships with each other" would "do more than anything else to enrich and embellish [women's] lives and to crown them with contentment."[28]

This Victorian emotional ethos created a climate in which "smashing" and physical contact between same-sex friends was permissible. Nineteenth-century gender ideology also supported intense, romantic female friendships. Because women were widely regarded as frivolous and asexual, close friendships between them could be viewed as unimportant, transient components of the interval between girlhood and marriage. In this context, physically demonstrative relationships could be accepted temporarily and even considered a form of preparation for eventual adjustment to the marriage relationship. Moreover, while nineteenth-century middle-class women did not necessarily experience the separation and isolation from men implied by the ideology of true womanhood and the doctrine of separate spheres, the beliefs represented by these concepts offered further cultural validation for a romanticized idea of female friendship.[29]

Hence physically demonstrative friendships and women's explicit references to such relationships clearly reflect a specific historical context that encompassed an extensive homocultural orientation. In this setting, young men also formed passionate, physically demonstrative relationships, although of shorter duration.[30] Such friendships may also reflect regional differences within that context, as in the case of romantic friendships experienced by young women in Southern boarding schools. While these friendships resembled those in other areas of the country, they were also compatible with specifically Southern customs of the period, such as permissive, affectionate child-rearing practices and the regular exchange of kisses between adult women.[31]

Contemporary scholars disagree with regard to the appropriateness of designating such friendships as homosexual or lesbian in the sense in which these terms are currently construed. The impossibility of documenting the exact nature of the physical contact between women in the past and of its meaning to specific individuals complicates the issue. It was not uncommon for nineteenth-century biological sisters to share a bed. References to friends sleeping together—as, for example, Lucy Stone and Antoinette Brown did—are compatible with both sororal and romantic models of friendship.[32] Furthermore, the physical dimension represents only one factor in a relationship. Thus, while young women in Southern boarding schools seem to have experienced physically demonstrative romantic friendships frequently, almost all of them eventually married as opposed to developing lifelong relationships with female partners. Again, this outcome may reflect regional social and cultural conditions, specifically the fact that female financial independence was even less feasible in the South than in other areas of the country. However, it also suggests that, for at least some young women, these relationships represented a source of comfort away from home or a temporary fad rather than a reflection of actual sexual preference.[33] For the historian of friendship, then, the effort to categorize particular nineteenth-century women's friendships in terms of a contemporary construction of lesbian identity seems less important than the need to acknowledge a physical dimension as integral to some friendships, to describe it sensitively, and to recognize its pertinence within the framework of Victorian emotional culture.[34]

An examination of one relationship in this category, Sarah Orne Jewett's friendship with Annie Fields, exemplifies the complexity of analyzing evidence regarding the nineteenth-century affiliations that historians have designated as romantic friendships. Fields was happily married to a prominent editor and publisher when she met Jewett, and her husband encouraged the friendship. After James Fields died in 1881, the women became inseparable companions. Their relationship illustrates the sort of affiliation that has been described as a Boston marriage. This type of life-long partnership between two women was not uncommon in the late nineteenth century. For the next two decades, until Jewett suffered a dis-abling accident, she lived in Fields's house in Boston for most of the win-ter, visited her own family in Maine in spring or early summer, and then spent most of the summer at her friend's seaside summer home. They en-joyed the intellectual stimulation and companionship of a wide circle of interesting literary friends.

Their letters reveal a reciprocal relationship characterized by flexible roles. Jewett appears to have been more emotionally dependent on Fields—frequently urging Fields to join her during her family visits—but she seems to have had greater authority when they discussed their writ-ing. The use of nicknames, childish language, and expressions of physical affection mark this relationship as a romantic friendship; scholars have debated whether or not it should also be categorized as lesbian. A letter from Jewett to Fields in 1886 offers a representative example:

Dearest Fuff—I am sorry that this letter will not get into the morning post and so you will not have a word from your affectionate and lazy Pinny this rainy day. I long to see you and say all sorts of foolish things, and to be as bold a Pinny as can be! and to kiss you ever so many times.[35]

Their circle of friends included Sarah Wyman Whitman, an artist and illustrator, to whom Sarah Orne Jewett also wrote what appear to have been love letters. Yet no evidence suggests that Jewett felt guilty or dis-loyal for expressing her love to Whitman while sharing her life with Fields. Furthermore, despite Jewett's use of affectionate, intimate lan-guage, no direct evidence documents physical expressions of affection in the context of her relationship with either Annie Fields or Sarah Whit-man. Parallel language, also without evidence of actual physical contact, appears in the correspondence between Lucy Stone and Antoinette Brown—for example, "Lucy Darling . . . O dear if you were only here so I could put my arm close around you and feel your heart beating against mine as in lang syne."[36] These similarities suggest that such letters may reflect linguistic conventions rather than actual behavior. As the author of a recent study of Jewett's life and work has observed, it is difficult if not impossible for the late twentieth-century historian to distinguish among the various "shades of sexual, nonsexual, and semisexual passion that the nineteenth century accepted as part of the normal spectrum of human emotions."[37] Hence any effort to define those feelings in terms of twentieth-century categories risks being an ahistorical misinterpretation.

Existing scholarship on pre-twentieth-century female friendship primarily emphasizes the strength of the bonds between white, middle-class American women and highlights the romantic language used by many to express their affection for one another.[38] For the most part, this literature portrays untroubled relationships rarely disrupted by any sort of friction or conflict between friends. Undeniably, women in the past helped each other cope with the demands of traditional female domestic roles and duties, as well as with less conventional problems. Furthermore, the social and cultural climate fostered and supported close, affectionate friendships. But the prevalent image of a golden age of female friendship raises two relevant questions for the historian to consider: First, does the paucity of evidence regarding conflict between friends necessarily prove its absence? And second, did strong, supportive, intimate female friendships have any negative effects on women's lives?

Recent studies in feminist history and the history of the emotions have addressed the issue of silence as evidence. This work has pointed out that Western culture has traditionally expected women to be silent in public and men to refrain from speaking about women. Historically, as a result, women have appeared to be absent from politics. Racism and poverty, as well as gender discrimination, have particularly silenced African-American women, so that they have been almost completely absent from the narrative of American history. Similarly, in accordance with prevailing discourses in particular periods, sexuality has been deliberately left out of some historical documents by their authors and censored from other sources by archivists. The kinds of things that people can and cannot say, or even think, about sexuality change over time. The same is true of the range of human emotions. But contemporary historians frame questions about past human activities and emotional experiences in the categories of late twentieth-century discourse. We need to recognize that silence is in effect constructed and thus to consider the context and purpose of its existence—that is, the provenance of historical sources—and to try to determine what it conceals.[39] From this perspective, the dearth of expressions of anger in correspondence between nineteenth-century female friends becomes more than just a reflection of the absence of this emotion.

Like the explicit discussion of same-sex intimacy, the silence about anger and conflict between friends may mirror the influence of Victorian emotional culture. Although that culture supported intense expressions of affection between women and encouraged loving relationships, it strongly discouraged expressions of anger and quarrels between family members, particularly spouses but also siblings and, by extension, close friends. Furthermore, the emotional culture sharply differentiated men from women. Thus it defined anger as specifically unfeminine and inappropriate in girls, although that emotion could be accepted in boys if they channeled it properly. Some evidence suggests that certain women who internalized the Victorian restriction on female anger may have converted the emotion into psychosomatic illnesses, such as hysterical paralysis and eating disorders.[40]

An intriguing allusion to this cultural stipulation appears in Elizabeth Cady Stanton's memoirs. Noting that she and Susan B. Anthony had often criticized one another's ideas and disagreed "hotly" over the years, Stanton observed: "To the world we always seem to agree and uniformly reflect each other. Like husband and wife each has the feeling that we must have no differences in public."[41] An interesting analogous comment in a letter from Antoinette Brown to Lucy Stone also addresses the issue of conflict between close friends. "O dear! Lucy I do wish we believed alike . . . but then we'll 'agree to disagree' as you used to say so often," she wrote.[42]

While it is impossible to generalize from the statements of two women, the reflections of Stanton and Brown clearly document the influence of the contemporary emotional culture. Their comments support the idea that if nineteenth-century female friends experienced anger with one another, they would probably endeavor to refrain from expressing it publicly or perhaps at all. However, an additional dimension further complicates the issue: It is also possible that friends did not actually feel angry with one another. If the dominant emotionology of a period actually affects the experience as well as the expression of a particular emotion, the predominant images of harmony and compatibility may represent accurate historical descriptions of many nineteenth-century women's friendships.[43]

Undoubtedly most close friends, like mothers and daughters in the nineteenth century, experienced at least minor tensions and occasional disagreements in the course of ordinary life.[44] Some examples suggest that, even within the framework of Victorian emotional styles, more substantial conflicts with serious ramifications could also arise. After fifty years of close friendship, Mary Cassatt and Louisine Havemeyer

quarreled bitterly in 1923 over the latter's perception that her friend
was challenging her integrity in a dispute about Cassatt's plan to exhibit a set of copperplates that had been printed and displayed previously. A year later, the artist declared that she had "broken off completely" with her old friend.[45] This disagreement escalated to the point
that it effectively ended their communication. Nevertheless, as her response to the news of Cassatt's death illustrates, the relationship remained important to Havemeyer. "While I am glad that Miss C. is at
last at rest," she wrote, "her death is a very, very sad loss to me. It is
the breaking of a lifelong friendship."[46]

A different sort of discord disrupted the long, close relationship between Sallie Holley and Caroline Putnam. These women, who met at
Oberlin College in 1848, devoted their lives to helping African Americans, first through antislavery activities and then as teachers. Holley was
the stronger, more domineering of the two. Originally as a mentor and
then as a loving friend, she challenged Putnam intellectually, supported
her financially, and encouraged her to become independent from her family and to develop a vocational identity. Her influence contributed significantly to Putnam's professional and personal growth, but other friends
saw Holley as overbearing and controlling. Eventually the relative power,
influence, and reputations of the two women shifted. Holley seems to
have resented her friend's increasing autonomy, and the women experienced some emotional distance in later years. Apparently Putnam denied
feeling resentment, preferring to seek reconciliation rather than to express
the anger she might have experienced, but Holley was more vocal about
her negative feelings.[47]

Both of these examples illustrate conflict over issues related to professional as opposed to domestic activities, and both portray difficulties between aging women. Certainly individual personalities, preferences, and
idiosyncrasies contribute to the presence or absence of disagreement between friends. However, the problems between Cassatt and Havemeyer
and Putnam and Holley suggest interesting hypotheses about other potential sources of conflict. Perhaps nineteenth-century women whose lives
centered on traditional roles and duties were less likely to have major disagreements with one another than those who pursued unconventional
lifestyles and thus experienced more personal autonomy. In some sense,
the bonds of womanhood may have been stronger between those for
whom marriage and motherhood defined reality. Finally, failing health

and other problems related to aging may have caused these women to overreact to situations involving close friends.

Examples of conflict also highlight the possibility that female friendship before 1900 incorporated an inherently negative component. Undoubtedly rejection or the cooling of affection on one side of a formerly intense and intimate friendship could produce anguish and insecurity, particularly in the context of an emotional culture that stressed the value of loving relationships. On the other hand, too many emotional demands by one partner could create pressure and anxiety for the other. Lee Virginia Chambers-Schiller addresses this question specifically as it pertains to the lives of single women in nineteenth-century America. She argues that just as the bonds of friendship influenced the development of female autonomy and facilitated independence and achievement, they also constrained women by conceptualizing their activities in terms of private vocations rather than professional careers. While friendship fostered self-esteem and individual identity, it did so, at least emotionally, within the confines of women's separate sphere, where work satisfaction remained tied to relationships and domestic values.

Chambers-Schiller also suggests that the constraints of intense friendships could contribute to the diminution of individual identity and the development of increased emotional dependence.[48] Because the sources typically offer silence rather than explicit discussion of any negative aspects of women's friendships, questions about conflict and tension are difficult to answer conclusively. Like the question of physical intimacy, these issues highlight the complexity of the interaction between the emotional culture, other social and cultural factors, and individual experiences of friendship.

Historical studies that document pre-twentieth-century women's reliance on close female friends for both emotional and more tangible support suggest that emotional distance, a lack of communication, and sometimes even hostility defined women's interactions with men, including husbands and fiancés. Such generalizations are based primarily on women's letters to one another, prescriptive literature, and legal definitions of women's status rather than on evidence that might document cross-sex friendships, such as correspondence between women and men. Hence they tend to discount the possibility of female-male friendship.[49]

Yet the historian cannot assume that cross-sex friendship was completely absent from female experience prior to 1900. The relationships of courting couples and spouses in nineteenth-century America encompassed heterosocial friendship as well as romance.[50] Most middle-class women in the past married and lived in families, and many raised sons. Those who did not have these experiences interacted with fathers, brothers, or other male kin. Thus they did not necessarily lack either models for candid communication with men or the inclination to relate to them as friends. Moreover, the male author of a popular nineteenth-century book on female friendship specifically praised the advantages of cross-sex friendship for men without wives "of good sense and good heart." Such relationships were better and safer, he observed, in cases where a disparity of age or circumstance precluded the development of love.[51]

At the same time, however, the American social and emotional culture of the past did not promote the development of platonic friendships between women and men, and such friendships were certainly not typical middle-class female experiences before 1900. The same ideology that fostered female friendship in eighteenth-century society mitigated against cross-sex friendship. Equating women with heart and men with reason left little common ground upon which they could meet as friends. Nineteenth-century prescriptive images of morally superior "true women," along with the patriarchal patterns of urban middle-class society, had a similar impact. Despite social and cultural constraints, however, a range of evidence indicates that some women before 1900 did experience friendships with men outside their own families.

One of the earliest examples of cross-sex friendship appears in the journal of Esther Edwards Burr, whose husband maintained a friendship with his wife's close confidante, Sarah Prince. Although most eighteenth-century men might have agreed with the individual who told Esther Burr that women were incapable of "anything so cool and rational as friendship," Aaron Burr apparently saw things differently. On several occasions when his professional duties required him to travel to Boston, he visited Sarah Prince, and he wrote to her independently to offer advice about a potential husband.[52] Yet as highly educated offspring of elite colonial New England families, the Burrs cannot be regarded as representative of eighteenth-century people. Their experiences do not typify gender dynamics in the colonial period. Furthermore, the fact that Sarah Prince's friendship with Aaron Burr in no way mirrors the intensity of her exchanges with his wife highlights the priority of female friendship. But the relationship between Prince and Aaron Burr clearly indicates that ideological impediments to cross-sex friendship in early American society did not necessarily preclude its existence.

Although the dominant emotional culture and the ideology of domesticity presented formidable obstacles to female-male friendship, such relationships could also develop in the nineteenth century. Middle-class gender ideology relegated women and men to separate spheres and rigidly assigned their roles within those spheres, but these prescriptions did not always parallel actual experiences. Urban women emerged from their homes to participate in the public sphere in various ways throughout the century, and those in rural communities never experienced a rigidly segregated female setting, a "separate sphere." Instead, the requirements of farm work structured relationships between men and women, and joint social networks counteracted gender separation in labor patterns. Couples typically visited with kin and neighbors together. At least some women sought mutuality in cross-sex relationships, while the agricultural economy supported joint as opposed to separate modes of activity. In this setting, then, women and men mingled economically, socially, and emotionally. For example, men could be found at quilting parties, sewing circles, and ladies' aid society socials.

This evidence does not imply the existence of gender equality, however. Women remained legally and materially subordinate in rural farm families. They gained access to land only through male relatives. Their efforts to overcome gender-based barriers did not necessarily result in the establishment of close cross-sex friendships, most of which developed between kin. Neighbors and family members closely monitored the interactions of unrelated women and men, and any hint of romantic involvement made a friendship unacceptable. Hence strong, supportive, and self-disclosing relationships between brothers and sisters were more common in rural communities, but friendships between non-kin occasionally succeeded.[53]

Other nineteenth-century settings could be more conducive to cross-sex friendships. In the artistic and literary communities, such friendships grew out of mutual interests, often those of male mentors and their female protégées. Thus Edgar Degas's interest in the work of Mary Cassatt, who studied and painted in Paris after the Civil War, launched a forty-year affiliation that endured until his death in 1917. The young American artist had great respect for her eminent French mentor. Degas often visited her studio to look at her work and make suggestions; at least once, as Cassatt recalled, he actually "worked on the background" of one of her paintings. "Most women paint as though they were trimming hats," he told her. "Not you." They also shared social occasions, and Degas bought her a puppy.[54]

However, periodic quarrels and estrangements disrupted their relationship. Occasionally Degas abruptly withdrew his attention and support, and Cassatt felt betrayed, but she accepted the parameters of their relationship. "I am independent," she told her close friend, Louisine Havemeyer; "I can live alone and I love to work." Hence the friendship endured, and Cassatt remained a devoted friend until Degas died during the dark days of World War I. "We buried him on Saturday, a beautiful sunshine, a little crowd of friends and admirers, all very quiet and peaceful in the midst of this dreadful upheaval of which he was barely conscious," she reported to Havemeyer.[55]

The Cassatt-Degas friendship incorporated an element of flirtation, but apparently it never involved a love affair. Moreover, Mary Cassatt did not see herself as dependent upon or subordinate to Edgar Degas. This friendship belies the facile, culturally constructed supposition of both nineteenth-century observers and later researchers who have assumed that women in such relationships were or are probably in love with their male mentors/colleagues and/or subordinate to them. As the relationship between Cassatt and Degas suggests, such an assumption more accurately mirrors the power dynamics and hierarchical ideology of patriarchal society than the nuanced complexity of actual historical experiences of friendship.

The mechanics of an earlier nineteenth-century relationship, that of Margaret Fuller and Ralph Waldo Emerson, further illustrate this issue. After their initial meeting in 1836, Fuller and Emerson were close friends for seven years, until she left New England. They continued to correspond until her untimely death in 1850, although the intensity of the friendship diminished. Emerson seems to have perceived himself as Fuller's mentor, but their correspondence suggests that they interacted as intellectual equals. His use of emotional language and exaggerated metaphors offers some support for the hypothesis that Fuller tried to entice him into a sexual relation or that they were both romantically attracted.[56] Yet both used similar language in letters to other friends, and they shared their extended dialogue on friendship with others as well, suggesting that they did not consider their comments on this topic private or personal.

Despite his use of flowery, extravagant language, it was difficult for Emerson to express his emotions openly. He found intimacy uncomfortable, while Fuller sought closeness in relationships and conversations. These differences, which clearly mirror the cultural dichotomy between "heart" and "reason," created a barrier in their communication: "There is a difference in our constitution. We use a different rhetoric. It seems as if we had been born and bred in different nations. You say you understand me wholly. You cannot communicate yourself to me. I hear the words sometimes but remain a stranger to your state of mind," Emerson complained, in terms that seem to anticipate similar late twentieth-century concerns.[57] Nevertheless, their relationship continued.

Emerson's response to Fuller's death capsulizes the friendship's significance for him: "In her I have lost my audience," he declared succinctly.[58] In one sense, this statement implies that he valued Fuller primarily as an audience for his ideas and insights rather than as an intellectual peer or a close friend. At another level, however, it alludes to the depth and breadth of communication intrinsic to strong and devoted friendship. Virginia Woolf made a strikingly similar remark nearly a century later, commenting that after her friend Katherine Mansfield died, there was no one left to write for.[59] Despite the difference in their genders, she and Emerson used almost identical metaphors to articulate their profound sense of loss in response to the deaths of friends who played central roles in their lives. Moreover, conflict was integral to both of these relationships.[60] Ironically, after Emerson meticulously collected Fuller's writings following her death, he and some of their mutual friends engaged in a destructive editing process that distorted her work. Furthermore, while he had praised her prose during her lifetime, he later denigrated both it and her personal appearance. This behavior suggests that, at least for Emerson, the bonds between them never completely overcame the barrier created by Fuller's "different rhetoric."[61]

Fuller and Emerson appear to have related to one another primarily as peers, but the friendships of other nineteenth-century literary women and men reflect more distinctly defined mentor-protégée roles. Although Frances Sargent Osgood was already an established poet when she met Edgar Allan Poe in 1845, he functioned as a mentor for her. The gossip of their contemporaries and the content of various poems they wrote intimated that the friendship also involved romance, but Osgood was married and tried to deflect the rumors about their relationship. Similar speculation circulated when Fanny Fern and Walt Whitman established a brief friendship in 1856, but no data support the idea that Fern, the mentor in this case, was in love with the unemployed poet she had befriended.

Nor does any historical evidence suggest that the fifty-year relationship between Lucy Larcom—the Lowell "mill girl" who became a teacher, editor, poet, and essayist—and her mentor, John Greenleaf Whittier, involved a romantic element.[62]

From the colonial period to the late nineteenth century, the friendships of some American women extended beyond the bonds of womanhood to encompass relationships with male friends, but cross-sex friendship represented neither a typical nor a frequent experience. It did not involve the sort of nurturance and mutuality that characterized relationships between female friends; nor did it play the same central role in women's lives. Social and cultural expectations discouraged the development of cross-sex friendships, and the potential for sexual involvement introduced further complications. At the same time, shared experiences in the domestic realm and in an expanding female world fostered gender consciousness and female community. As women's sphere extended progressively to encompass church-related activities, educational institutions, and voluntary charitable and humanitarian associations, various affiliations beyond the home and family provided increasing opportunities for the establishment of friendships with female peers.

In the last quarter of the nineteenth century, additional changes further altered what one scholar has termed "the social geography of gender" as middle-class women began to participate in new kinds of work, extended educational experiences, and a rapidly proliferating club movement.[63] These developments were part of a set of broader social and cultural transformations that would eventually have a significant impact on women's lives and alter some aspects of their friendships. But on the eve of the twentieth century, middle-class American women continued to cherish and preserve their connections with female friends. They consciously recognized the importance of those bonds in their own lives, and in the context of an enduring Victorian emotional climate, they articulated that recognition, along with their warm and affectionate regard for one another.

2

"The Other's Facsimile"

Young Women's Friendships, 1900–1920

As Mary Pratt Sears celebrated her twentieth birthday on August 21, 1884, she reminisced poignantly about a close friend who had died several years earlier. "In forty minutes I shall really be twenty! It will be my fourth number that Fanny never had, but as I grow older, she seems to grow older too," Mary wrote to her cousin. "I remember her writing to me on my fifteenth birthday about its being the first birthday we had ever had apart, and now there have been four. Do you suppose she has thought about it at all today?"[1] These sentimental thoughts suggest that, like their predecessors, adolescents and women in early adulthood at the turn of the century continued to care deeply about their relationships with one another. Mary Pratt Sears, whose own health was delicate, also lost two other young contemporaries, and she remembered each as an important part of her life. She was not atypical in this respect.

Although the United States experienced a range of social and cultural changes that affected women's lives as modern America came of age in the late nineteenth century and the decades preceding 1920, young women's friendships resembled the characteristic Victorian model. Occasional suggestions of a transition in the nature of friendship are discernible, but adolescents and college students continued to seek and prize close female friends. Moreover, the strong bonds of friendship formed in college remained important to young women and could ease their transition into adult life.

The persistence of female friendships characterized by intense affection (sometimes expressed physically), mutual support, and interdependence reflects the endurance of Victorian emotional culture, with its emphasis on love and self-disclosure. Victorian emotionology remained dominant in American society throughout the nineteenth century and in the early decades of the twentieth, although some discussions in the prescriptive literature hinted at changing views. The volume of advice literature devoted to emotional standards declined between 1900 and 1920, which may reflect the continuing relevance of mainstream Victorian views. However, the treatment of some specific emotions suggested revisionism and foreshadowed new themes that would reshape the dominant emotional culture after 1920.[2]

In the decades prior to the emergence of a new emotionology, popular periodicals addressed both the general topic of friendship and the specific subject of women's relationships with one another from a variety of perspectives. This literature articulated a blend of traditional and more recent views. Some discussions clearly reflect earlier influences, such as the Western cultural emphasis on the value of friendship, the valorization of male friendship, and the contrasting nineteenth-century image of the unique character of female friendship. Other commentary suggests the impact of structural changes and the development of new attitudes about friendship in the context of early twentieth-century American society. Thus, even though Victorian emotionology remained dominant at the turn of the century and beyond, the ideology of friendship took on a slightly new tone.

General discussions of the topic often defined friendship in male terms and incorporated a perception of its decreasing importance in American society. In this vein, one author lamented that "men have innumerable acquaintances, but few friends." Another decried the death of the "art of friendship" and the rise of mediocre, utilitarian relationships: "We live, alas, in the suburbs of each other's hearts." Interestingly, this commentator noted that women as well as men have succumbed to "acquaintanceship as opposed to friendship." Probably in response to perceptions of this sort, readers were reminded that new friendships could bring vitality, meaning, harmony, and joy to their lives, and they were urged to expand their circles of friends. One writer who mourned the decline of close friendships between men in modern society complained testily that women "have pushed themselves or been pushed into place as [men's] companions." In a review of recently published books on the topic, another described friendship as "a necessity to normal souls" and asserted that no one can have too many friends. Although it was acknowledged that impulsive anger could damage or destroy a friendship, readers were assured that relationships can be rebuilt if participants recognize their value, and that friendship can survive absence and even death.[3]

Literature that centered specifically on women's relationships often portrayed their capabilities and performance as friends in positive terms, reflecting earlier distinctively Victorian images of female friendship. In 1900, an article in *Harper's Bazaar* declared that women's friendships "are among the most elevating, stimulating and satisfying experiences of their lives." Citing several examples of such relationships, the female author asserted that close friends should share at least some similar "pursuits and aims" and that their interactions should be characterized by equality as opposed to distrust, envy, and jealousy. In tones reminiscent of typical nineteenth-century emotional prescriptions, she concluded, "Friendship is fed from an inexhaustible source, and they who belong to one another here may well hope to continue the intercourse of love and loyalty beyond the stars."

Other writers held similar views. Stressing the vast benefits of friendship as an educational, broadening, ennobling, and satisfying experience, one stated dramatically, "We live for our friends, and at bottom for no other reason." A particularly interesting article reported the conclusions reached by a male author with the help of "two wise, kindly, and gracious ladies" whom he consulted. None of the three could think of more than one or two examples of "the best and highest kind of friendship" between two men or between a man and a woman who were not in love or married. Hence they agreed that "in the emotional region, many women, but very few men, can form the highest kind of tie," that is, true friendship; they decided that marriage satisfies male emotional needs.[4]

Various negative images of women's relationships with one another balance the positive images conveyed in late nineteenth-and early twentieth-century periodicals. An article that characterized friendship as one of the "supreme privileges of existence" also labeled friendships between women as neither "perfect" nor as "apt" as those between men. Indeed, the author maintained, female friendship "has often been proved a danger and a delusion" because it can involve "fatal extremes of self-abnegation." Another writer declared flatly that "the sisterhood of women is inconceivable." Women cannot cooperate with one another, this author stated, because they remain unfinished people until they marry; attractive women are particularly antagonistic and "naturally treacherous to one another." However, after middle age, a woman begins to care more about female friends: "She has survived [men] and returned to her own." One author asserted that the traits women admire in one another are "the very ones which most women largely lack and which they most admire in men." Thus he concluded that friendship "in its very highest sense" cannot exist between two women.

Female friendships were indicted on other grounds as well. One critic questioned the worth of such relationships on the grounds that a woman receives the most important part of her education, her knowledge of "womanly arts," not from "girlfriends" but from her grandmother. Another deplored the sort of "groundless intimacy" between "girls" that leads to silliness and laxity and interferes with important relationships; this writer identified only three friendships in a woman's life as significant—those with a mother, a husband, and a daughter. In contrast to commentators who firmly discounted the existence and/or value of real friendships between women, a more moderate individual observed that although classical philosophers agreed that women are temperamentally incapable of friendship, he was not sure one way or the other.[5]

The prescriptive literature addressed practical issues as well as abstract and evaluative conceptions of female friendship. References to letters from readers suggest that concerns about making and keeping friends were widespread in the culture of the period. Individuals who wanted to make friends were advised to be open-minded, interested in other people, forgiving, and inspiring. One writer stressed the need to avoid "self-consciousness," apparently construed as an undue emphasis on personal appearance; she maintained that "in 9 cases out of 10," women noted historically for their ability to develop friendships have been "plain, if not ugly." Young working women were cautioned to choose new friends carefully and to learn something about fellow workers before accepting invitations from them, because "bad" girls could easily misguide them. Parents were told not to worry about intense friendships between adolescents, since such relationships diminish naturally as young women mature; furthermore, "a girlish friendship is certainly more desirable than a premature love affair." Indeed, even "passionate and romantic friendship between a young girl and a woman some years older than herself" could be beneficial if the older woman "has a fine character." If not, however, parental intervention was advised to be appropriate.[6]

A 1901 article by a Smith faculty member suggested that college friendships could be as significant for young women as they were for young men. Although relationships between college students cannot all resemble that of the proverbial David and Jonathan, the author argued, high forms of friendship are possible in college. "Contact with art and thought" can teach young women "that the highest loyalty is dissociated from jealousy." College also can provide a respite from the constant wait for "*the* man," the author counseled, and students can find comfort in belonging to the college "crowd." Here again, nineteenth-century echoes resonate: "But whatever the form or circumstance, in whatever apparel they come, friends are messengers of the mighty gods, and whoever is without one may indeed 'quit the stage.'"[7]

In another example, an ode to the noble ideals of friendship, the author described her disappointment that a childhood friend did not share her passionate commitment to their relationship in adulthood, and expressed her realization that this relationship had not reached the Emersonian ideal of unselfish dedication to fostering one another's development. Concluding that mature people can make friendship a less "personal," "higher and lovelier thing," this writer urged readers to keep their ideals of friendship high. Another personal analysis of female friendship recounted the author's recognition that "any friendship which means happiness only for the two involved in it must be a mistake." To be meaningful, a relationship must incorporate "unselfishness, consideration, and the desire to be of service." While boys learn friendship "naturally," girls need to be instructed against "giving all their love and confidence to any friend before being persuaded of her worth." If women understand that "the gift of a friend demands a gift in return to the world," she concluded, the bonds between them "may be among the greatest blessings of life."[8]

As some of the preceding sources show, late nineteenth- and early twentieth-century periodical literature clearly reflects the influence of Victorian emotional culture as it pertained to women's relationships with one another in particular. Thus observations concerning women's special abilities as friends, the significance of college friendships, and the value of close relationships between young women as a substitute for premature heterosexual involvements recall nineteenth-century views and attitudes. Similarly, both implicit and explicit allusions to gender differences in the context of friendships mirror earlier ideas and socialization practices.

However, other images of female friendship—and of friendship more generally—present a more complicated picture. Negative evaluations of women's capacities as friends suggest continuities with the traditional Western cultural valorization of male friendship. At the same time, such attitudes differ significantly from nineteenth-century ideas about the beauty and perfection of close relationships between women. References to readers' anxieties and questions suggest that friendship may have become more of an issue for young women than it had been for their eighteenth- and nineteenth-century predecessors, such as Esther Burr and Sarah Prince or Lucy Stone and Antoinette Brown Blackwell, who could take for granted the bonds of womanhood. These references, as well as the discussions of the declining importance of male friendship and friendship in general, reflect aspects of mature industrial society, particularly the disruption of the domestic sphere and a growing emphasis on impersonality.

Other clear evidence of change in the ideology of friendship can be seen in discussions about the necessity for married couples to develop friendships, views of marriage as the highest form of friendship, and a distinctly new link between impersonality and friendship. Some contemporary readers probably found one writer's praise for a close friend's impartiality and restraint surprising: "My best friend is so because she is impersonal. She accepts me as I am and suggests neither changes nor improvements." To earlier middle-class American women, the notion that one's best friend should not give advice would have been virtually incomprehensible.[9]

Like the contemporary periodical literature, the tenor of friendships between adolescent and young adult women during the period 1900–1920 reflects the continuing influence of Victorian emotionology, along with the impact of several other social and cultural factors. Educational settings continued to provide opportunities for the formation of female friendships. Secondary and junior-high schools enrolled increasing numbers of young people, particularly girls, during the first decades of the twentieth century. These institutions, along with more traditional boarding schools, fostered close relationships. While in the past young women often spent only a year or two in female academies or seminaries, a growing number now completed four years of secondary education, resulting in prolonged and concentrated school associations that invested adolescent friendships with a quality of intensity reminiscent of earlier relationships.

Ida Sophia Scudder, for example, suffered over her perception that other girls at boarding school were "cool" to her and lamented the loss of "my precious Baby," a friend who withdrew from school because her mother was ill. "The day has of course been lonely as they all are now and I long more than ever to have someone love me," she observed plaintively after her friend's departure. "Oh, that I could find a new true friend!"[10] Letters from "Baby" indicate that their relationship survived both the latter's absence and Ida Scudder's departure for India, where her parents were missionaries. Reminiscent of the tone of earlier nineteenth-century interchanges, these letters gush with extravagantly affectionate language and incorporate various explicit references to apparently physical expressions of love, as in a wish that "if we could be together to night [*sic*] we would 'Spoon' and no mistake and for once Snookie you wouldn't be very far behind in the line of that blissful occupation yourself. For if you wouldnt [*sic*] spoon I would."[11] Correspondence from other friends also reflects a romantic tone. One young woman especially regretted Ida's departure for India because "you were one of the first girls whom I knew and loved here in the Seminary." Another, apparently not even a really close friend, found herself "nearly heartbroken." "I never knew I loved you so before and now I can think of nothing else," she wrote to Ida.[12] As in the case of earlier nineteenth-century friendships, it is impossible to ascertain the extent to which relationships like these incorporated actual physical closeness in addition to affectionate language.

While adolescent friendships typically involved expressions of love, a highly acceptable emotion in Victorian culture, they also encompassed less positive feelings such as insecurity and envy. Young women often worried about being excluded by friends. In a telling reference to an emotion evaluated by the contemporary culture as both negative and characteristically female, one individual wrote to two peers traveling together in Europe, "I AM NOT jealous that you're together." However, she readily admitted to the fear that "you like each other better and that I'm left-out." Similarly, Ida Scudder resented the intrusive presence of her roommate's close friend: "I am so provoked at myself but Anna Lee is in here so much to see Mittie and they spoon and fuss so that I am jealous," she confided to her diary.[13]

The intricacies of friendship could be very troubling for young women in the throes of adolescence. Marion Taylor agonized over several crushes on female teachers and worried about her propensity to quarrel with other girls. She belonged to a secret club, and then, with one other club member, formed a *"very* secret club . . . for the purpose of confidential confidings." Marion wondered if she and her confidante had trouble with their relationship because they were too much alike: "Half the time Ruth and I get along just grand, and are certain we're made for each other and the rest of the time we're stiff and . . . afraid we'll be nice to each other," she observed. "It's a good thing we don't see each other any oftener than we do or we'd never get along at all. She's so sure of herself and determined and bossy."

When Ruth received a pin for scholastic achievement and won a spelling match, Marion found herself "jealous and sour and sulky."[14] Eventually a new friend replaced Ruth. "I go around with Henrietta mostly now. . . . Henrietta is the congenial girl I've longed for," Marion wrote. "She is a kindred spirit. Henrietta is more congenial than Ruth and her disposition is far superior. . . . Oh you can't understand how I enjoy her, diary!"[15] Despite frequent disagreements, this introspective adolescent valued friendship highly and cared passionately about having a "chum."

While adolescent friendships might be fraught with difficulty, they could also serve as an important source of support for young women. The ability to confide in a close friend made it possible for one individual to cope with her father's serious illness. Despite her mother's desire not to share the family's problems with other people, she felt that she had to "unburden" herself to someone. "You know that feeling of a weight being lifted especially when someone as near and dear as you is made the participator of your trials and pleasures," she wrote to her friend Maida Herman. "It is awful to see Dad so weak and to know how much he suffers and he is so patient, so uncomplaining." Another friend of Maida's shared her feelings about a difficult situation of a different sort. The specifics of the experience are not clear from her letter, but the memory of a distasteful episode with a male acquaintance troubled this young woman. "Such an awful, sensuous creature. I *can't* even talk about him now without all my primal instincts rising up and fighting inside me," she confessed.[16]

Young women cared deeply about their friends' judgments and wanted to be reassured about their good opinions. The friend who turned to Maida Herman for support when her father was ill wondered anxiously if Maida found her spoiled: "Answer immediately as I want to know your opinion. I don't think I am a society girl in the least. If you do tell me on what you base your decision. Write at once—I need it," she demanded.[17] Another friend expressed similar concerns. "I promise you Maida, I am not the shallow experienced girl you think me," she wrote from boarding school. "I am beginning to realize that there are other things in life than mere frivolities. You were right when you said I am not a 'thinking girl' but I am trying to be."[18]

Not all adolescents engaged in this sort of soul-searching in their relationships with friends. Those who attended coeducational high schools (as opposed to single-sex boarding schools) began to display a new tendency that would increase in the decades following 1920. As one young woman explained it, their discussions focused on boys "endlessly, chiefly on the great problem of whether or not we should allow them to take our arm when they took us home."[19] While these young women continued to consult and confide in each other about important issues, then, the nature of those issues was starting to change.

Like Marion Taylor, some young women experienced conflict with friends and developed transitory affiliations. For others, friendships formed in adolescence endured as lasting and valued relationships. Rachel McClelland received numerous letters from her Dobbs School classmates and kept in touch with these friends in later years. Early letters suggest that affectionate relationships and "crushes" formed an integral part of her school world, as they did for Ida Scudder. Nancy Marshall wondered why Rachel didn't "adore" a particular young woman at Dobbs as she did. "Sarah [Rachel's sister] says you haven't a sign of a crush and just won't get one," she commented. Another school friend described the size of the bunches of violets "that some of the girls give to their crushes; the violet part is easily the size of a basket ball! What do you think of that?" she inquired.[20] Subsequent correspondence reflects a transition in Rachel McClelland's friendships to a more social, heterosexual orientation, as suggested by descriptions of male callers, parties, dinners, and rumored engagements.[21] Nevertheless, her relationships with women friends continued. Years later, one friend commented on the endurance of adolescent friendships as she apologized for her negligence as a correspondent: "Please try to continue to think of me as a real friend, for you know as I grow older I realize more and more that school friends and friends of early girlhood are the ones that count most in the long run."[22] As an adult, Rachel McClelland valued these enduring relationships, too, often expressing her affection for friends of long standing through gestures that resembled those of earlier nineteenth-century women, such as handmade gifts or her own paintings. This generosity overwhelmed one recipient of a painting, who declared, "I was so touched I nearly cried. I don't know when I have been so pleased."[23]

The friendship of Josephine Peabody and Abbie Farwell Brown also displayed traditional overtones, although their correspondence contains no evidence of intensely romantic feelings. Josephine initiated what would become a thirty-year relationship when she invited Abbie to tea in 1891. "Don't stand on ceremony, please," she urged. "I can be as ceremonious as anyone, but what is the use of wasting time?" As their friendship developed, these young women exchanged valentines and gossiped about new hats and mutual acquaintances. Apologizing for her negligence as a correspondent at one point, Josephine explained that the news of another young woman's engagement "struck me dumb—and resulted in mental paralysis."[24] But this friendship was anchored by a more substantial component, also reminiscent of nineteenth-century women's activities—a mutual interest in writing.[25]

From the early days of their acquaintance, they read and critiqued each other's creative efforts. "Where are those poems?" Josephine asked a few months after they met. "Will you send me a rhyme now and then? Shall we be a Literary Association: Let us!" A note on the envelope that accompanied this query, apparently appended later, says succinctly: "Absolutely the Egg of the friendship." Subsequent exchanges support this characterization. Josephine described one of Abbie's sonnets as "quite out of the beaten track of fancy and there is a certain delicate little fragrance about it." When she discovered that *New England Magazine* had published one of her poems and one by Abbie in the same issue, she was delighted: "Great mirth shook me this evening. . . . If you get more money than I do, you must go halves: I won't stand it. What shall we buy?" she exclaimed. On another occasion Josephine was impressed by a story her friend had written. "It astonished me. . . . a stunning idea," she wrote.[26]

Growing opportunities for middle-class women to pursue higher education created extended opportunities for the development of close relationships. Like those of adolescents, turn-of-the-century college friendships, particularly among students at women's colleges, exhibited characteristics similar to the Victorian model. The phenomenon of "crushes" or "smashes," typically based on a younger woman's admiration for an older student and occasionally involving an older student and a faculty member, either with or without an erotic component, continued to be a common occurrence at Vassar and Smith, for example. Apparently students accepted such relationships as a part of the college experience.[27] At the same time, contemporary American attitudes toward such interactions began to reflect the influence of European research on homosexuality. Articles and prescriptive literature warned about the dangers of homosocial intimacy among middle-class adolescents and post-adolescents, presaging an impending transition to an emphasis on heterosexual relationships and a redefinition of intimate attachments between women as improper and unacceptable.[28]

Martha Vicinus has suggested that "smashes" or "raves" permitted young women to express their love and desire through symbolic acts rather than through actual physical closeness or even friendship in the typical sense. Thus distance deepened the pleasure of this phenomenon, as in the practice of sending flowers anonymously to the object of one's affection or making her bed secretly.[29] In 1918 Katherine Bement Davis, a social scientist, surveyed 2,200 women, most of whom had graduated from college around the turn of the century. Her data revealed that intense same-sex friendships were common in both coeducational and women's colleges. However, these relationships were more prevalent in the latter, where the intensity of living close together and the emphasis on dormitory life may have fostered stronger emotional bonds. The survey's respondents differentiated between emotionally close relationships and those with erotic components, whether or not those feelings were expressed, but they also reported experiencing both types. As in the case of earlier intimate friendships, then, it is inappropriate to categorize the relationships of these late nineteenth- and early twentieth-century college women in terms of contemporary constructions of homosexuality and heterosexuality.[30]

The experiences of Miriam Van Waters offer an interesting illustration of the complexity of this issue. Van Waters had two close female friends as an adolescent, one of whom she kept in touch with when she went to college. Although she had a heterosexual social life at the University of Oregon, she relied extensively on female friends. By her senior year, she had formed a very strong attachment to an individual named Rachel. When a letter from this young woman left Van Waters feeling "too full of emotion to talk about it," she sent it home for safekeeping. "There are certain kinds of people whose friendship is sweeter than life," she told her mother. Two years later, she still cared enough about Rachel to send her a box of wildflowers. Van Waters's romantic rhetoric distinguished this

affiliation from her other friendships at this time, including one with Elizabeth Woods, who would remain a lifelong friend. The fact that she
shared both Rachel's letter and her feelings about it with her mother reveals the innocence that could still accompany college women's crushes
and romantic friendships in the first decade of the twentieth century. And
it underlines the importance of interpreting such relationships within the
specific historical contexts in which they developed.[31]

Although strong bonds developed within the female communities at
women's colleges and coeducational institutions, social and economic differences could create friction in both settings. The Wellesley community
experienced a heated debate about the role of college societies in fostering snobbishness and cliques, and it was not unusual for individual students to be intolerant of other young women's backgrounds. For example, Jane Cary, who entered Wellesley in 1910, found it difficult to like
her first roommate. "My room mate is a Quakeress, and I can't go her
[sic]," she wrote to her mother. "I shouldn't say that, she's all right but
I'm not smitten, I get rather tired of 'Thank thee,' and 'thee' this and 'thy'
that, some people could use it without offense, but I think she's rather
proud of it. How-ever [sic] she's a good girl and I'll stick it out." Jane experienced feelings of insecurity and inferiority because she had to wait on
tables for two years to earn her board; she felt more comfortable later,
when she lived in a cooperative dorm where all of the students had jobs.[32]

Friction between the male and female segments of the student body at
coeducational colleges and universities was not unusual. The cultures of
some institutions relegated women to the status of second-class citizens.
Distant and hostile male attitudes could make female students feel uncomfortable, although this was not always the case. Moreover, college
communities did not accord the same importance to women's and men's
interests and activities. Lillian Moller's academic record qualified her for
Phi Beta Kappa membership at the University of California, Berkeley, in
1900, for example, but she was denied election on the grounds that while
a "girl" did not need this honor, it could make a real difference to a
"boy's" future.[33]

Various factors also divided women on both single-sex and coeducational campuses. A student could find herself excluded from activities on
the basis of religious, racial, or ethnic identity. Thus a 1910 Wellesley
graduate recalled that "no matter what their popularity or ability, Jew-
esses were never elected to high office either in class or general student organizations." The growth of sororities promoted similar exclusivity at

other institutions. At Berkeley these organizations discriminated against Jewish students, while African Americans were virtually excluded from campus life there. Religious and racial prejudice existed at the University of Chicago, too, and pronounced class divisions also separated wealthier, urban female students and less affluent young women from rural backgrounds. In an effort to combat this problem, national sororities were banned at Chicago, but the students organized secret clubs to replace them.[34]

Although such divisive factors contributed to an increasing complexity in the texture of female friendship, for many young women the establishment of close relationships with other students still represented a major benefit of higher education. Dorothy Mendenhall, who had spent her childhood primarily in the company of people older than she and had never had a close female friend before college, remembered that "perhaps at Smith, more than actual study, my contact with girls my own age and the making of a few close friends, were the most valuable part to me." She grew particularly fond of Margaret Long, "a unique person from the start of our acquaintance." Margaret had beautiful clothes but never wore them. She did little work and avoided social occasions. She "adored" Dorothy and would have lavished "all her worldly possessions . . . as well as her affection" on her friend, who described her as "one of the staunchest, most honorable women I have ever known."[35]

Despite initial feelings of inferiority due to her financial circumstances, Jane Cary also developed close, warm friendships with "the nicest bunch of girls." Jane even enjoyed having an upset stomach, she told her mother, because her friends "dusted my room, combed my hair, squeezed orange juice into a glass, made toast and have done everything under the sun." In turn she willingly nursed friends who felt ill and comforted those who suffered from homesickness. Jane was delighted when other young women admired her Christmas gifts and the pillow her mother made for her room, and she liked to invite friends for a "spread" when boxes of food arrived from home. On one occasion, her guests were particularly impressed by her hospitality; they had "never seen or heard of such a box; they haven't stopped talking about it yet," she reported happily. Reflecting on the value of her college experience many years later, she stressed that her Wellesley friends had "made life fuller, richer, and happier."[36]

In addition to nursing one another through minor physical ailments and gloomy moments and sharing homemade delicacies, college friends could provide important support in cases of lasting emotional distress.

One young woman, deeply troubled over her parents' impending divorce, found comfort in sharing her problems with friends at Smith. Initially reluctant to discuss family problems, she finally decided to tell three close friends why she had been ill and worried throughout the school year, even though she feared the news might change their feelings for her. She reported sadly that she had tried to "fix things up without having the disgrace of divorce on our heads, but I've given up hope," and she enumerated specific worries: How would her little brothers be affected by their parents' difficulties? Would her father would die of apoplexy, or her mother of grief? Should she have stayed home rather than spending a year at Smith? She lamented that she no longer had any confidence in marriage now that she realized that couples could live together for twenty-five years and then "blast" their lives and those of their children. This young woman was greatly relieved to learn that her friends did not reject her. She reread one friend's letters over and over and drew strength from the sympathy and understanding of all three, assuring them, "It's the greatest pleasure I have now[,] hearing from you girls."[37]

As female students at coeducational institutions expressed increasing interest in the opposite sex and challenged earlier, more conservative codes of behavior, references to male friends suggest that those who attended women's colleges also had some heterosexual social life. Nevertheless, female friendship remained an important focus for them. Students still attended all-female campus parties, where younger women asked upper-class peers to dance. According to Jane Cary, this meant that "we got the ones we wanted." Young men visited Jane at Wellesley, but apparently such visits did not necessarily constitute a significant event, nor were they regarded as essential. "Weeks go by when I don't even see a man," she observed nonchalantly in her junior year.[38]

When heterosexual relationships did become a major issue, college women confided in one another. One was glad to report to her friends that despite the presence of mistletoe, she had not been kissed at a party where "nearly every other girl was in the room." In a letter to her close friend, Maida Herman, this same young woman insisted that there was no reason she could not be friends with "Dr. Bernstein." "*I don't want you to worry* about my future for so far it has not gotten beyond *my* control," she advised. Another friend also complained about Maida's disapproval of her relationship with a young man. "The part that troubles me in your letter is that you seem to side with [my parents] and practically infer I should give up Lee," she protested. "I'm glad you wrote me though, only please explain your attitude. Has this cleared up things at all? I hope so."[39] These exchanges reflect the traditional closeness and sharing of confidences that characterized female friendship—eighteenth-century young women had discussed men and marriage, too. At the same time, however, an increased emphasis on these topics foreshadows the growing importance that would eventually be placed on heterosexual relationships and the accompanying potential for conflict between loyalty to female friends and other commitments.

Despite suggestions of new priorities to come, female friends remained very important to adolescent and college women at the turn of the century and beyond. Like previous generations of young women, they continued to express affection for one another and to articulate more general thoughts about friends and friendship. One individual described such feelings simply but eloquently:

Every time I see you and am with you I like you better and I love to be with you. You have some sterling qualities which few girls nowadays possess and I admire you for them. Please do not think that I am flattering you for that is not in my line. I just want you to know how much I have grown to like you and I hope that we will continue to be good friends and that our friendship will always strengthen. Lovingly Aimee[40]

Extravagant protestations of affection, such as "For heavens sake write me everyday or I shall die my chum. . . . O! Darling! I am dead for want of you. It is awful to miss someone so much," and "You know I love you better than any girl in this whole world except May," link late nineteenth- and early twentieth-century friendships with earlier interactions.[41] Less effusive, more introspective reflections also suggest a connection to traditional attitudes. Thus, for example, the statement "We are the others [sic] facsimile in fact a part of the other" resembles Aristotle's vision of a friend as "another self."[42] More casual observations also imply that young women invested the acquisition of friends with major significance and thought seriously about the process, as Jane Cary's appraisal of the process illustrates: "Isn't it queer—some of one's friends select one without any help; now Helen, I never would have thought of her for a friend, if she hadn't been so nice to me and done all of the making friends part."[43]

As young women entered adulthood and acquired new responsibilities, they often preserved and nurtured relationships established in adolescence or their college years. Abbie Farwell and Josephine Peabody maintained close communication despite extended journeys abroad, poor health, and other obligations that precluded regular visits. In response to Abbie's description of a European trip, Josephine replied, "The chills went down my own back, at the mention of chills down yours, when you saw the Irish coast." She also felt chills "down my romantic spine to breathe that actual breath of Stratford" when she found a flower from that city in another of Abbie's letters. Josephine wanted Abbie to approve of Lionel, her fiancé, and was relieved to hear her "amended opinion of mine Elect, for it would hurt me seriously to feel that you did not see him in a congenial light." She shared the particulars of her wedding plans with her friend, reporting traditional details about dressmakers, gowns, the ring (crafted by the groom himself), and the couple's gifts for one another, as well as the very untraditional promise by the minister to leave out "every vestige of . . . Obey-phrases for he heartily agrees that the thing is a barbaric remnant."[44]

Abbie and her mother were in Europe when the wedding took place, so Josephine sent some incense for them to light on the day of the marriage and asked that they say a prayer. Her friend's "exquisite message of flowers" pleased the happy (if exhausted) bride, who confided that her new husband was "the most inconceivably care-taking guardian who ever encumbered himself with a Cinderella to cherish every minute in the day"; she declared that both Abbie and her mother "must love him beforehand," although they would meet him soon.[45] Josephine's marriage did not impede this relationship; her letters now included regards from Lionel. Abbie served as godmother for the couple's first child and offered to help with the shopping when her friend was ill. The dialogue about writing remained important to both women, and even the exchange of valentines continued.[46]

Mutual intellectual interests also linked Annie Lyman Sears, the sister of Mary Pratt Sears, and Frances Rousmaniere. Annie never enrolled in a formal college program, but she attended lectures, occasionally took courses at Harvard, and tried to study independently while she taught kindergarten in Waltham, Massachusetts. She longed for opportunities to be around people who thought about intellectual subjects and hoped that Frances would visit frequently while she was pursuing doctoral studies. "Perhaps through your being in Cambridge," she wrote, "I shall get a little more of the University atmosphere." Annie was interested in her friend's work and relished the fact that their relationship enabled her to have "a taste of student Bohemia. . . . the life I suppose we both have dreamt of in the past." She advised Frances to devote three years to her thesis in order to avoid fatigue, and she commented that it would be fun to travel together "to Oxford or some other strange interesting seat of learning!" Many of Annie's letters discuss intellectual matters; she often sought Frances's opinion on academic and philosophical issues or asked her to explain a particular concept or idea. "Do you see any reason for separating knowledge and action as much as the Pragmatists do?" she inquired after reading *The Jungle*. When a Harvard professor whose seminar she attended invited her to read part of her term paper, she wondered if Frances would have declined, as she had, because she had heard that male students objected if "a woman and an outsider" took up an evening.[47]

Annie's letters reveal that she thought about more traditional female concerns as well as esoteric academic topics. Early in their relationship, she reflected on the importance of keeping in touch with friends. "While I agree with you and Emerson that often we must live on trust in regard to our friends," she commented, "yet experience seems to show me that if friends never meet or exchange a line for a long time, so they really know little about each other's daily life, they do inevitably in spite of themselves drift apart." Later, after a visit to Mount Holyoke, where Frances had acquired a teaching position, she wrote, "I am glad that I can picture your life so much better now, both at your classes, in your apartment and at your jolly little meals, as well as somewhat in the actual college life. Please remember me to your two friends. . . . don't get overtired for that spoils all."[48]

Annie clearly recognized that women's lives were changing and perceived the conflict between traditional and new experiences. On one occasion she inquired about Frances's aunts. "I feel so sorry for them," she wrote. "There seems to be unhappiness in store whether we belong to the old type or the new; and in spite of all the gains I can't help feeling that this world is not made for women. . . . That would hardly be the opinion of the modern society young girl, would it?" she asked.[49]

Like other young women, Annie was excited by the news of her friend's engagement. "You cannot think how much I wish I could see you, and know a little what this new life means to so dear a friend," she replied. "I want to hear from you what Dr. Dewing is like as you get to know him more and more." As the wedding date approached, she wondered if it would be hard for Frances to give up her academic life and thanked her for "the glimpses of semi-Bohemian college life" their friendship had provided. "You will know that I am thinking of you all these days . . . wishing all good wishes, praying that it may be truly the best life for you, as I believe that it will be," she said.[50]

As in the case of Josephine Peabody and Abbie Farwell Brown, this friendship survived the marriage of one participant. Annie's letters continued to address both typically female subjects and broader concerns. She appreciated the photographs Frances sent and hoped her gift of a tea set for the children had arrived safely. She shared news about her sisters, brothers, and cousins and discussed current events. In one letter she commented on the brief Christmas truce during the first year of World War I: "It seems such an irony to think of the German armies singing 'Silent Night' and then going on fighting." In another, she wondered if women would ever be viewed as persons in their own right. "That is what I care for, not the vote," she declared, "though it may help a little in social reforms perhaps."

It would not have been unusual for female friends in previous generations to discuss current events; even in the eighteenth century, Esther Burr described matters such as militia training and threats of Indian attack in her letters to Sarah Prince. But Annie Sears's comments about personhood and women's rights highlight the influence of new ideas and a new level of gender consciousness that would have bewildered Burr and Prince, as well as their nineteenth-century successors. This new frame of reference did not alter the importance of female friendship for Annie, however. Thus she was delighted to learn that Frances liked the book she had finally managed to write: "You could not say anything I should like better about my book," she assured her friend. And she continued to comment on the value of friends, noting, for example, "Friendship seems to me about the best thing this life gives us, and I should be sorry to neglect my friends or run the risk of getting separated from them."[51]

Rachel McClelland's correspondence offers similar evidence of the importance young adult women placed on their relationships with one another. Rachel's friends frequently expressed their appreciation of her thoughtful and supportive friendship. "There are some things and people that one is rather apt just from knowing them so well—to take for granted, but I am beginning to appreciate my 'blessings' (meaning the nice McClelland family)," one correspondent noted. "I may not be a good letter writer, but I am just as fond of you as if I were! Love, Esther."

This individual, the same one who commented about the enduring value of adolescent friendships, consistently apologized for her negligence as a correspondent while reiterating her regard for Rachel. She acknowledged the latter's frequent letters and postcards and thanked her for "letting me into your daily life the way I love" despite her own lack of response. "Deeply I appreciate it, and my stolid, selfish silence does not mean I am unmindful of your true comradship [*sic*]. . . . You know I never forget you and never shall." At the same time, she thanked Rachel for her Christmas gifts and described some "romantic additions" to her life, including a poet and "one old friend in a new guise." Her reluctance to write letters may simply reflect a personal idiosyncracy, but it also hints at the development of a new, casual style of behavior that contrasts distinctly with the diligence of nineteenth-century women as correspondents. Nevertheless, this friend provided empathy and affectionate support for Rachel at crucial moments, as when she confronted her father's serious illness: "You tell me your philosophy has failed you. . . . A person just has to have courage, that's all," she wrote. "I wish I could see you and talk to you, not that I imagine that you would be cheered by my presence, but you would know, at least, how much I sympathize with you."[52]

Rachel's friends sought each other's approval when they chose to marry. One young woman hoped that Rachel would approve of her fiancé "because he is so perfect and I simply adore him." "So please try to like him," she pleaded. Another wanted to share her happiness and regretted that she could not invite Rachel and her sister to the wedding, "for you are two of our oldest friends, and a friendship like that does count for so much," she wrote.[53] Later, these friends and others offered Rachel help and affection when her brief marriage foundered as a result of her husband's emotional illness.[54]

Like Rachel McClelland, other young adults maintained friendships formed in boarding school or college; these relationships survived and flourished. Alice Duryee, who pursued missionary work in China following her Smith graduation, rejoiced when her college friend Elizabeth McGrew received a graduate fellowship. She appreciated Elizabeth's letters and waited eagerly to receive them: "To say that your letters are a joy is putting it mildly, and I have just been rereading the long one from Muskoka with renewed pleasure. And the way you have written regardless of equal returns from this end deserves a crown of glory," she wrote. "From the recipient of the letters you have more thanks than can be written down for I never realized quite in the same way before what a joy friends are." Alice shared the news of her sister's engagement and her own happiness about the forthcoming marriage. In response to the news of Elizabeth's plans to marry, Alice replied, "Oh Betty I am so glad, so glad that the greatest happiness that I think a person can have has come into your life or rather it is only beginning. . . ." She wanted a photo of "Mr. Kimball" and suggested that the couple travel to the Far East for their honeymoon.[55]

Despite the geographical distance between them and their different lifestyles, Alice and Elizabeth kept in touch regularly and managed occasional visits. Alice was "exceedingly pleased" to learn of Elizabeth's impending motherhood. "I have planned already what I am going to bring your baby," she replied. "My dear, aren't we getting old, to think of me looking forward to the coming of your baby as calmly as if it were the entering of a new freshman class." She was equally delighted when Elizabeth's second child arrived and very proud to serve as his godmother.[56]

Alice continued to express her affection for Elizabeth and her family and her appreciation of their friendship in letters, giving no hint of the approaching tragedy that would end this relationship. In ill health, apparently due to overwork, Alice jumped overboard into the China Sea from a ship en route to the United States, where she was to be treated for "neurasthenia with increasing melancholy brought on by acute insomnia that she kept to herself until too late." According to one of her sisters, who wrote to thank Elizabeth "for loving my Alice" and to ask if she would accept some of the latter's possessions, the friendship had held a very important place in her life: "Your photograph with your children was the very last thing Alice took any pleasure in—the only Christmas gift she opened herself and it stood in her chiffonier till she left my home," she reported sadly.[57]

Dorothy Mendenhall also valued the friendship of Smith classmates as a young adult. As a medical student and then an intern in Baltimore, she lived with Margaret Long, the young woman she had admired so much in college. Although she had not known Rose Fairbank well at Smith, she grew very fond of her as well in Baltimore, where "she became a dear friend and we were closer than other girls because of our previous years in the same class at college."[58] As these comments indicate, the experience of attending the same college could forge strong links between young women and serve as the basis for the development of friendships after graduation.

Friends played a central role in the life of another Smith graduate, Azalia Emma Peet. Like many earlier American women, she and her friends shared a commitment to church-related activities. Azalia drew vital support from these friends when her mother died, but found it difficult to sort out her feelings about them and to cope with their feelings of jealousy, as well as her own. "The regulation of ones [*sic*] friendships do surely require much tact, much patience, a good deal of love," she observed. Her relationship with one friend, Patty, involved a special intensity: "In my heart of hearts," Azalia confided to her diary, "I fear I covet her love and *all* of it. . . . she has been a friend when I sorely needed friendship. And too she has intuitively denied me the physical part of friendship which in the past has been disastrous."[59] The dimensions of this relationship are difficult to ascertain. The diary reveals that the two young women "slept together" on several occasions and that Azalia "craved Patty's demonstrative love." It also records Azalia's dismay after her friend declined to accompany her to a party and then miraculously recovered from a severe headache when a young man and his "auto" arrived.

Azalia was disappointed because Patty did not share her religious zeal, but she was also strongly influenced by Patty's opinions of the missionary society meetings they attended together. "Patty was always my interest thermometer," she observed.[60] This diary blends clear evidence of continuity in the intensity and importance of female friendships with an indication of the impending transition to an explicit stress on heterosexual relationships. Furthermore, Azalia's enigmatic references to the physical dimension of her relationship with Patty provide an additional graphic illustration of the challenge of interpreting historical evidence concerning romantic friendships.

Anita Pollitzer and Georgia O'Keeffe, two talented, energetic young women who met in 1914 as students in the School of Practical Arts at Teachers College, Columbia University, experienced an intense friendship as kindred spirits, apparently without a physical dimension. When Georgia left New York to take a teaching job, the relationship became a fervent correspondence. They avidly discussed their teachers, peers, commitment to art, hopes and aspirations, and efforts to understand the meaning of life. For Georgia O'Keeffe, her friend's letters were "like drinks of fine cold spring water on a hot day." Driven by "nervous energy that makes people like you and I want and go after everything in the world," she relied on their correspondence for stability. "Anita—I feel all sick inside—as if I could dry up and blow away right now," she declared. "Write me quick." Similarly, Anita felt "keyed up" for an entire day after receiving a letter from her friend. "You write letters exactly like yourself, and I love them," she told her. She wondered whether Georgia enjoyed her letters as much as she relished Georgia's. The reply was a resounding yes: "I just want to tell you lots of things. . . . I haven't found anyone yet who likes to live like we do," Georgia assured her.[61]

They often discussed mutual acquaintances, both male and female, and analyzed their own relationship. Anita was very supportive when Georgia shared the details of her interactions with "a man I don't know what to do with." At one point, Georgia warned her friend not to "expect too much of me for your bubble is bound to burst if you do." Anita's response was equally direct: "I know what you are—I really don't expect anything else." Their shared artistic vision gave this friendship a special quality. Astounded by the impact of a series of drawings Georgia had sent her, Anita described her reaction vividly: "I tell you I felt them! . . . They've gotten past the personal stage into the big sort of emotions that are common to big people—but it's your version of it."

Anita remembered Georgia's remark that she would rather have Alfred Stieglitz's favorable opinion of her work than that of anyone else and proceeded to show the drawings to him. Recounting his positive reaction, Anita reminded her friend of that comment and told her, "It's come true." Georgia's response seems to have anticipated the profound impact that Anita's intervention would have on her life and career. "There seems to be nothing for me to say except thank you—very calmly and quietly. I could hardly believe my eyes when I read your letter this afternoon. . . . It makes me want to keep on," she wrote. "I am glad you showed the things to Stieglitz—but how on earth am I ever going to thank you or get even with you—"[62]

Anita's action on her friend's behalf culminated first in Stieglitz's professional mentorship of Georgia and eventually in his marriage to her in 1924. Although their friendship continued, its intensity and intimacy diminished. Hints of this change appear in Georgia's descriptions of her responses to letters from Stieglitz. In almost the same glowing terms she had used about her correspondence from Anita, she reported, "Stieglitz asked about you—I think I never had more wonderful letters than he has been writing me—and isnt [sic] it funny that I have you to thank . . . his letters Anita—they have been like fine cold water when you are terribly thirsty[.] I would like you to read them but some way or other—they seem to be just mine."

Georgia expressed similar feelings on another occasion: "Im [sic] enjoying his letters so much—learning to know him the way I did you— Sometimes he gets so much of himself into them that I can hardly stand it." Anita was glad to hear that Stieglitz wrote to her friend, but she sensed a growing distance between herself and Georgia. They corresponded less frequently. Anita wrote that she wished she could view Georgia's work alone and then have an opportunity to talk to her so that they would "know each other again."[63] In this case, unlike in other examples from this era, the marriage of one woman decisively altered the relationship between female friends. This situation clearly distinguishes Pollitzer and O'Keeffe from earlier women for whom female friendship remained central despite the presence of husbands and families. Nevertheless, while the tone of their interactions changed, they kept in touch and continued to see one another occasionally. After Anita was married, Georgia's letters included greetings to her husband. And at a certain level, the connection between the two women remained deep and strong, though it had been modified.[64]

Like Anita Pollitzer, Helen Tufts provided crucial support, albeit of a different sort, for a close friend, Helena Born, who had fascinated her from the beginning of their acquaintance. Helena was an unconventional individual whose radical views and vegetarian eating habits marked her as "too much of an oddity" for Helen's parents to understand. The friendship blossomed nevertheless, and Helena was grudgingly received at the Tufts home. She introduced Helen to the work of Walt Whitman, and Helen taught her to ride "the wheel" [a bicycle]. As a twenty-third birthday gift, Helena made a flannel nightgown for her devoted friend. But her anarchist sentiments continued to cause problems. "Papa has boiled over about some of Helena's views; so Helena is not coming up home again for a while, and I am not on speaking terms with him," Helen recorded angrily on October 6, 1897. Her parents eventually relented and had a "frank talk" with Helena, but Helen feared this represented simply "the patching up of a truce" as opposed to any real understanding on their part.[65]

A potentially serious crisis arose when Helena fell in love with William Bailie, a married man with six children. Not surprisingly, this liaison provoked serious disapproval on the part of their mutual acquaintances, but Helen supported her friend's choice. "I do not feel jealous," she wrote. "I am sure of Helena's love. I shall back them up, though I feel as though I were standing over a mine, people are so easily horrified." Interestingly, although Helen's parents certainly did not condone the couple's plan to live together, her mother considered them "responsible to themselves," and her father "sympathize[d] with the love they have for each other."[66]

Three years later, when Helena became terminally ill, Helen provided vital support once more, caring for her friend and sustaining her anguished lover. Even Mrs. Tufts helped to nurse the frail young woman. After Helena's death, Helen notified Helena's father, dismantled her apartment, packed her possessions, and paid the doctor's bill. She also fulfilled her promise to Helena to look after William. Together they scattered Helena's ashes at Walden Pond and then read Whitman. They also finished the book that Helena had been writing, which was published on May 11, 1902—her birthday. In an interesting, almost Hollywood-like epilogue to this devoted friendship, Helen and William fell in love and lived together for several years. They were married after his wife had finally agreed to a divorce.[67] Thus in a sense, just as she had helped complete her friend's literary work, Helen also completed another unfinished part of Helena's life. Like Anita Pollitzer and Georgia O'Keeffe, Helen Tufts and Helena Born confronted very different problems from those typically encountered by their Victorian predecessors, but the importance of female friendship in their lives links the generations. And in a curious fashion, Helen's relationship with the man her close friend had loved represents a modern translation of a common traditional practice: the marriage of a man to his dead wife's sister.

These young women were not unique. Despite hints of change in the prescriptive literature and in the behavior of some young women, the experience of female friendship remained a pivotal force in adolescence and young adulthood. Even where specific circumstances and social and cultural trends presented distinct contrasts with a more traditional Victorian social milieu, female friendships continued to display patterns similar to those in earlier periods. The growing number of young, middle-class women who interacted as coworkers in offices and places of business— as opposed to educational, religious, or domestic settings—retained strong emotional ties with each other. Thus, for example, white-collar employees in Chicago often lived in boarding houses with childhood friends from their hometowns and enjoyed shared activities, such as dressing up in costumes for theme parties, including "Kid Parties" and "Old Maid" or "Spinster Parties." Although these women were independent, single, and salaried, their intimate friendships closely resembled nineteenth-century relationships.[68]

Why did young women's friendships at the turn of the century and in the early twentieth century continue to reflect the characteristic Victorian model? What accounts for the continuity between female adolescent and young adult relationships during this period of major transformation and those of earlier eras? A number of social and cultural factors converged to sustain the formation and maintenance of strong bonds between young women from the turn of the century to 1920. While they spent increasing amounts of time outside the domestic setting, they also had extended opportunities to enjoy the company of peers in educational settings that supported a sense of female community—high schools, women's colleges, and coeducational universities. Moreover, the traditional settings of church and school were supplemented by a new context for female interaction: the workplace. As both clerical jobs and sales positions in department stores were increasingly filled by young, single, middle-class women, these positions were redefined as women's work, in theory and in practice. For example, by 1900, women constituted over a third of all clerical employees, and twenty years later, they formed the majority.

The feminization of such occupations meant that they were conducive to the maintenance of a sense of female community. Thus old friendship patterns that had evolved in the private sphere could be transferred to new, feminized venues in the public sphere. Furthermore, for at least some young women, an increasingly sophisticated level of gender consciousness also served to foster the bonds of female friendship. Finally, at least three related reasons explain the continuity in the nature of women's relationships with one another. Victorian emotional standards were widely disseminated from early childhood on and found unqualified acceptance in mainstream, middle-class society. In addition, the emphasis on intensity in these standards gave power to this emotionology.

Nevertheless, occasional suggestions of a transition in the nature of women's friendships are discernible in both the prescriptive literature and some women's experiences. Intimations of ambivalent feelings about the physical demonstration of affection and other clues also herald the emergence of new expectations and priorities that would redefine the structure and meaning of female friendship in the period after 1920. This transition reflects the impact of a series of structural developments—major technological advances; the rise of larger, more formal, bureaucratic organizations; new arrangements in work and leisure; and increased impersonality—that accompanied the maturation of an urbanized, industrial American society. Birthrates declined significantly (particularly among the middle class), geographic and social mobility increased, and white-collar jobs proliferated. Traditional communities, defined geographically in terms of place much as they were in colonial America, gradually gave way to a new form of community defined more by experience and interaction. These trends elicited ambivalent responses as efforts to accommodate to change contrasted distinctly with an impulse to maintain earlier patterns. Thus in the early years of mature industrial society, American culture manifested a definite tension between tradition and innovation.[69]

A succession of dramatic transformations in women's lives that peaked around the turn of the century accompanied the broader structural, social, and cultural transformations of the late nineteenth century. The disruption of the equilibrium of nineteenth-century domesticity and family was accompanied by the beginning of the deconstruction of nineteenth-century women's culture, as traditional female authority in the domestic sphere started to erode in favor of outside experts on matters pertaining to the home. The novelty of the choices available to them significantly altered the expectations and aspirations of American girls and young women. For some, this landscape clearly provided viable alternatives to marriage and traditional motherhood, as the large number of single, white, middle-class American women at the turn of the century attests. Even the majority, who did not adopt unconventional lifestyles, began to embrace broader horizons and to display a growing sense of personal independence, as can be seen through fashion innovations such as shorter skirt lengths and flamboyant hat styles and through untraditional social behavior such as public cigarette smoking.[70]

Contemporary observers of the American social scene found this growing female independence distressing. Some critics feared that the family was breaking down and attributed the problems they observed to the negligence of the so-called new woman, whose selfish pursuit of higher education and a career prevented her from fulfilling her appropriate roles as wife and mother. Late nineteenth-century physicians decried what they perceived as the willful misdirection of limited female strength and energies from reproductive capacities to exhausting and unnecessary intellectual activity. Other commentators found the new woman vulgar and unfeminine.[71]

These cultural images exaggerated the characteristics of the new woman and her threat to the American family, but they also highlighted the development of a distinctly untraditional female mindset and an increase in instances of equally unconventional conduct. Certainly all middle-class young women did not reject domesticity in favor of financial independence and unconventional manners and morals. However, many college women did adopt a distinctly new sort of behavior—a definite tendency not to marry—based on the conscious choice of autonomous professional lives over the restraints of family life.[72] These alterations in female expectations and activities reflected a movement away from domesticity and tradition and toward a more public presence for women. Like all social transformations, this shift occurred gradually. By 1920, the "female world of love and ritual" no longer defined the lives of middle-class American women. Nor did its values define the friendship styles of young women.

3

"Boys in Particular"

Young Women's Friendships after 1920

When Yvonne Blue met Phoebe Jacobus in 1931, she liked her immediately, although Phoebe was neither as well dressed nor as "immaculate" as she might have been. The two young women discovered that they had much in common, and their friendship blossomed quickly. Both craved activity and excitement and feared that life after college would be dull and conventional. Yvonne valued the relationship particularly because she found that she could talk to Phoebe "as I have talked to no one else before in my life. . . . we discuss everything in general and boys in particular with entire and perfect frankness. It is a good thing to have an outlet."[1]

While the exchange of confidences between female friends certainly does not distinguish the post-1920 era from previous periods in the history of women's friendship experiences, Yvonne Blue's comments reflect a distinctly twentieth-century emphasis on "boys" as the most important topic of communication between young women. Her observations about other friends suggest a similarly untraditional, frankly pragmatic attitude that contrasts sharply with the romantic views expressed by earlier young women about their relationships with one another. "I go with Adele because she likes me and is jolly, with Maryellen because she gives me the adventure I crave, with Lucile because she is brainy, with Lillian because she understands me in some ways," Yvonne noted in her diary. At the same time, she observed nostalgically that only Val, a high-school friend, could provide "everything." "I think Grace I like next best," Yvonne continued. "But she lacks the spirit of wildness, the adventure and craziness of Val, and those I know that have that—like Maryellen—are really wild and unrefined and not nice."[2]

As these analytical, unemotional reflections suggest, the intensity of young women's friendships decreased and the emphasis of their interactions shifted during the decades following 1920. The convergence of several significant social and cultural influences produced a distinctly twentieth-century friendship model. Adolescents, college students, and young adults still wanted and needed female friends. But the combined impact of at least five factors—changing emotional standards, rising consumerism, a trend toward reliance on expertise, the pressure of the heterosexual imperative, and the stigmatization of homosexuality—resulted in a revised script that structured their relationships in new ways.

The expectations and priorities heralded in late Victorian prescriptive literature began to crystallize in the 1920s in the form of a new emotional culture that stressed more cautious emotional management. Although Victorian emotionology had maintained that certain negative emotions should be controlled, love was not among them. Intense expressions of love and affection—between mothers and their children, men and women, and same-sex friends (especially female)—had remained acceptable, and indeed had been encouraged. But the subsequent revision of emotional norms resulted in a post-1920 culture that stressed restraint in all emotional areas, including those that Victorian culture had defined as positive, such as familial love. This revision also encompassed a reduction of emphasis on gender difference in emotional socialization. While emotional standards from the 1850s on had clearly reflected the separation of male and female roles in their definition of gender-based emotional goals, now women as well as men were expected to manage their feelings.[3]

Transformations in individuals' actual emotional experiences are far less accessible to the historian than alterations in cultural norms and written emotional expression. Emotional experience changes slowly, and the infinite variety of individual human temperaments and predilections adds further complexity to the issue. However, compelling evidence indicates that the new emotional culture profoundly affected people's attitudes, beliefs, and behavior and influenced social institutions and conventions in important ways. For example, the genre of romantic love letters declined significantly. Partially a response to the accessibility of new means of communication, particularly the telephone, this development probably also reflected a perception of Victorian emotionally expressive language as inappropriate. The same trend toward emotional neutrality appears in correspondence between female friends.[4] The absence of extravagant expressions of affection between couples or friends does not necessarily mirror a major change in emotional experience, yet emotions historians increasingly discern potential meaning in silences. Thus the possibility of a connection between expression and experience cannot be discounted, particularly when the paucity of emotional display in a specific period contrasts distinctly with evidence from other periods, as it does here.

Cultural prescriptions concerning friendship changed significantly in the larger context of altered emotional standards. The prescriptive literature, which became less philosophical and more expertise-oriented generally, proffered fewer articles on friendship than in prior decades. Where periodical articles and advice books addressed friendship, they often linked the topic with new concerns about the importance of conforming to group norms and cultivating a pleasing personality. This focus mirrored a change of emphasis from "character" to "personality" as the ideal modal type in the post-1920 context of an emerging American culture of abundance. For example, parents of adolescents were instructed on the importance of peer acceptance and approval for the future well-being of their offspring.[5] While the importance of friendship might be acknowledged in the literature, the dangers of intense emotional attachment were also emphasized. Both the tone and quantity of this literature, then, reflected the broader cultural effort to replace emotional intensity with moderation and restraint.

Although the prescriptive literature devoted less attention to female friendship than it had in earlier periods, aspects of this theme still appeared in women's magazines. Some commentary reflected traditional attitudes. One author regretted the selfish absorption that caused her to neglect devoted friends who had tried to help her cope with her sister's death. Another extolled the virtues of childhood friendships, "almost invariably the deepest, the most abiding, and the most precious," and claimed that, with the exception of love between husband and wife and mother and child, nothing in life was more beautiful than friendship. She strongly disputed the idea that women lack the capacity for real friendship. Still another writer stressed the importance of devotion to friends and examined the pressures that threaten "the stout fabric of friendship."

A clearly unemotional, more analytical tone characterized other commentary. One article argued that women unconsciously dislike one another because they depend on men for economic survival; hence they regard other women as potential rivals for all that they desire. The author concluded that the few who can be friends either "are economically independent or they are, through idealism, sufficiently evolved to be free of rivalry."[6] Another article maintained that the impulse to share confidences with friends should be avoided on the grounds that revealing embarrassing secrets or giving advice can damage a relationship irreparably. A writer who lauded meaningful friendships that continue to grow insisted that those that provide "an emotional crutch" offer no benefit. In stark contrast to nineteenth-century images of lifelong friendship and enduring support, she contended that a relationship that serves as "a mutual Wailing Wall" should be discarded; when a friendship is "outgrown," it should be left behind. The author of an article on how to select friends combined traditional criteria with a pragmatic approach; she advised women to proceed slowly and carefully, choose age peers of good character from nice families, maintain high standards, and hold out for the best choice.[7]

Although vestiges of earlier views highlighting the importance of female friendship can be discerned in this material, the combined influence of new emotional standards and the twentieth-century emphases on expertise and heterosexuality is clear even in literature authored by women. Most discussions of friendship considered aspects of male-female interactions or of men's relationships with one another, not friendships between women. An anonymous, "happily married" female author maintained that few women want to associate only with other women, since men's richer experiences make them more interesting companions. Even nuns seek the company of God, she observed. Yet in order for women to view men as ideal companions, they must correct "the conviction that we are inferior to them." One article offered readers of *Good Housekeeping* five examples of model friendships, all male. Another advised new brides to downplay female friendship, ration the amount of time devoted to visits and phone conversations with a "best friend," and refrain from inviting her to every dinner party. "A happily married woman does not need [the] kind of exclusive friendship of adolescent 'best friends,'" the author admonished readers, "and neither, for that matter, does a happily grown-up woman who has not yet married."[8] The obvious contrast between this sort of commentary and the standards for female friendship espoused in Victorian society clearly underlines the changes imposed by the new emotional culture.

A distinctly new and undeniably instrumental approach to male friendship surfaced in various forms also. A series of articles in *Rotarian,* the Rotary Club's magazine, celebrated friendship: Topics included potential links between the organization's program of fellowship and brotherhood and the prevention of war, the utility of friendships as a means of job advancement, and rules for maintaining friendships in business. This series also incorporated more traditional ideas, such as the value of friends in times of adversity and the importance of continuing to cultivate new friends. Various other publications also instructed readers about male friendship. One article advised men to refer to St. Francis and his beliefs about brotherhood as a model. Another discussed the effects of friendships among political leaders.[9]

The post-1920 prescriptive literature suggests that the new emotional culture had major implications for the experience of friendship in general and for women's friendships in particular. A related emphasis on consumerism in the early twentieth century had a similar impact. In a world of increasing abundance, advertisements—often targeted toward women, who were becoming the primary consumers—incorporated emotional as opposed to utilitarian appeals. The inherently individualistic ethos that defines a consumer economy fostered attachments to goods, not other people. In a cultural climate that discouraged intensely emotional connections with their peers, young women, for whom dolls and other toys had become an emotional focus in childhood, might well be inclined to pursue similar attachments with objects as they moved into adolescence and beyond.

The heightened cultural emphasis on heterosexual relationships and a concomitant stigmatization of passionate same-sex attachments fostered by the dissemination and popularization of Freudian ideology also influenced friendship patterns. Young women absorbed Hollywood images of heterosexual love and read novels that promoted a similar conception of romantic attraction between the sexes. At the same time, they assimilated the increasingly negative connotations ascribed to female intimacy. The ideal of companionate marriage, in which love, sex, and friendship blended, implied that the emotional support and companionship that women (and men) had found previously with members of their own sex would be provided by their spouses. From the 1920s on, the amount of time women spent with men increased. They also attained greater freedom of emotional and sexual expression with men. In this context, close female ties began to appear old-fashioned, if not abnormal, to women themselves as well as to the wider society.[10]

An additional category of change specifically affected young women as the rise of a strong youth culture displaced adult influences in important ways. By 1930 over half of all American girls of high-school age were in secondary schools, and 10 percent of college-age women were enrolled in institutions of higher learning. Hence young women were spending more time with peers than had any prior generation. For many, this meant that peers played a more important role in the process of self-discovery and the development of self-esteem than either family or religion. At both the high-school and college levels, the lives of white, middle-class students were structured according to a system governed informally but rigorously by peer oversight and centered on heterosexual dating. The availability of a growing selection of commercial entertainments and the ability to drive facilitated the rise of dating and offered young people new freedom from adult supervision.[11]

On coeducational college campuses, fraternities and sororities formed the center of this peer social structure. By the 1930s, approximately 30 percent of college students belonged to these organizations. Although other groups of students, linked by shared interests, also functioned on campuses, fraternities and sororities formed the heart of campus peer culture and produced the campus queens and heroes. This culture stressed conformity, submerged individuals into the group, and downplayed commitments and interests that failed to serve group needs. College women often devoted large quantities of time and energy to the pursuit and enjoyment of dates and social life in accordance with these standards. Belonging to the "right" sorority facilitated encounters with appropriate young men; sorority "girls" were expected to date only fraternity men, sometimes only members of particular fraternities. Hence affiliation might be sought as much for prestige and conformity as for the opportunity to build friendships. The interactions of sorority "sisters" frequently consisted mainly of activities related to planning heterosexual encounters: arranging dates for one another; discussing hairstyles, cosmetics, clothing, and appropriate sexual conduct; and sharing the details of ensuing experiences. Although sororities were not present in women's colleges, in this setting as well, heterosexual conquests took precedence over female friendships. Sororities, dances, clubs, and clothes also consumed the energies of many middle-class high-school girls.[12]

*

The friendship experiences of young women in the post-1920 period, then, distinctly reflect the dominant social and cultural influences of the era. The pursuit of popularity consumed their energies in both high school and college. Adolescent friendships often focused extensively on discussions about "boys" and dates, while the necessity of conforming to peer group standards could determine how young women treated one another. Diaries and correspondence suggest that concerns about personal appearance and emerging sexuality captured much of the attention of girls in their teens in the context of the cultural pressure for heterosexual interactions. Yet friends still played a major role in young women's lives, and their relationships incorporated elements of traditional female friendship, particularly during the period before their own biological and social development corresponded to the demands of the heterosexual imperative. A complex equation of change and continuity characterized adolescent friendship styles, but the nuances of their relationships in the decades after 1920 increasingly mirrored the distinctive qualities of the new setting.

When Dorothy Smith was fifteen, she had no interest in boys: "If it weren't absolutely necessary to get married before getting children I wouldn't care a bit about getting a husband," she declared in 1919. She enjoyed the time she spent with other girls "when I see them," but she had no special friend upon whom she could rely, and this bothered her. "What I like is to have at least one girl who will run into [*sic*] see me of her own accord and not have to be invited," she confided to her diary. "I can't remember one single time when anyone has done that except when I'm sick and the worst part of it is that they think I'm having a fine time, continually and don't particularly need their companionship, that is why I'm so crazy for boarding school." This young woman particularly valued her relationship with a friend who was going on vacation, and she wrote a "train letter" for her: "I hope it won't be the last I see of Jean," she commented, "for she's a dear girl and I love her in spite of her great reserve and undemonstrativeness."[13]

Yvonne Blue, a precocious and imaginative individual who wrote stories and poems, recorded similar thoughts in the prolific diaries she kept from the age of eleven. Comprehensive, articulate accounts of her social life, opinions of other girls, and feelings about herself provide a detailed, intriguing picture of middle-class adolescence. Yvonne and her friends formed secret clubs, played imaginary games, shared books, hosted "luncheons," spent the night in one another's homes, and occasionally read parts of one another's diaries. Yvonne was especially fond of Bobbie, a friend who seems to have shared her vivid imagination and creative bent. Together they wrote descriptions of imaginary people, burned the products of their collaboration, and saved the ashes to scatter in the country some day in order to reveal "the secret of two girls' imagined dreamfolk and of their eternal youth and beauty." They planned to go to college and then to be "reporters together on some paper, till we get enough money to go to Europe and Asia." Along with another friend, they stalked a mysterious male classmate, who never spoke to either of them. On one particularly "wonderful" night, Yvonne stayed at Bobbie's house, and they made fried cheese sandwiches at 1:10 A.M. In the morning they did exercises with scarlet sashes tied around their waists, ate breakfast at a waffle shop, and then went to school. After spending Christmas Eve at Bobbie's, Yvonne commented happily, "Nothing in the whole world is more fun."[14]

Not all of Yvonne's friendships were as harmonious. Frequent negative comments about another friend document a typical love-hate relationship between two fussy early adolescents. Thekla was no fun; she was "very, very conceited." She bragged about her nonexistent ability to turn cartwheels, she hinted for an invitation to dinner, and she visited twice in one day and "went home mad both times." Furthermore, she was "pretty but awfully loud and boy-crazy." Yvonne was annoyed when Thekla gave her a photograph inscribed "Worlds of love to my best friend Yvonne, from Thekla." She summarily dismissed this notion: "I don't think I'm really her best friend. I hope not because Bobbie and Ginny are mine and always will be."[15]

Like Dorothy Smith, Yvonne first professed disinterest in the opposite sex, and she disliked it when adults talked to her about boys. Yet by the age of fifteen, like others in her generation, she had changed her mind on this subject. Along with a growing interest in young men, Yvonne and her friends developed profound concerns about personal appearance and weight as they moved through adolescence. (Yvonne also lost confidence in her literary abilities at this time.) "Our new passion is self-improvement," she reported to her diary after she and Bobbie had made a list of rules to guide them in this process. Hoping to lose twenty pounds during the summer before her senior year in high school, she dieted so rigorously that for a short time her eating patterns resembled those of a young woman suffering from anorexia. Yvonne was not alone in her concern about weight: Her friend Val complained about "going on fasts" that made her sick.[16]

This heightened self-consciousness about appearance reflects the cultural insistence on female slenderness as a gender-based requirement that linked a moral imperative with contemporary fashion standards. While dieting had become part of the American cultural landscape around the turn of the century, the prescriptive literature explicitly constructed obesity as a female issue in the decades after 1920 and placed responsibility for this problem squarely on women.[17] In the context of both this concern and the cultural stress on heterosexual social life, adolescent friendships could easily evolve into concerted mutual efforts, including diets, to ensure the ability to attract boyfriends.

Although elements of Yvonne's interactions with her friends mirrored specific contemporary developments, other aspects evoked earlier adolescent friendships. Her emotional response to the news that three of her close friends were going away for the summer had a distinctly nineteenth-century ring. "Val, Ginny, and Margaret Artman are going to Europe for sure, and I feel as if another nail has been put in my coffin," she declared melodramatically. "Margaret Artman has promised to write me long, long letters, and I really believe she will, for she has something a little like a crush on me . . . She thinks I write better poetry than Val or Ginny." Yvonne feared that she could not live up to this reputation, but soon found herself "deep in the composition of Margaret's first letter." When the recipient of that epistle pronounced it "the most perfect letter I have ever read," an astonished Yvonne did not know what to make of Margaret or of her sixteen-page answer.[18]

Like Yvonne Blue's experiences, those of Beth Twiggar incorporated elements of traditional and newer friendship patterns. Her diaries suggest that Beth had internalized the heterosexual imperative and that it complicated her friendships with other young women. At the same time, however, she cared about having female friends, sought their good opinions, and even admitted to developing "crushes." She enjoyed an especially close relationship with her friend Mavis. They smoked, gossiped "nonmaliciously," and discussed weighty matters like the "absurdity of marriage, the idiocy of certain conventions, the disgustingness of the ways and means of babies, our possibilities pro and con love affairs, and tommorrows [*sic*] lesson in Ancient history." Beth was pleased that Mavis's new bedroom would be "very cute" and "as private as mine." But in an obvious reflection of the influence of consumerism, she also pronounced herself "livid with jealousy" because her friend was going to have blue sheets.[19] However, this relationship involved more substantial issues than interior decoration. Beth felt that she was totally dependent on Mavis— "I am her slave"—and was hurt because the latter did not reciprocate her devotion with the same intensity. She suffered when Mavis was angry with her, lamenting that school and other activities "arnt [sic] going to be worth a kick in the pants if she's not there with me in spirit."[20]

In this case and in at least two others, Beth's friendships closely resembled those experienced by young women in previous generations. Like Yvonne Blue, she used the earlier term "crush" to refer to these relationships and described analogous behavior. Thus, when she found herself attracted to an individual, she stared at her, envied other girls who knew her "intimintly," and blushed in her presence. Yet unlike her predecessors, Beth felt uncomfortable about her feelings: "After all it is foolish for one girl to fall in love with another," she observed. "For thats [sic] what a crush *really* is!" Later she admired an older girl and was thrilled to hear that the girl had asked Mavis about her. Eventually she and Mavis began to "go around" with this person and one of her friends. But in a distinctly twentieth-century fashion, Beth wondered whether the older girls were just using them "for some boy-achieving purpose."[21]

This instance and others also highlight the degree to which the twentieth-century issue of "boys" could permeate adolescent female friendship. When a young man said something nice about one of Beth's friends, although she thought the compliment was deserved, she decided not to tell her "because she knows enough nice about herself now!" Beth wished she had a boyfriend to write about in her diary and deplored the fact that since "Herbert has defunct [sic]," she had no one. When she phoned a friend and discovered Herbert was visiting her, she was appalled: "Its [sic] an awful thing to discover a boy who took you to a dance and necked you as though he'd never seen a girl before is at another girl's house," she lamented. Though she blamed both her own shortcomings and her friend's "intrigue" for this disaster, she conceded that "it is a woman's right to take a man away from another girl if she can."

In the same vein, Beth remarked that another young woman would sacrifice a girlfriend instantly in favor of a man. She herself cancelled a date with Mavis in order to go out with a boy, and although she understood Mavis's angry reaction, she assumed that the latter would have done the same thing. Ironically, Beth was surprised to learn that her friend

Bertha regarded her as "a boycrazy [sic] flimsy, artless creature, without the slightest conception of that which is really beautiful or worthwhile"; nevertheless, she had always "thought of [Bertha] in exactly the same words."[22]

The preceding examples illustrate both change and continuity in the texture of adolescent friendships during the 1920s. Young women wanted their female friends to like them, but often that desire was directly linked to a more pressing need for male approval. They still experienced "crushes," but these did not preclude an interest in "boys." Furthermore, female friends might judge each other in terms of their success with the opposite sex.[23] Thus Beth Twiggar was devastated when a blind date from West Point never called or wrote to her again, but the worst part was deciding what to tell her friends. "I wonder—if I could lie. Say he came . . . Would I forfeit my chances of Heaven, such as are not dead already?" she conjectured. The response of friends also figured prominently in Beth's evaluation of a more successful heterosexual encounter: When she reported necking with a young man who was ten years older than she, "the girls were thrilled." Their reaction pleased her enormously: "I like having girl friends," she noted. "It helps a lot!"[24]

Edythe Weiner also acknowledged the pragmatic value of female friendship. As a high-school sophomore, she realized that friends could be useful in attracting the attention of the right boys: "If only I were in with a popular crowd of girls, it would help loads, I know," she confided to her diary. She recognized another link between friends and members of the opposite sex as well. "I seldom get a crush on a boy unless some other girl has a crush on him. Then I first begin to notice him, and find hidden beauty in him," she observed. These comments clearly distinguish Edythe from her counterparts in earlier generations, as does her response when a friend was chosen to be a cheerleader: "Without being inspired by jealousy," she remarked, "I can truthfully say that [Mary] was the *worst*, almost, of any of the candidates." Yet she responded with warm enthusiasm when she received another friend's photograph. "I'm crazy about her—she's adorable, and the picture is simply darling," she exclaimed.[25]

Helen Laprovitz's adolescent insecurity about her abilities and appearance was compounded by the fear that other girls didn't like her because she was Jewish. Thus at one point she told her diary, "After school talked with the girls. I can feel the curse of those Gentiles in my Jewish blood." Although she seldom experienced overt bigotry, Helen apparently felt a generalized sense of exclusion. Her closest friend was also Jewish, and they discussed the implications of this shared social identity at length, linking it to a definition of appropriate boys to pursue as well as to their own perceived status and popularity.[26] While Helen's friendship experiences were mediated by her perceptions of the impact of her Jewishness, her diary, like those of other young women in the 1920s, reflects a strong desire for female friends along with the requisite interest in young men.

Many letters and diaries suggest that similar friendship experiences typified female adolescence in the decades between 1920 and 1960. These sources document the power and influence of the peer culture and the importance of "girl friends" in that framework. They also illustrate the priority placed on heterosexual social life and its role in the structuring of young women's friendships. Thus, for instance, Jane Emmet often discussed her friends when she wrote to her parents from boarding school, commenting at length about which girls she liked.[27] Helen Snyder pasted pictures of her friends and listed their names in her junior-high-school memory book. Her diary documents a close friendship in high school. Frequent entries record the time she spent with Janet—"supper with Jan and remained all nite," "talking about everything—silly and otherwise," and "Jan and I downtown in typical small town Sat. nite manner." Occasionally Helen also noted her friend's activities, as in "Jan went to Pittsburgh."

Yet one evening in 1933, at the end of her senior year, she declared, "We're slowly coming to the parting of the ways. She's too different and too smart. Lonesome as hell." The following day she again predicted the demise of the relationship: "Yep—we're on the wane—I can see it." Most likely it was the unsettling prospect of graduating and moving on while her closest friend, who had another year in high school, continued to live the life they had shared in a small, western Pennsylvania town that seemed to threaten their friendship. Nevertheless, after a summer away from home, Helen continued to go "down to Jan's," and the relationship endured. Another diary entry also hints at the sort of angst that could disquiet a graduating senior as she contemplated leaving her high-school friends: "Talked a long while to B. today. She's quite nice. We could have been swell friends—maybe tho, it's much better as it was."[28]

Helen's references to informal gatherings, dances, and casual interactions describe the relatively unsophisticated heterosexual social life that typified a small-town high school. Like other young women, she thought male friends were important and regretted that she had no serious romantic interest in high school. "Wish I were nerts [i.e., nuts] about someone," she confided to her diary.[29] Adele Siegel, who was the same age as Helen Snyder, experienced a more sophisticated and social adolescence while growing up in the New York area. Adele wrote extensively about both male and female friends in her diaries during 1930 and 1931. She felt secure about her status with peers of both genders. At the age of fifteen, she made lists of boys she liked, boys who liked her, and what she liked about them.[30]

Adele Mongan also wrote about boys constantly. In 1945, after seeing *Wuthering Heights,* she articulated her vision of a romantic future:

I'd love to live as wildly and as fully as Cathie and Heathcliff did though not as full of hate. I worry often about whether *I can* ever love a man passionately as lovers do or must I be content with a soft half-love. . . . I just want to love someone completely, and I'm afraid that maybe I never will. I want to be wild, strong and fresh as the moors and I mean to become so and thus prepare myself for loving.[31]

While Adele dreamed of a great love, she sought the approval of female friends and valued their potential capacities to facilitate heterosexual interactions. Adele was distressed when her friends misunderstood her attempts to be funny; although her mother had warned her about this behavior, she had refused to listen until she found out that her peers reacted negatively. Then she made a concerted effort "to act nicely," and her mother noticed immediately, which also bothered her. "It goes to show how horribly I must have been acting lately that just being fairly decent makes such an impression," she lamented.[32]

Adele and her friends all read *Seventeen Magazine:* "I hardly know any girl who does not get it," she reported. Like Beth Twiggar and her friends, Adele's crowd smoked, and they worried about how to conceal this activity from their parents. When one friend's mother found a package of cigarettes in her daughter's pocket and wanted her "to promise never to smoke again till she's 18 or 21 she was too mad to decide which," Adele "made a hiding place in last years [sic] diary by cutting out the centers of the pages" and left her cigarettes there in order to avoid a similar fate.

Adele's conversations with friends covered a range of weighty matters. In an exchange concerning marriage and family life, the other girls were "agin it," but Adele disagreed. "They think the beginning of having a baby (martial [sic] relations I guess you call it) is disgusting but I don't know," she observed. A friend's revelation distressed Adele—she didn't want children because her own mother "went crazy when John was born"—but a discussion with another young woman intrigued her. Their conversation touched first on religion but soon "turned to the absorbing topic of sex. She explained to me what fuck means, and we talked about various other things," Adele reported.[33]

One particular entry in her diary offers an especially interesting illustration of the power of the heterosexual imperative in mid-twentieth-century culture and the nature of the pressure adolescent girls could face in this context. "Mother was telling me today how Ursula O'Keefe always had 3 or 4 boys walking her home from school & she wonders why I don't. ([A]t least she didn't come right out & say so but that's what she meant)," Adele wrote. "Well so do I wonder," she continued, "but I wish she wouldn't because it makes me feel sorry for myself which is silly. I've got the notion that I'll make myself famous and thus in some way wipe out the stain (of unpopularity) on my honor. I guess I'm more juvinile [*sic*] than I think."[34] These observations reveal Adele's discomfort over the implied criticism in her mother's remarks. They also highlight the extent to which adult women, themselves targets of contemporary prescriptive instructions regarding heterosexual interactions, reinforced the cultural message that popularity with the opposite sex defined a critical component of female adolescent experience. This maternal complicity helps to explain why young women allowed dating to define much of the content of their relationships with one another and to take precedence over female friendship.

Adele Mongan's mother was not unique in her interest in her daughter's social life. "I woke up this morning to hear Mom say, 'I hope to gosh she gets a husband who's worthwhile,'" fifteen-year-old June Calendar recorded in her diary. "She [is] actually worried about me getting married—If people would only trust me to my good taste—" This entry and others document a consistent pattern of maternal effort to promote June's success with the opposite sex. While Adele explicitly objected to her mother's comments, June accepted her mother's input. Nevertheless, when the message that heterosexual social life was the most important category of interaction came from one's mother, it could have a powerful impact on the nature of one's commitments to female friends.[35]

By the 1950s, popularity with the opposite sex represented the *raison d'être* for preadolescents as young as ten years old, the age at which Annie Dillard started dancing school in Pittsburgh in 1955. Her close friend had to go to "Jewish" dancing school at the same time. From that point on, Dillard and her peers were "on some list. We were to be on that list for life, it turned out, unless we left," She recalls. In conjunction with the so-cial obligations implied by membership on the list, "intricately shifting [female] friendships" involved extensive discussions of "hair" and "other girls." While Dillard was a success in this social setting, she found it un-comfortable.[36] Twelve-year-old Ruth Teischman had similar feelings: "Tonight I was talking to my mother (I was very frustrated). I was telling her all my problems about being popular with the boys." Her mother, like the mothers of Adele Mongan and June Calendar, took those problems quite seriously and had definite ideas about how they should be solved. "We talked about the dance and she told me I should ask the boys to dance, and I should stay near the boys," Ruth wrote in her diary. "I told her it wasn't so easy."[37]

Ruth Teischman was right: It wasn't easy at all. Adolescent girls in the post-1920 decades confronted a complicated set of tasks. As all young women do, they faced the "developmental work" created by profound bi-ological, cognitive, and psychological changes.[38] They also encountered a specific set of social and cultural influences that constructed their roles as women in very particular ways, as well as structuring their expectations about friendship and their interactions with one another as friends. The message came through loud and clear: Popularity with boys was the ulti-mate goal. By mid-century, that message had a monumental impact on its recipients. According to the author of a recent study of adolescence in the 1950s, "For girls who lived through it, just hearing the word 'popularity' is enough to generate a cold sweat."[39] While the focus was on attracting dates, affiliations with popular girls could enhance the possibilities for heterosexual success, which could then be reported to female friends. By the time adolescents moved on into college and early adulthood, they had solidly internalized both the new twentieth-century emotionology and the cultural imperative regarding heterosexual relationships. Hence their friendships mirrored those influences as they entered the next phase of their lives.

The "college girl" of the 1920s and beyond represented a new phenome-non. The aspirations and behavior of the three preceding generations of female students had evolved from the so-called new woman's dedicated, serious pursuit of higher education to a transitional model that combined traditional and new values. But the age of "flaming youth" produced a unique, modern college woman. In the framework of the revised emo-tional culture and the emphasis on heterosexual relationships, she expressed her individuality through the combination of frivolity and rebellion that defined the image of the flapper. This young woman smoked, drank, and danced; she bobbed her hair; and she used cosmetics. She also embraced the cultural mandate regarding heterosexual companionship, and she acted on it in a new and daring fashion. While late nineteenth-century college women had found a large measure of fulfillment in relationships with one another, this post-1920 college generation focused on "boys, boys, boys," a logical response to the cultural proscription of female intimacy.

Although the end of the flapper decade and the beginning of the Depression had a sobering effect, fraternities and sororities still flourished. Many female students of the thirties continued to enjoy campus life and to conform to the expectations of the dominant peer culture with an exuberant disregard for the harsher realities beyond. A 1937 study reported that college women talked about personalities, sex, careers, and religion, in that order; apparently they did not talk about female friendship as frequently. Ironically, during this decade a college woman risked expulsion for staying out all night with a man, but she could also be dismissed for having too "intense" a relationship with another woman.

For a brief period during World War II, young women were encouraged to enter traditionally male fields such as science and engineering. However, the 1940s also witnessed a decline in female educational aspirations. The message of the postwar years was unambiguous: The ultimate goal of attending college should be marriage, preferably guaranteed by a tangible sign—an engagement ring acquired before graduation. By 1952, an advertisement for Gimbel's department store captured the priorities of many female students accurately: "What's college? That's where girls who are above cooking and sewing go to meet a man so they can spend their lives cooking and sewing."[40]

Even in this context, a young woman's first experiences of college life could be profoundly affected by encounters with female friends. Virginia Foster arrived at Wellesley in 1921 and was absolutely delighted with her assigned roommate, Emmie Bosley. "She was lively and vivacious and attractive," she recalled. "It was just a mutual meeting of the souls; we adored each other. It couldn't have been a happier combination." Virginia was glad that Emmie's family was not exceptionally wealthy—"They were like me—they went with all the rich people and were part of the society group . . . so they always had to worry about money too." She also liked the fact that she and Emmie had similar relationships with their respective sisters: Each regarded her sibling as more beautiful and more popular. Clearly this fortuitous friendship contributed importantly to Virginia's enjoyment of college life. "Wellesley was sheer delight to me," she recalled. "I never felt so well or so happy in my life."[41]

Margaret Mead experienced a similar happiness when she transferred to Barnard in 1920 after an unsatisfying first year at DePauw. "I found—and in some measure created—the kind of student life that matched my earlier dreams," she remembered. "In the course of those three undergraduate years friendships were founded that have endured a lifetime of change." She and her friends, whose ages varied, lived in apartments together and adopted a group name, the Ash Can Cats. Margaret invented a kinship system for the group, designating some members as parents, some as children and grandchildren, and even one as a great grandchild. In addition to their being linked "by ties of temperament and congeniality and by a common interest in literature," she noted that some of the group

also were children of our period. . . . a generation of young women who felt extraordinarily free—free from the demand to marry unless we chose to do so, free to postpone marriage while we did other things, free from the need to bargain and hedge that had burdened and restricted women of earlier generations.

While these were her closest female companions, Margaret also enjoyed other friends, whose interests included more conventional activities like dancing. They were not compatible with the Ash Can Cats, but she valued their friendship as well.[42]

Margaret Mead described her friends as rather unsophisticated regarding matters of sex. They learned about homosexuality from gossip about faculty members and "worried and thought over affectionate episodes in our past relationships with girls and wondered whether they had been incipient examples"—a clear reflection of the influence of contemporary cultural norms. With regard to heterosexual social life, they agreed among themselves to an explicit rule against canceling plans with a female friend in order to go out with a man.[43] This declaration of loyalty to female friendship distinguished these young women from many of their peers, for whom the pursuit of sisterhood was decisively displaced by the quest for heterosexual popularity, if not by outright competition for dates.

The behavior of Margaret Mead and her friends contrasts starkly with that of a young woman who reassured her parents about the imminent termination of her relationship with another girl's boyfriend: "We both realize that we have no right because of Clara. Don't worry, Mother, I'm still fighting and as soon as we get back to school and he can be with her again we'll just naturally forget each other."[44] Most young women probably did not find themselves in this situation, but it is evident that many placed a higher priority on heterosexual social life than on female friendship. "I have met some very nice girls and of course some pills," Jane Shugg wrote breezily to her parents early in her first year at Wellesley. "The social life on the floor has been dull as dull can be," she noted on another occasion. Two of her friends had "no bright hopes for the future"; another had, as usual, two "steady" men; a third had one boyfriend; and Jane was probably going to break off her current romance. "To keep ourselves from getting too low," she reported, "we have had numerous birthday parties and just parties."[45] While earlier college women had looked forward to dormitory parties as special occasions for fun and friendship, now such events apparently served more to console and amuse female students in the absence of dates or heterosexual gatherings.

Jane Shugg made no secret of the fact that marriage represented her overriding ambition. In response to her parents' concern about the amount of time she was devoting to social life during her senior year, she complained, "No one seems to remember their youthful days or maybe those who wanted to get married were in the minority. Heaven forbid that *I be a career girl.*" Though at the moment she believed she would be "forced into [becoming] one," this would "*definitely* be *second* choice." Since she had failed to meet any "eligible young men" in Detroit so far, it was unlikely that going home to pursue a career there would help her find a husband, even though she still had nine more years before she turned thirty. Finally she stated angrily, "This urge or desire which you think so peculiar is a fairly universal one and none of us want to loose [*sic*] it."[46]

Certainly all young women in college did not manifest the single-minded commitment to the quest for a husband that Jane Shugg articulated. For some, as for Margaret Mead, female friendship continued to define the college experience in vital ways. Helen Snyder's diary consistently documents the pleasure she derived from the new acquaintances she made and the fun she had with two young women in particular during her four years at the University of Pittsburgh in the 1930s. From the beginning of her first year, their friendship enhanced her college life. "Had lunch with Maxine and Doris. Everything is nicer now—associa-

tions and everything," she told her diary. "Lunched with Doris and Maxine and lots of fun," she noted a few months later. Helen felt especially
comfortable with Doris because they had a great deal in common: "We
seem to enjoy each other so much," she noted. They studied together, visited each other's homes, and shared family occasions. When Helen's
brother came to town, Doris's parents invited him to dinner also. After
her friend had surgery, Helen expressed great relief: "Doris is back. What
else could have made me so lonesome before?" she wrote. "I missed her
terribly. But she's back and it's o.k."[47]

She also continued to value her earlier relationship with Janet, who
eventually went to college in Philadelphia. They corresponded regularly
and spent time together when both were home for vacations. It was ex-
citing for Helen to meet her friend at the airport after a trip: "Marvelous
thrill. Saw Janet come in from Kansas City on a big silvergrey [*sic*]
plane—T.W.A. lines. She looks grand and enjoyed it all." She liked
"Janet's Burt" and observed that her friend talked "*beaucoup de B. qui
est très gentil.*" When Janet invited her out to lunch, they "talked 'Burt,'"
and Helen concluded that "everything looks like a marriage will be forthcoming."[48]

The cultural emphasis on the importance of heterosexual social life
made a strong impression on Helen, who worried constantly about her
own deficiencies in this area. She "discussed our mutual unhappiness—
discontent or whatever it is" with Doris. When the latter was invited to
an important interfraternity social event, Helen "was so thrilled it
could have been me. Gee, but I'm glad," she wrote. "Couldn't even fall
asleep last nite thinking 'bout it." But vicarious pleasure had its limitations, and on another occasion she complained bitterly, "It isn't college
not to go out and have dates. I don't know why I'm so miserably un-
popular." For this young woman, the pressures of the contemporary
heterosexual peer culture were exacerbated by other contemporary developments. Her family experienced serious economic difficulties as a
result of the Depression, and college expenses presented a real problem. For Helen, financial constraints compounded the insecurities
about popularity and dating that most college girls experienced. Thus,
for example, buying a new dress for a dance posed a difficult, almost
insurmountable problem.[49]

College students' relationships with both female and male friends
could be complicated by other factors as well. Earlier generations of
young women (and men) who pursued higher education had generally

shared similar social backgrounds; individuals whose racial, ethnic, or re-ligious heritages set them apart from the majority of their fellow students were often excluded by the latter. As increased social mobility and immi-gration resulted in a more heterogeneous student population in the decades following 1920, disparaging allusions to the backgrounds of peers of both genders multiplied. Such remarks indicate that social prej-udice strongly influenced the choice of female friends, as well as male companions, for many college women during this period. Apparently the social selectivity of the sorority system also contributed to this situation: According to one dean of women, "A very deplorable practice in sorori-ties is to select girls who dress well and rate well with men."[50]

The sources offer numerous examples of this type of prejudice. Vir-ginia Foster was horrified to find herself seated at the same table with a "Negro" girl. Although she feared her father's reaction to her decision and wondered if she should have "stood by Southern tradition and gone home," she chose to accept college rules and eat at the table to which she had been assigned. She remembered that other girls experienced the same conflict between the traditions of their upbringing and the desire to stay at Wellesley. "I didn't become friends with the Negro girl, but I was pleas-ant," she recalled. Nor did she make friends with the "foreign girls," al-though she had to get used to the presence of Chinese and Indian students as well. "My friends were the white Southern girls and my roommate and her sister," Virginia recalled. Yet she also remembered that the incident with the African-American student triggered the beginning of a doubt in her mind, eventually leading her to question what she had been raised to believe.[51]

Yvonne Blue found herself attracted to a wide variety of people be-cause they were interesting, bohemian, and intellectual. Yet frequent ref-erences to the class and ethnic backgrounds of friends and acquaintances demonstrate the degree to which social prejudice determined her choice of friends. Disparaging her friend Lillian as "common" and Lillian's school as "Flunker's Paradise," Yvonne observed that she herself would not associate with the "poor whites, Negroes, Jews, Chinese and what have you" who went there. On the other hand, she prized the friendship of two other young women because she felt like "a smart northshore so-ciety girl" when she was with them. Jane drove a "roadster," and Alice's grandfather was a millionaire who lived in Lake Forest. After a lunch date with them and four other young women of similar background, Yvonne wrote, "I love to mingle with that sort of group—it makes me feel that

I've accomplished so much since my high-school days when not even the lowliest Jew would play with me."

Yvonne would have liked Grace, another friend, better if her family were more like Alice's, but unfortunately they were "common German immigrants." It would also have helped "if [Grace] dressed nicer and used make-up and if her feet were not so big and if most of her friends were more attractive. It's terrible but it's true," Yvonne concluded. She described a new acquaintance whose father was the American consul in Milan as "very Greek looking, and built on a large scale, like those Caryatids—I think you call them, who hold up the Eretheum [sic]." Although Yvonne really did not like this young woman, she found it "rather nice to know her," so she decided to continue the friendship. She complained to her diary about another young woman, who had invited herself and her family for tea, noting that a mutual friend described these people as "*nouveau riche* without the money."[52]

The same sort of snobbish attitudes influenced Jane Shugg's college friendships. Early in her Wellesley career she accepted a blind date for a dance and was appalled to find that the event was sponsored by a Jewish fraternity. Since the girl who had arranged the date didn't "look Jewish," Jane had never suspected this possibility. Fortunately, no one else found out about this event, she assured her parents, "so my chances of dates from Gentiles aren't comprised [sic]." In another letter home, she listed the names of her close friends and reported that the floor she lived on was a good one: "At least the five of us are not Jews and are quite congenial." When school started the following year, Jane was happy to see all the "gals" again and relieved to find what she considered a nice crowd in the house—"not many Jews and no Seniors." Another blind date in her junior year worked out a bit better: "He grad. from U of D and is Catholic but aside from that everything is favorable," Jane declared.[53]

While students at women's colleges did not encounter the friendship issues raised by sororities, the policies and attitudes of these organizations could significantly influence the friendship experiences of young women at other institutions. Margaret Mead recalled that her exclusion from sorority life at DePauw had a tremendous impact on her, because it marked the first time she had ever confronted "unacceptability," which she attributed to her unfashionable dress and her church. In part because of this traumatic experience, the friendships she established at Barnard assumed great importance in her life.[54] Helen Snyder could not afford to join a sorority, and she experienced great anguish when she had to decide whether or not to attend a rush party, even though she knew that she would be unable to accept an invitation to join the group.[55]

Five sororities at the University of Chicago rushed Yvonne Blue, who was convinced that she would not be asked to join any of them. She professed to be uninterested in membership, but accepted an invitation when it arrived. At the pledge initiation, the other girls kissed her and told her they were glad she had joined. Yvonne felt embarrassed because they were not her "type." Although they adopted "an attitude of great familiarity" that she felt she could not "live up to," she realized that she actually liked it. Pleasantly surprised when she accepted an invitation to dinner at the home of one of the members, she found that she even enjoyed playing bridge, which she had never done before.[56]

Yvonne's high-school friend Val was rushed by a number of sororities during her first semester at the University of Arizona. She felt sure that she could not make people like her, although she made a good first impression, and this posed a serious potential problem. "It's a swell place (if you don't join the wrong sorority)," she told Yvonne. Before she left for Arizona, Val had dreaded all the cute girls and the "datay" [date-oriented] atmosphere and had hoped to have a frumpy roommate. Yet by her sophomore year, she belonged to a sorority and was going out quite a bit. Still, conforming to the mainstream campus culture did not eliminate her anxiety: The boys were dumb, her sorority sisters objected when she accepted a date with a Sigma Nu, and then the date was not a success. Although she "sort of" liked dancing, she found dances "agonising in a way." Eventually she concluded that she was not "collegiate," though she was glad to have the chance to see what college life was like.[57]

Even as distinctly new, twentieth-century features characterized post-1920 college women's friendships, these relationships could still incorporate vestiges of earlier patterns. Martha Lavell, a first-year student at Mills College in 1927, enjoyed a "Baby Party" at which participants dressed in costumes and played children's games, an event reminiscent of gatherings enjoyed by earlier generations of college women. During her year at Mills, she especially valued the friendship of one thoughtful and articulate young woman, to whom she attributed her own mental awakening. Their conversations ranged from serious intellectual and philosophical questions to the distinctly twentieth-century issue of "whether there were any boys who didn't insist on petting." This relationship resembled earlier close friendships to some extent, but it manifested an unmistakably modern tone.

Like her turn-of-the-century predecessors, Martha Lavell worried about having friends. She compared her "happy times" at Mills with the isolation she felt after she transferred to the University of Minnesota. Later, she found it easy to make friends as a graduate student at Smith and wondered how she had managed to conquer what she described in distinctly twentieth-century terms as the "crushing feeling of inferiority" that had troubled her previously. That feeling recurred occasionally, as did a sense of doubt and concern about her sexuality. Even after she consciously decided to "become aggressive" because she could not "endure another year with no men companions," Martha described herself as "greatly susceptible to an attraction for women," which she knew was not "normal."[58] These observations document the pressure and anxiety that a young woman might experience if she found it difficult to conform to cultural prescriptions for social life. They also illustrate the sort of anxiety about homosexuality expressed by Margaret Mead and her friends.

Yvonne Blue's friendships, like those of Martha Lavell, blended older features with distinctly twentieth-century characteristics. Despite her frankly critical and often unkind appraisals of her friends' qualities, lengthy passages in Yvonne's diaries attest to the importance she attached to her relationships with other young women during her college years. She suffered because Val's letters from the University of Arizona made "her seem a complete stranger." Since Val was "an Alpha Phi, and popular and co-edish like a girl in the movies," Yvonne feared that they would be "as far apart as the poles and completely uninterested in each other" when they met again. They had been close friends for seven years "and liked each other all the time," so this possibility really troubled her. "Oh I hate it—I hate it," she exclaimed. "Val can't help it so I'm not mad at her—this is a sad but very resigned farewell to an actuality. . . . pretty soon neither of us will ever see or think of the other at all . . . because that's the way things happen." Val's efforts to reassure her—"Why if I got so I had twenty five dates a week I'd still think the same of you! Good heavens! There is not anybody like you, Yvonne! Don't *you* still like me?"—proved unsuccessful. Another friend who had experienced a similar situation offered sympathy, but also gave pragmatic advice that would have horrified a typical Victorian young woman: "It hurts to see a friendship die, but there's not much you can do about it. . . . Shed a proper tear or two and look for something even better," she counseled Yvonne.[59]

As Yvonne grew estranged from Val, she relied more on other friends. Behaving in a manner reminiscent of traditional friendship practices, she shared her diary with a young woman who was so impressed that she started her own diary and dedicated it to Yvonne. On the other hand, Yvonne found Lucile, an unconventional friend, fascinating because she dated "old" men and had affairs with married professors, but Yvonne also found it hard to respect her. When a mutual friend decided to "drop" Lucile, Yvonne pondered the possibility that she would have to side with one or the other: "If it came to a choice between Lucile and Grace I would want to choose Lucile but I would pick Grace. I like Grace better, but Lucile stimulates and interests me and one hates to give up a relationship like that," she concluded dispassionately. In a conversation that distressed both young women, Lucile questioned Yvonne's failure to warn her about this situation. "Lucile said that she gave everything in friendship and . . . that if . . . someone said a word against me she would instantly stand up for me," Yvonne noted contritely. Earlier young women might also have agonized over a misunderstanding that seemed to threaten their friendship, but this situation was resolved in a thoroughly modern fashion: The conversation ended when Lucile declared that if she had not had a date in fifteen minutes, she would have cried.[60] A college woman in a previous generation would never have made such a statement. Nor would she have written admiringly, as Yvonne did about another friend, "She's unbelievable! She has a hole in her dress so she got a boy's fraternity pin merely to hide it. She keeps poison in the bathroom so she can commit suicide when she feels like it."[61]

An uncommunicative roommate created a dilemma for Mary Sill, who started college at Smith in 1949. "I don't quite know what to *do about* Maggie. She is quite cold and sometimes almost rather unfriendly," she observed. A friend surmised that Maggie was jealous because Mary had so many dates, so Mary decided to keep quiet about her "social affairs," to leave her roommate alone, and to "hope for the best." They continued to share a room through the fall term, but eventually moved into two single rooms. When Mary told Maggie that life would seem strange without her, the latter "only said that we would both be able to study better." Mary accepted this rather distant and perfunctory response dispassionately, commenting only that the girls on the floor had welcomed her when she moved to her new room.[62] The tension with her roommate concerned her, but her unemotional tone and Maggie's equally detached attitude reflect the impact of the emotional culture of the period as well as the declining emphasis on the centrality of female friendship. The degree to which they also reflect the young women's actual emotions is of course impossible to ascertain.

Another example highlights the complexity of the issue of congruence between the expression and experience of emotion when cultural norms limit expression in specific ways. Jean Nearing also described her interactions with friends in a matter-of-fact manner, but female friendship definitely played an important role in her college life in the early 1940s. Jean liked the girls she met at the beginning of her first semester at Wellesley, although she wished that she knew "some of the boys." Soon she found other, more compatible students with "a lot more depth to them than many of the girls on [her] floor," who never talked seriously about anything. "All they ever do is laugh and giggle about nothing," she complained. She and one of her new friends, Jo, concluded that "there were some of the girls that weren't worth much." Jean thought that she and Jo were "kind of a lot alike. She's in about the same financial situation we are I guess," she told her parents, "and she hasn't been spoiled[,] having *five* other brothers and sisters."[63]

In her sophomore year, Jean was pleased to be living in the same residence hall as her new friends. When some members of this group couldn't get rooms in the hall for the following year, she and her roommate agreed to move to another location: "You can imagine how awful it would be if we were separated," she wrote. "We thought it was more important to be all together than to be in the house we wanted as our first choice." This sentiment and other comments suggest that Jean valued female friendship in much the same way as earlier young women had. She described birthday celebrations and visits from other girls' families, and she was glad to report that one friend liked a birthday gift she had chosen and "thanked me seven times." She was thrilled with her Christmas gift from another friend—"there was nothing I'd have rather had," she declared. And she was equally delighted when "the girls" gave her "some awfully nice things" for her own birthday.[64]

Nevertheless, a modern accent clearly distinguishes Jean's relationships from more traditional female friendships, including those of her mother, Jane Cary, who preceded her as a Wellesley student. In addition to particular language conventions, including references to "nice kids" and the use of the adjective "swell," a reduction in emotional intensity is apparent. Thus when a friend apologized profusely for canceling plans to go to Boston with Jean because another young woman and her parents invited her to a football game, Jean nonchalantly "told her gee whiz I'd have done the same thing." Similarly, although she was sorry to learn that Jo had not come back to school for their junior year, her response was not particularly emotional: "I have heard that Jo isn't back—flunked out I guess—I'll miss her as she is a good friend."[65]

Certainly the degree of emotionality manifested by any individual reflects her own personality as well as the prescriptions of the larger emotional culture. Although Jean Nearing's letters refer to dates and young men, she seems to have maintained a balanced perspective even on this highly charged topic.[66] Yet other young women's comments consistently reflect a high degree of anxiety, particularly with regard to heterosexual relationships. Yvonne Blue's frantic social life constantly distressed her. She felt ashamed of herself "for indulging in the greatest American sport" with a young man she found very attractive, but feared that something was wrong with her, since although she thought it was wrong, she actually didn't feel that it was. She enjoyed going to parties in artists' studios with a group of "Bohemians," but worried about the potential consequences of her actions and feared she might end up "at the clinic," especially after a female friend said that her behavior was "disgusting"—she had been drunk and "simply terrible."[67]

Yvonne's emotional reaction to her indiscretions with men impelled her to confide in her friend Phoebe, who assured her that the anguish would fade and advised her not to stop going to the parties. Phoebe understood how it felt to wake up in the morning with a bad taste that comes not from your stomach but from your "mind," and she suggested that they should both try to dislike the men "that try to make you cause if thats [sic] all they want you for they're really not worth while having." Pledging her support—"you can always depend on me to be your pal"—Phoebe assured Yvonne that her indiscretion would never be revealed: "I'm burning the letter now so there will never be any danger of its falling into the wrong hands," she promised.[68] This interchange suggests that an overall diminished emotional intensity did not prevent young women from confiding in female friends when they were troubled. It also underlines a distinct contrast between Yvonne and Phoebe and their predecessors before 1920: While earlier young women might have faced similar moments of regret, most likely they would not have discussed their sexual conduct, even in the context of close friendships.

❊

A brief examination of young women's relationships during the transition from college to mature adulthood will complete the picture, revealing the presence of familiar themes as well as a subtle suggestion of movement toward new priorities. With the completion of formal education, friendship settings changed; the constancy and immediacy of peer interaction in classrooms and college residence halls ended. Moreover, young adults no longer moved directly into a shared domestic world that fostered and facilitated female friendship. Instead, many pursued independent lives for a period before marriage. But relationships with high-school and college friends often endured, and new friendships developed, often in work settings. Men continued to provide a major focus of discussion. Although they were often separated geographically, college friends shared news of dates, engagements, marriages, and eventually the arrival of babies. Where distance was not a factor, friends might visit informally, share apartments, or attend concerts and plays together. As with younger women, conflict occasionally surfaced. Yet friendships could also assume new importance in the post-college years as women moved into the adult world and confronted major life choices.

Echoes of earlier friendships infused Eleanor Coit's relationships. "Did ever girl have so rich and sweet a friendship as yours?" her friend Eleanor Olcott wrote in response to Coit's thoughtful bon voyage gifts. "I nearly wept over the blue tulle and your thinking of such a tiny detail of me and my belongings. . . . It's most fetching and just what the dress needs." Eleanor Coit's Y.W.C.A. colleague, Alice Burbank, gratefully acknowledged receiving the "hairnets" she needed and confided the news of her hospitalization for emotional difficulties in 1921. "You don't know, old darling, how much you are meaning to me these hard days, just knowing you are you. I am leaning on you hard." Marjorie Paret, another coworker, wished that Eleanor was traveling with her in Poland in 1920, "to laugh with her over the funny times and talk over the difficulties and act as 'father confessor.'" Paret confessed from Poland, "This is the first time I've ever been really away from friends, and it's awfully hard." In a more modern vein, she also reported smoking a cigarette shortly before a professional meeting and said that she had "degenerated" in other ways—"I've grown to need the companionship of men—an awful confession for a confirmed old maid like me, isn't it?" Because she had not found a "pal" among the women she knew there, she would have liked to find "one really nice" American man to fill that role, but so far all potential candidates had been "disappointments."[69]

Gladys Bell, a teacher in a small, western Pennsylvania community, pondered a friend's advice as she confronted her doubts about marrying the fiancé to whom she was engaged for the second time. "Even tho' Elsie surmises that I shall be severely disillusioned in my contemplations, I still hope that there are others who can be just as devoted and trustworthy as she and *her* husband," she wrote in her diary in 1925. Later that year, Bell anxiously recorded Elsie's pregnancy—"Surely she'll survive it"—and finally noted happily, "Dear Old Elsie's got a baby boy. And how she does love it too." A year earlier, however, tension and conflict had threatened this relationship. At that point, Gladys Bell described her friend as "a confounded big deceiver" and regretfully resolved to be "guarded" in all interactions with her. The friendship continued, however, and in 1932, Bell recorded a visit from "Elsie and her gang," pronouncing her friend the "same good old kid."[70]

Young adult women shared minor problems as well as more significant concerns with one another. When Dorothy Smith complained in a letter about being asked to make potato salad, Josephine Crisfield loyally supported her friend's interests. Although Josephine accepted the chore of catching, boiling, and picking ("not to mention eating") crabs as a part of her own life in Savannah, she thought that Dorothy's impending departure for Paris, where she planned to continue her musical education, should have exempted her from such mundane domestic tasks. "The idea of your making potato salad is just too hideous," she exclaimed. Later, she welcomed Dorothy's letters from Paris and urged her to send a photograph of herself "and the boys you see mostly." Marriage and impending motherhood prevented Josephine from visiting Dorothy in Chicago in 1928. "How can I take a trip with you," she wrote plaintively the following year. "I am nursing a baby but it is not by choice. That is a mother's duty it seems and I used to think people had babies and preferred to nurse them. That is incorrect. I think everybody hates it," she declared frankly. Although delighted to hear about Dorothy's forthcoming marriage and plans for a European honeymoon in 1930, Josehphine was expecting another baby and could not be at the wedding.[71]

Beth Twiggar wanted to continue her college friendships, but her first Skidmore reunion was a disappointment. "It was my last reunion, as well as my first," she declared in 1935. She found it difficult to interact with friends "in a body" and disliked the "girlish chatter" that interfered with real conversation. Several months later, the news of a close college friend's engagement made Beth feel "queerly out of things where Honey, who has been such a large part of my daily living is concerned." While she knew all the details of her friend's three previous "loves," she had little information about Honey's latest romance because they had seen little of each other since leaving Skidmore. Beth thought that all college friends must experience the same "trite dismay" as their ties weakened following graduation, and she felt a loss: "For Honey has been an education, a joy, and a responsibility; she has been strength and laughter to me. I'll be the poorer when she's gone."

Beth also worried about her relationships with new friends. She was distressed when she learned that Elsa and Helen, whom she had met through her job, had privately appraised her current boyfriend and pronounced him probably "nil." And she was humiliated when they told her directly that she was boring, failed to face reality, and behaved "like the baby of the family." Nevertheless she gladly supported Elsa through the two weeks preceding her father's death, holding her hand, providing handkerchiefs, and running errands for her.[72]

Harriet Hardy's experiences offer an interesting comparison to those of Beth Twiggar. Her journals from medical school in the 1930s consistently record the satisfaction she found in her friendships with other young women. "The day was happily ended by dinner with Emily—her quiet sincere loyalty, her honest easy way of looking at life combine to make a good companion," she wrote on one occasion. A week later, Hardy described another friend as "a rare companion, marvelously uncomplicated and straight in her outlook." She also reflected on the mystery of friendship in general—"God alone knows what the subtle charm of communion between spirits here on earth is but it has a potent hold on me. . . . I wish for everyone friends."[73]

Two decades after Harriet Hardy expressed these sentiments, Mary Sill contemplated the task of telling the young woman with whom she shared an apartment that she intended to make different living arrangements. "I have never felt particularly at ease with Faith," she noted. Although she knew the decision would hurt her roommate, she really did not mind losing this friendship. Mary had more in common with Ruthie, a friend whom she could consult about important matters concerning men and dating. One letter from Ruthie offers a striking contrast to earlier correspondence between female friends and symbolizes the sort of changes manifested in young women's friendships by the mid-twentieth century. Not only was Ruthie's letter devoted to the issue of whether Mary should consider moving to San Francisco to be with a young man, but the advice it contained conveyed the opinions of Ruthie's boyfriend, not those of the putative female adviser.[74]

While the preceding examples do not offer a comprehensive survey of post-1920 young adult friendships, they highlight some components of such relationships and suggest some general patterns. Like those of their younger counterparts in high school and college, the friendships of women in early adulthood reflected both traditional and modern influences. Thoughtful gestures and the exchange of confidences might be balanced by unemotional interactions and an ever-present focus on heterosexual social life. For some individuals, as for women in earlier generations, female friendships remained a major source of satisfaction and support. For others, such relationships could provoke anxiety, as new activities and choices altered the frequency and settings of their interactions. As in any historical period and stage of life, the unique characteristics of individuals, their socialization experiences, their childhood interactions, and the contemporary social and cultural milieu influenced the structure and style of young adult friendships after 1920.

In 1936 Willa Cather made the following observation in a preface to a collection of essays: "The world broke in two in 1922 or thereabouts, and the persons and prejudices recalled in these sketches slide back into yesterday's seven thousand years."[75] This melodramatic declaration overstates the case for change in American society in general and exaggerates the degree to which female friendship was transformed in the twentieth century. However, while it does not address the nuances of historical change, Cather's assertion is relevant to the history of women's friendships because it highlights the post-1920 era as a social, economic, cultural, and technological turning point. The relationships of adolescents, college students, and young adults who came of age between 1920 and 1960 resemble those of their predecessors in some ways. Yet they also reflect the imprint of structural changes, alterations in the emotional culture, and other powerful influences that include an orientation toward abundance and consumption, an explicitly articulated cultural preference for heterosexual relationships, and an increasingly extended exposure to a powerful peer culture. As young adults matured and assumed additional responsibilities in the context of family life and, for some, professional life, their friendship styles also reflected that combination of influences. At the same time, as the following chapter demonstrates, the concerns and priorities of mature adulthood would produce a somewhat different model of female friendship.

4

"The Staunchness of Female Friendship"

Adult Friends, 1900–1960

In 1937, a pensive and vulnerable young wife reflected on the disintegration of her marriage and the difficult decision to seek a divorce from her second husband. "My friends have been wonderful," she wrote in her diary. "And my faith in the staunchness of female friendship has once more expanded. I *know*—I know how they have helped me."[1] These observations highlight one woman's recognition of the supportive role of friends in the context of a specific crisis in her life. But they also define a major leitmotif for women's friendship experiences more generally throughout the first half of the century. As they moved beyond adolescence and college life through the stages of adulthood, many middle-class American women enjoyed the support of loyal female friends across a spectrum of experiences. At the turn of the century, their friendships often resembled those of their nineteenth-century counterparts. Conventional wives and mothers, as well as individuals whose lives followed less traditional paths, might share their deepest personal interests and values with female friends, rely on them for moral support of various kinds and even financial assistance, and maintain close contact over many years.

At the same time, intimations of a more casual attitude toward friendship between 1900 and 1920 suggest a contrasting theme that developed further in the succeeding decades. As the new century unfolded, adult women's friendships would also manifest some generational change in response to the social and cultural trends of the post-1920 period. Yet the accent on change after 1920 was far less pronounced in the case of adult

97

relationships than it was for younger women. While the friendship choices and priorities of adolescents and college students unequivocally mirrored the new emotional culture, particularly the dominant heterosexual imperative, those of women past the stage where dating typically defined the crucial *raison d'être* exhibited a more textured quality.

To some degree, married women's friendship patterns reflected the influence of the same twentieth-century cultural prescriptions as the relationships of their younger contemporaries. Unlike their predecessors in earlier periods, wives and mothers now perceived a conflict between their family responsibilities and domestic obligations and their relationships with female friends; as a result, the latter assumed a distinctly lower priority. At the same time, however, such women still maintained contact with friends, even when they rarely met, and many eventually acknowledged the importance of these bonds. Generational change can also be discerned in the friendships of single and professional women, but its impact is less clear in these subgroups. Although two discrete periods are apparent in the friendships of younger women between 1900 and 1960, then, the pattern becomes more complex in the case of adult relationships. Here, despite some evidence of generational shifts after 1920, continuity rather than change defines the dominant theme.

The category of post-1920 adult women encompasses individuals who came of age in the first two decades of the century—or even earlier, when Victorian culture still prevailed—as well as those who matured after 1920. In her memoirs, Lillian Hellman, born in 1905, alluded to the complexity engendered by this generation gap:

By the time I grew up the fight for the emancipation of women, their rights under the law, in the office, in bed, was stale stuff. My generation didn't think much about the place or the problems of women. . . . (Five or ten years' difference in age was a greater separation between people in the 1920's, perhaps because the older generation had gone through the war.) . . . I was too young to be grateful for how much I owed them . . . in the war for equality.

As Hellman's comments imply, the women of her generation grew up with different priorities from those of their predecessors. Even though female friendship remained important to both her peers and their older counterparts, other differences, such as nuances of language, distinguished their relationships. This discrepancy in style highlights a potential source of generational conflict for younger and older women during this period, and it also identifies a source of possible confusion and misunderstanding for the historian engaged in the task of analyzing change and continuity in women's friendship experiences. Even for women who were primarily products of Victorian culture, however, friendship did not remain a static experience removed from contemporary influences. Hence the range of interactions that comprised adult female friendship throughout the first half of the twentieth century reflects the coexistence of enduring traditional elements along with some new friendship qualities.[2]

The nineteenth-century world of domesticity and female companionship certainly did not define the experiences of adult women during the two decades before 1920, but their friendships reflected unmistakable elements of the earlier Victorian friendship style and the separate female culture and community that supported the achievements of turn-of-the-century feminism.[3] Those who had reached adulthood at the turn of the century continued to preserve traditional images of friendship and to maintain close female networks composed of both kin and unrelated friends. Thus, for example, as a middle-aged woman, Mary Pratt Sears devoted herself to her friends and voiced her feelings in flowery and expressive tones. "Our own friendship, dear Julia, with its manifold roots, is a beautiful and holy flower," she wrote to her cousin and close companion, Julia Lyman. "It hardly seems as though we could share more than we do of memory and love." Both her language and the closeness of her friendship with a family member reflect a distinctly nineteenth-century flavor. Julia's sister, Ella Lyman Cabot, whose own extensive network of friends encompassed former students and other women (and men as well) of diverse ages and backgrounds, compared this relationship to those of Ruth and Naomi and Jonathan and David, pronouncing it "like the friendship of a classic age."

Cabot herself enjoyed the loyalty and esteem of countless devoted friends with whom she corresponded regularly, and their letters frequently reflect the same Victorian fervor as those of Mary Pratt Sears. "How wonderful is friendship and how precious! I count upon it more than you can realize," Louise Amory wrote to Cabot. "Darling Ella, Richard [Ella's husband] once wrote that friendship like Marriage is a Sacrament—It is! My love to you both always."[4]

Frances Crane Lillie would probably have agreed with these sentiments. A physician with a large family and a devoted husband, she also sustained an intense relationship with a close female friend, Ellen Gates Starr. An extensive collection of letters to Starr and a memoir by Lillie's daughter document the centrality of this friendship in Lillie's life. She shared her deepest religious feelings and a strong commitment to the poor with Starr, who served as her daughter's godmother and as a model for her own life's direction. Like Esther Burr and Sarah Prince and numerous other eighteenth- and nineteenth-century women, mutual religious convictions bound these women together and solidly anchored their relationship. Lillie's husband disliked religious discussions, and she seldom spoke of her strong religious feelings to anyone but Starr. Despite the opposition of family members and other friends, she followed Starr's example in her decision to convert to Catholicism, a choice that had a profound impact on her life.[5]

Religion also played a role in the friendship of Anna Allen Tracy and Mary Helen Humphrey, who met as teachers in the American Missionary Association School for "colored" children in Lexington, Kentucky, and kept in touch for more than fifty years. While the correspondence of Ella Lyman Cabot and her circle and that of Frances Crane Lillie and Ellen Gates Starr projects a definite Victorian quality, Tracy's letters to Humphrey blend traditional qualities with evidence of new influences. Prior to her marriage, she wrote frequently, often using Rosalind, a special nickname, as her signature. Her letters resembled those of earlier correspondents in both tone and content. When Humphrey faced surgery, Tracy offered to help in any possible way—financially as well as personally. "Please feel that you can call upon me unreservedly for everything . . . if I am needed I will be up on the next train. You shall have all the comfort you can get out of my presence," she assured her friend. Along with domestic topics such as clothing, obligations to aging relatives, and interactions with sisters and friends, Tracy also discussed aspects of her settlement and mission work as well as books and magazine articles she had read. Not surprisingly, the details of her engagement and marriage to Edward Tracy at the age of thirty-three filled a number of letters.

As a wife and mother, Tracy found it more difficult to set aside the time for correspondence; her evenings belonged to her husband. He was not interested in letter writing himself, she told her friend, though he enjoyed hearing Humphrey's replies to his wife's letters. Unlike her Victorian predecessors, Anna Tracy grew progressively more dilatory as a correspondent. She frequently apologized for her negligence, citing the press of family obligations. "You must have a letter for New Years [sic] if Charlotte's dresses remain too short and the house does not get dusted," she pledged on one occasion.

1. Winslow Homer, *Backgammon*, 1877. Fine Arts Museums of San Francisco, Achenbach Foundation for Graphic Arts, Gift of Mr. and Mrs. John D. Rockefeller 3rd, 1993.35.15.

2. Mary Cassatt, *The Tea*, ca. 1880. M. Theresa B. Hopkins Fund, Courtesy Museum of Fine Arts, Boston.

3. John Singer Sargent, *Venetian Interior*, ca. 1882. Carnegie Museum of Art,
Pittsburgh, Museum purchase 20.7.

4. Mary Cassatt, *Young Women Picking Fruit*, 1891. Carnegie Museum of Art, Pittsburgh, Patrons Fund.

5. William Merritt Chase, *A Friendly Call*, 1895. National Gallery of Art, Washington, D.C., Chester Dale Collection.

6. Sir Luke Fildes, *An Alfresco Toilet*, 1899. Board of Trustees of the National Museums and Galleries on Merseyside, Lady Lever Art Gallery, Port Sunlight, Wirral, Merseyside, United Kingdom.

Right: 7. John Sloan, *Three A.M.*, 1909. Philadelphia Museum of Art, Gift of Mrs. Cyrus McCormick.

8. John Sloan, *Sunday, Women Drying Their Hair*, 1912. Addison Gallery of American Art, Phillips Academy, Andover, Massachusetts.

9. Maurice Sterne, *Resting at the Bazaar*, 1912. Museum of Modern Art, New York, Abby Aldrich Rockefeller Fund.

10. Elizabeth Bishop and Robert Lowell in Rio de Janeiro, Brazil, August 1962. Elizabeth Bishop Collection, Vassar College Libraries, Special Collections.

11. Helen Snyder (*left*) and Janet Oppenheimer, Uniontown, Pennsylvania, c. 1930.

Left: 12. Helen Snyder Weinberg (*left*) and Janet Oppenheimer Landis, Pittsburgh, c. 1961.

Below: 13. Helen Snyder Weinberg and Arnold Weinberg (*right*) on vacation with Janet Oppenheimer Landis and Burton Landis at Camp Tamiment in the Pocono Mountains, c. 1972.

14. Marilyn Blau *(left)* and Marcia Lustgarten in front of 1231 Sheridan Avenue in the Bronx, c. 1945.

15. Marcia Lustgarten's (*right*) fifteenth-birthday surprise party, with Marilyn Blau, 1957.

16. Marcia Lustgarten Hammer (*left*) and Marilyn Blau Klainberg at their "hundredth birthday party" celebrating fifty years of friendship, January 1992.

17. Linda Weinberg (*left*) and Mary Jo Lazear, 1951.

18. Linda Weinberg (*right*) and Mary Jo Lazear at Carnegie Library, Pittsburgh, 1952, *Pittsburgh Press*, February 3, 1952.

19. Linda W. Rosenzweig (*left*) and Mary Jo Lazear, August 2, 1964.

20. Linda W. Rosenzweig (*left*) and Mary Jo Lazear, Christmas, c. 1992.

21. Linda W. and Richard Rosenzweig (*right*) with Mari S. and Bill
Gimbel, Pittsburgh, November 1970.

22. Linda W. Rosenzweig (*right*) and Mari S. Gimbel, Wellfleet,
Massachusetts, August 1998.

23. Amy Rosenzweig (*right*) and Norma Savitt at
Amherst College, 1987.

24. Jane Rosenzweig (*left*) and Denise Meyer at Oxford University, 1993.

Though she traveled periodically from the Midwest to New England where her friend lived, Tracy found it virtually impossible to arrange to visit Humphrey. Once, when she was in Connecticut to visit a daughter at college, she chose to schedule a trip to the Metropolitan Museum (which she hadn't seen in over twenty-six years) rather than to stop in Simsbury to see her friend. Explaining this apparently nonchalant, almost cavalier choice in a matter-of-fact tone, she wrote, "I fear the frosts make you too inaccessible, you are busy teaching and my time is very limited . . . so I guess we shall have to postpone our gossip until next June. It will seem queer to be in such a small state as Conn. and not see you. I shall miss it."

Tracy was anxious for her daughter Charlotte to visit Humphrey. "You have so many colonial treasures to show her, as well as a renewed acquaintance on both sides," she wrote to Humphrey. This relative urgency offers a striking contrast to her own apparently casual attitude toward their reunions.[6] Evidently she saw no inconsistency between her inability or unwillingness to schedule an occasional trip to her friend's home and this effort to preserve the bonds of friendship in a fashion that echoed the habits of nineteenth-century mothers, who often sent daughters for extended stays with their own close friends. Even as late as 1939, Tracy could not incorporate a visit to Simsbury with one to her daughter's home in Massachusetts.

Nevertheless, Humphrey managed to visit the Tracy family at regular intervals, though her friend sometimes had trouble scheduling these visits as well. Yet the latter clearly valued their relationship. Their warm, lively correspondence continued, as did Tracy's use of the signature Rosalind and their annual exchange of Christmas gifts, until Tracy's death in 1947. A poignant letter from one of her daughters to Humphrey attests to the enduring bonds between the two women. "I ordered flowers for you—It was a big basket of long stemmed asters (predominately) white with pink edges. They look as if they could have been picked in your Connecticut garden," she told her mother's old friend. "This basket was placed just a little apart beside the piano. . . . When the minister comes back in the fall he is going to write out one of the poems he read. If he does I'll send you a copy. . . . With much love—Barbara."[7]

Various factors undoubtedly account for the apparent disparity between the efforts of these two women to preserve their relationship. It would not be unusual for a single woman to have more time to spend with friends than one with a husband and children. And as an independent individual with fewer personal responsibilities, Mary Helen Humphrey may have been more committed to the friendship. Although she too cared about the relationship, Anna Allen Tracy obviously felt less free to devote herself to friends. Differences in health, energy, finances, and so forth may also explain their behavior. The evidence clearly indicates that both women valued the relationship, but Tracy's choices and actions also mirror the early stages of the evolution of a twentieth-century friendship style in which the intense devotion to female friends displayed by nineteenth-century women would be not only challenged by a new emotional culture but also displaced by married women's other commitments.

Nevertheless, between 1900 and 1920, hints of change were offset by strong continuities, even among women whose lifestyles clearly contrasted with those of their nineteenth-century predecessors. Margaret Sanger, a far less conventional individual than either Frances Crane Lillie or Anna Allen Tracy, relied on female friends for financial backing and for introductions to influential potential patrons who might support her work in the birth control movement. She also shared her most personal concerns and feelings with them. She complained bitterly to her friend and benefactor Juliet Rublee, for example, about the "devilish and cruel" activities of Mary Ware Dennett, her competitor in the movement, and confided her dissatisfaction with her second husband, Noah Slee. To Dorothy Brush, another supporter and close friend, she expressed the sense of loss she experienced after Slee's death and reported the details of a casual, six-year affair with a young painter, whom she described as fun "but not for keeps."

Sanger and Brush traveled together, sometimes accompanied by Rublee, whose utopian vision of their joint mission to humanity extended far beyond the effort to foster reproductive freedom. "Darling—we must hurry—hurry—hurry—to pass B.C. [birth control] on to others so that we can work for this other, super, bigger thing which will make men and women into Gods and Goddesses," Rublee wrote to Sanger. "B.C. was a necessary step, but useless unless we can also create finer human beings spiritually and mentally. . . ." Few nineteenth-century women viewed the interests they shared with friends in such grandiose terms as Rublee envisioned, but many would have identified with Dorothy Brush's feelings about her friendship with Sanger. "They said that David and Jonathan had a love 'passing the love of women,'" Brush declared. "Well I love you passing the love of men, I really do . . . no one has ever understood me as well as you do, or has been as dear and patient and kind and considerate and thoughtful."[8]

Neither Mabel Dodge nor Gertrude Stein would have compared their relationship to the classical model of friendship symbolized by David and Jonathan, but for a very brief period, it too suggested an intensity of connection reminiscent of the tone of earlier female friendships. As art collectors and salon hostesses heavily involved in the literary and artistic communities in New York and Paris respectively, these women shared many interests. When they met in Paris in 1911, Dodge had been married, widowed, and remarried, and she would eventually marry a third time; Stein's partnership with Alice B. Toklas was four years old. Mabel Dodge recalled the beginning of their friendship: "She [Stein] and I had taken to each other in Paris. I seemed to amuse her and she was always laughing her great, hearty laugh at me." Their correspondence began formally with Dodge addressing her new friend as "Dear Miss Stein," but the tone quickly changed to a more personal one, mirrored in letters addressed to "My Dear Mabel" and "Dearest Gertrude" with affectionate closings such as "Much love to you always, Gertrude" and "Love, Mabel."[9]

Early in their acquaintance, Stein gave a copy of *The Making of Americans,* a long novel in progress, to Dodge, who became an informal literary agent for her in the United States. "To me it is one of the most remarkable things I have ever read," Dodge declared after reading the manuscript. "There are things hammered out of consciousness into black and white that have never been expressed before—so far as I know." This fulsome praise, reminiscent of Anita Pollitzer's youthful response to Georgia O'Keeffe's work, sparked the rapid development of what appeared to be a close friendship, although Dodge was clearly more committed to the relationship than Stein. After three years, the friendship cooled noticeably in the spring of 1914. Stein grew increasingly distant, but Dodge continued to write occasionally and made a final effort at reconciliation when Stein came to the United States for a lecture tour in 1934. The latter pointedly avoided seeing her, however, and the evidence suggests that they had no further contact before Gertrude Stein's death in 1946.[10]

Mabel Dodge blamed Alice B. Toklas for the failure of the friendship. "I felt that it was Alice's final and successful effort in turning Gertrude from me—her influencing and her wish, and I missed my jolly fat friend very much," she remembered. Despite the ostensible warmth of the tie between them, Stein evidently viewed the relationship in a casual, instrumental fashion, completely antithetical to the Victorian approach to friendship, although Dodge's commitment had involved a strong emotional investment. This imbalance certainly accounts in part for the path of the relationship. If Dodge was correct in her appraisal, jealousy and resentment on the part of Alice Toklas also contributed significantly to the friendship's demise, a circumstance that invites comparison with the constraints that obligations to husbands and children could impose on women's relationships with female friends.[11] In this sense and in other respects, although Mabel Dodge and Gertrude Stein led eccentric, unorthodox lives, their interactions resembled the friendships of their more conventional contemporaries. Common interests drew them together, and for a time at least, their correspondence reflected the language conventions of the period. While it lasted, the relationship met specific needs for both women. Dodge provided encouragement, praise, and publicity for Stein. The latter offered very little in the way of overt emotional or concrete support in return, but she apparently furnished some inspiration and personal validation for Dodge.

The brief interlude of closeness experienced by Mabel Dodge and Gertrude Stein offers an interesting illustration of the blend of mutuality and asymmetry that often characterizes the bonds of friendship. Dodge and Stein were unusual individuals, but even among more conventional women, in any historical period, personality differences and idiosyncrasies can result in an imbalance between the investment or contributions of the partners in a relationship, as the experiences of Anna Allen Tracy and Mary Helen Humphrey illustrate. Still, despite differences of this type and variations in lifestyle, the friendships of women who matured in the first two decades of the twentieth century were characterized more by enduring support and caring than by superficial instrumentality.

This tendency consistently marked the interactions of unmarried women, even when their relationships also reflected the growing emphasis on the importance of heterosexual social life. Thus Eleanor Coit enjoyed the esteem and warmth of affectionate friends who admired her work in the Y.W.C.A. and labor movements as well as her personal qualities. "Don't forget about the little flirtation you are to have—or a big one if you like. That's one of the things a vacation is for. And anyone as attractive as you are need have no difficulty, as you know, if she just has an inviting gleam in her eye," one friend wrote to Coit, who was en route to Europe in 1935 at the age of forty-one. "I think you are a whiz of an executive and a marvellous person, and I love you," she continued, combining traditional sentiments with unmistakably contemporary language and advice. "Much love for you dear, and do please be *frivolous* in Sweden," another friend declared. "I can quite understand why the language barrier might be quite trying, but all hail to the many men! . . . And do remember that you are *not* too old. You have many years that might be very happily married years."[12]

Jeannette Rankin, the first woman to serve in Congress and a dedicated peace activist, also enjoyed close, supportive relationships with female friends. While her life and career commitments certainly reflected post-Victorian influences, echoes of earlier friendship styles combined with evidence of twentieth-century influences in her letters to personal friends, as when she exhorted them to "write long emotional letters against war" to "Senators, Congressmen [*sic*], and the President." Rankin's letters to her friend Flora Belle Surles and the latter's companion mentioned the same sorts of things discussed by nineteenth-century Victorian correspondents and expressed her feelings in warm, affectionate terms. "Living in the glow of your love and care was a great joy," Rankin wrote after a visit with them. "I'm very grateful for the happy time and am looking forward to seeing you again before long. Lovingly Jeannette." Rankin offered both moral support and more mundane assistance to another friend, who was a missionary teacher in Turkey during World War II. "I know you are working hard and doing a good job. . . . you are such a joy in this world I hope you don't ware [*sic*] yourself out during this stupid war," she told Harriet Yarrow, adding that she was sending a "nylon blouse . . . that you might find useful for every day."[13]

A similar warmth pervades the letters of Sarah Norcross Cleghorn, a writer and poet, to Elizabeth Kent, who taught English at Russell Sage College. In 1936 Cleghorn was delighted to accept her friend's invitation to visit her class as a guest speaker, but she doubted that she had said anything worthwhile to the students; she particularly liked Kent's Russell Sage colleagues, "who were so undeservedly nice to me." Like earlier friends, these women interacted with one another's relatives and close companions. Thus Cleghorn acknowledged Kent's thoughtful gift of flowers to her aunt and sent her love to her friend's "delightful mother and to Miss Rose [probably Kent's companion]." The news of the latter's sudden death elicited a letter of condolence reminiscent of earlier missives: "knowing . . . how Miss Rose was in your home, and was a daughter to your dear mother—Oh! Elizabeth, I tremble for your mother, and my heart aches for you," Cleghorn wrote. Perhaps the most graphic illustration of the persistence of traditional aspects of female friendship in this relationship appears in the twenty-two sonnets about religion, faith, and death that Cleghorn wrote for Kent, possibly around the time of the death of "Miss Rose."[14]

The preceding examples offer clear evidence of continuity with earlier patterns along with some suggestions of change in the friendship styles of women who had matured before various developments in the post-1920 period significantly altered the social and cultural landscape. The resonance of those new developments can be discerned in the lives of both groups of women, but their impact on the experience of friendship was more pronounced among those who grew up in a post-Victorian world. As in the case of adolescents and young women, the cultural stress on heterosexuality and companionate marriage challenged the centrality of female friendship in the lives of adult women in the decades after 1920. At the same time, the twentieth-century revision of Victorian emotionology diminished the emotional intensity of friendship in general, while rising consumerism diverted a portion of middle-class women's emotional energies toward the acquisition of material goods.

Several other trends in mature industrial society altered the terrain of women's friendships in the post-1920 period. The proliferation of women's organizations around the turn of the century reflects the impact of a general trend toward impersonality and organization. This development produced a major new venue for middle-class female friendship. While the intimate sororal relationships of the nineteenth century were anchored primarily in the domestic setting, women's interactions increasingly occurred in a broader context of shared intellectual interests, social commitments, and for a select group, professional contexts. This development suggests that by the 1920s, for some women at least, clubs and groups may have displaced more intimate relationships and moderated the traditional tendency toward fervent self-disclosure. Some evidence also indicates that as leisure activities generally became more organized and group oriented, female friendships took on a more superficial character.[15] The 1920s also witnessed the disintegration of the self-conscious female community that had fostered friendships in the context of Progressive reform efforts and the battle for suffrage. Finally, influences such as the growth of geographic and social mobility and the availability of the telephone resulted in decreased face-to-face visiting between friends. While the latter development facilitated communication at another level, it reduced the need for the sort of lengthy, self-disclosing correspondence through which earlier women built and maintained close relationships.

Yet even as these factors imparted a new tone to mature women's friendships after 1920, other influences contributed to the persistence of traditional elements in their relationships. Despite affiliations and activities outside the home, most middle-class women still shared the experiences of marriage and domesticity. While they had internalized the heterosexual imperative, many found the reality of married life disappointing in comparison with the ideal of companionate marriage, and female friends could be a source of support and comfort for them, as well as for those who did not marry.[16] Moreover, despite youthful experiences of the sort of social liberation personified in images of flapperdom and flaming youth, middle-class American women's continuing subordinate status united them. At the same time, earlier liberating experiences may also have fostered a sense of personal agency that enabled women to transcend cultural prescriptions. Hence, although new developments affected the friendships of women of all ages after 1920, powerful factors of particular significance to the relationships of mature adults preserved the continuity between their interactions and those of eighteenth- and nineteenth-century female friends.

Like Anna Allen Tracy in the previous generation, other women found that the obligations of marriage and child-rearing dictated more limited commitments to female friends. Elsie Hagemann Noetzel, born in 1924, remembered that she and her best friend through junior and senior high school had expected that they "would always be there for each other forever." However, although the friend served as maid of honor in Noetzel's wedding, she did not hear from her again until her fiftieth anniversary. But friendships interrupted by marriage and the accompanying home and family duties might resume when these responsibilities lessened. Several young women, who were dating friends of Noetzel's future husband, also became her close friends, and they were her bridesmaids. They were too busy to get together more than a few times a year while raising their families, but later "these same girls (now women)" became "closer than ever," and for Noetzel their friendship was "a precious blessing." This experience suggests that the advent of the "empty nest" phenomenon helped shape mature women's friendship experiences after 1920, as did the gender gap in longevity, which had a similar effect.[17]

Alumnae magazines, round-robin letters exchanged by college and high-school classmates, and regular reunions of high-school friends over long periods offer other evidence that despite the pressures of the heterosexual imperative, friendships formed in the adolescent and college years, both before and after 1920, might remain strong in succeeding decades. While their expressions of regard projected a less emotional tone than the language used by earlier women, mature adults often reiterated the significance of long-term, supportive female friendship.

Letters submitted to the Wellesley *Record* in response to requests for news at intervals coinciding with class reunions indicate that college relationships continued to be important to women in the class of 1908. In 1923, Bertha Scott wrote that she was impressed by the solidarity of the class and their lasting interest in news of their friends, as well as by the dedication of the class officers who kept the correspondence going. "And surely nothing else so surely revives our youthful hopes and enthusiasms as contact with the friends of earlier days," she noted. "Incidentally, nothing in the world, however, can make you feel quite so old and unnecessary as to go back to Wellesley without some of your old friends." Hence she humorously advised classmates visiting the college at any time other than a reunion to "be sure to telegraph every friend near Boston to act as personal escorts. Otherwise you'll be depressed for a year by the pitying stares from the bobbed-hair infants, and you'll feel almost certain that you really belonged to the class of 1884." Lillian Wye Pike, a classmate who planned to attend the 1908 reunion in 1928, wondered what her husband would do while "Georgia Henry Whipps and I renew our youth. . . . I can hardly wait to see you all in June," she wrote. Twelve years later, Pike listed among her current activities "the best hobby of all, realizing the real value of friendships." In the same letter she commented that her years at Wellesley and her affiliation with "fine 1908" stimulated "the round of my days."[18]

A round-robin correspondence between 1943 graduates documents the existence of similarly strong ties in a later generation of Wellesley graduates. Letters from Mary Falconer Bell to the nine classmates who participated in the correspondence describe her experiences in war work, her marriage and family, and her reaction to her twentieth college reunion. She wrote about topics with which earlier generations of women would readily identify—for example, her enjoyment of her grandson—and also about distinctively twentieth-century concerns, such as her growing desire to either find a job or go back to school. The regular exchange of letters with Wellesley classmates was a source of enduring pleasure for this woman. "I've reread Robin and find it all so delightful—each and every letter[—]that I have to sing a little song not of sixpence but of joy that I have such good good friends," she declared in 1946.

Later, touched by the lasting ties with her classmates, she confided that her son had been in prison for two years.[19]

Eighteen women from Wooster College's class of 1930 communicated in the same fashion for a period of more than fifty years. As late as 1989, although six original members of the group had died, the others continued to exchange notes, clippings, and photos every week or so. When a round-robin envelope arrived, each woman removed her own earlier contribution, added something new, and mailed the package on to the next person on the list. The only divorced member of the group was gratified to have the unqualified support of her friends. "When I told them my husband and I were separated, they accepted it even though divorce was still uncommon," she recalled. Another member's expertise in social work enabled her to provide vital assistance to a classmate whose son was born with a developmental disability.

As they grew older, illness became a concern for these women; they worried about one another, and if a letter did not arrive on schedule, anxious phone calls followed. "I always try to include something funny," one participant observed. "We've seen so much illness and pain, we need a good laugh." Although they lived too far apart for regular gatherings, the memories of bridge games, concerts, and other activities at Wooster, where they had all shared a large house from their sophomore year on, continued to unite the surviving group members.[20]

There is little to distinguish the lasting ties enjoyed by these post-1920 friends from those of women who had matured slightly earlier, such as Rachel McClelland Sutton, whose relationships with her boarding-school classmates reflected the same strong attachment throughout mature adulthood. Their letters document an enduring feeling of connection to one another and to the Dobbs School where they met. Frequent references to class reunions and other events at the school appear in their correspondence. Although she had read about Sutton's activities in the Dobbs newsletter and heard about her from another friend, one woman wrote that "friends do need to get together once in a while to pick up loose threads and get a fresh start so to speak." Another was delighted to hear that both Rachel and her sister would attend "the Dobbs luncheon" with her: "You don't know how happy I will be to see you and Sarah! Won't it be fun to all be together again? I can hardly wait!!"

When Sutton's friend Esther Morgan McCullough went back to Dobbs to attend graduation in 1931, she felt the presence of earlier generations of students. "Through the silence comes to me the ghost footsteps of the old girls. All time seems one. . . . the girls graduating Wednesday . . . are vivid and noisy but the others are more poignant and just as alive—even those who have gone further away from Dobbs than just into the world," she wrote. Two friends wrote to Sutton about the retirement of a teacher, "one of the last people we know at Dobbs," and one reported on another teacher's funeral. Esther McCullough found the reunion luncheon in 1943 "a little sad" because attendance was small due to rationing, but she was glad "they did not break the long chain of reunions by giving it up."[21]

Rachel McClelland Sutton faithfully remembered her friends' birthdays and other occasions as her Victorian predecessors did—with cards, notes, and handmade gifts, including her own paintings. But in twentieth-century fashion, her friends were not always prompt correspondents, nor were they as thoughtful as she was. Nevertheless, they supported Sutton as she coped with her husband's mental illness, his hospitalization, and their subsequent divorce. Esther McCullough offered to visit the ailing ex-husband if it would be helpful and provided information about "a new stuff they have given certain cases of nervous breakdown similar to Bill's with good results," along with the name of a doctor to consult. Another friend wrote sympathetically, "No one can be blamed for being mentally ill any more than physical illness." This sort of whole-hearted support would not have surprised earlier generations of middle-class American women, but some of the contexts in which it was proffered would have dismayed them—as in the plight of the individual who wrote to Sutton from Reno, Nevada, "I am out here getting a divorce for 'mental cruelty,' the nearest thing to incompatibility there is."[22]

Like Sutton and her friends, later generations of secondary-school classmates were linked by enduring bonds. Six teenage girls who pledged lifelong friendship in 1944 still continued to fulfill that promise forty-four years later. Because they all lived close enough for frequent reunions, they managed to meet four times a year for lunch or dinner. Anyone unable to attend a gathering participated through a phone call to the assembled group. One member attributed the durability of their connection to the facts that they never talked about one another and that they accepted one another. Another explained their lasting friendship in terms of the traditional support of female friends: "All one of us has to do is get on the phone to the other and say 'I need you,' and that person drops everything—no questions asked," she stated simply.[23]

Not all women enjoyed renewing old ties, however. Frida Semler Sebury's comments on this subject suggest that even those who came of age before 1920 might have untraditional views about the value of an enduring network of female friends. "I never see a 1908er. Something in me has a horror of female gatherings," she observed in 1933. "I went to our last 1908 breakfast and ran away after the second course. These coy, plumpish women being all girls together is too much! If I had known I would have to keep telling the story of my life, I would not have gone to college," she declared.[24] Dorothy Smith Dushkin, a 1925 graduate, did not actually share Sebury's views, but she expressed ambivalence about attending her thirtieth commencement reunion at Smith. "Seeing college classmates after 30 years was not too unfavorable. Many I had no recollection of—some looked as I expected they would and most of them didn't know me either now or then," she wrote in her diary. Still, she was glad to have three "best friends" there and to learn that one of them would receive an honorary degree.[25]

Certainly other less candid women had thoughts like those of Sebury and Smith, but they did not necessarily choose to put them in writing. Moreover, those who responded to requests for news, attended reunions, and participated in round-robin correspondences with high-school or college friends represent a self-selected segment of the larger middle-class female population, many of whom probably had no interest in maintaining the sort of long-term friendships documented by evidence of this type. Thus the essential continuity between post-1920 friendships and earlier relationships reflects the absence of explicit expressions of indifference as well as the endurance of traditional views.

Some long-term relationships offer particularly striking evidence of the complicated interaction of traditional qualities with more contemporary influences that characterized women's friendships after 1920. Janet Oppenheimer Landis attributed the fact that her friendship with Helen Snyder Weinberg endured for more than seven decades in part to "our love of reading and our imaginations," but also to the fact that their husbands "found common grounds and so even tho we were 300 miles apart we could maintain contacts with no problem." Moreover, Landis observed, "this was really unusual for girlhood friends as they easily drifted apart due to their husbands' boredom." Such an observation would have appeared virtually incomprehensible in a Victorian context. Her emphasis on the role of husbands in the maintenance of female friendship clearly mirrors the influence of twentieth-century culture, but her reaction to the death of her friend conveys an undeniably timeless quality that would have evoked instant recognition in earlier periods: "I feel as if part of my life has gone," she commented. "We were good friends for over 70 years and that cannot ever be replaced."[26] (See figures 11, 12, and 13.)

Women born in earlier decades also consciously recognized and acknowledged the potential conflict between marriage and friendship. Some accepted the culturally prescribed order of priority. Apologizing for her tardiness as a correspondent as Anna Allen Tracy did, another woman cited her busy household "with three meals a day to be gotten, a big garden to be cared for, and the hundred and one odd things that turn up to be done during a day. I do all my own washing and ironing too, and it's really amusing what a difference it makes in my attitude toward clothes," she observed.[27] Others were less sanguine about the primacy of marital obligations. "I hope somehow we can all be together again—Life shouldn't break off, to my mind, into a complete change when one marries. How can one cut off all one's former contacts?" Esther Morgan McCullough wrote to Rachel McClellan Sutton. "Roger is so understanding about it, too, and encourages me. We both have separate friends, as well as friends in common and I never feel married, unless I'm very tired or Mother reproves me. . . . I don't feel attached or dutiful or any of the things we should!"[28] Louise DeSchweinitz, a physician, subordinated her career to the needs of her five children, but she maintained her own friendships as well as those she shared with her pediatrician husband. "We had friends in common," she recalled, "but I kept up a lot with college friends and childhood friends because I am a letter writer."[29]

These comments imply that the cultural image of companionate marriage as the vehicle for complete emotional fulfillment did not necessarily reflect the desires or experiences of individual women. Dorothy Smith Dushkin enjoyed a harmonious, companionable personal and professional relationship with her husband and found satisfaction in her children. Yet she also felt a strong need for close friendship with other women. "Why shouldn't I be able to speak clearly and unembarrassed to my friends?" she asked. Dushkin viewed this desire as one component of a full life, while at the same time she thought of herself as having "certain tendencies to homo-sexuality." This description may represent an accurate assessment of her emotional and/or physical needs. But it also suggests an effort to account for the discrepancy Dushkin perceived between her persistent desire for female friends and the cultural image of friendship as superfluous after marriage.[30]

Other women did not enjoy the sense of companionship and shared mutual interests in marriage that Dorothy Dushkin found with her husband. For those who discovered that the reality of married life bore little or no resemblance to the culturally prescribed ideal, female friendship could play an even more crucial role. During the 1950s, Patricia Frazier Lamb and Kathryn Joyce Holwein shared their most personal concerns in a frank correspondence that documents the particulars of their marital difficulties and extramarital involvements, their reactions to childbirth and parenting, and their responses to the world around them. Their letters reiterate a mutual recognition of the significance of their friendship as a source of support and stability that neither woman could find in her own family life. "You are the only light in my life, I sometimes think, from the outside world," Lamb wrote to her friend. Both experienced devastating loneliness and isolation as young wives trying to survive in relationships with uncommunicative mates. "When I think of the Barrett-Browning concept of married love I carried with me at twenty, I have to either shudder or laugh," Holwein observed on one occasion. "Life is often so terribly at odds with one's image of life, and I often think we live more in the irreal [*sic*] than the real."[31]

The rhetoric of this correspondence and the candid discussion of intimate matters locate this friendship in the middle of the twentieth century. Indeed, the revelations of profound unhappiness, unsatisfactory sex, and bitter disillusionment anticipate the unveiling of the "feminine mystique" and subsequent late twentieth-century feminist developments. Evidence of strong disagreements between Lamb and Holwein, some of which concerned the relevance of feminism to their personal problems, also reflects the relationship's modernity. Yet its importance to both participants links it firmly to the relationships of eighteenth- and nineteenth-century women.

Their disagreements did not disrupt the bonds between Patricia Lamb and Joyce Holwein, but the experiences of other women clearly indicate that severe tension could intrude on and fatally weaken even the ties of long-term friendship. Dorothy Thompson's relationship with Rose Wilder Lane initially resembled earlier female friendships in its closeness and its importance to both women, though they rarely saw one another. While their confidential exchanges typically focused on distinctly modern concerns, Thompson assured her friend, "Rose, your letters are the chief joys of my life." She sought Lane's advice as she contemplated marriage, read and critiqued the latter's stories, and urged her not to become discouraged over the absence of real love in her life. "You have a very great gift for friendship," she wrote. "There may be some providence that keeps you from being immersed in a great and wholly successful love—which would almost certainly shut all the rest of us out of your heart." Although she had not heard from her in four years, Lane responded warmly when Thompson turned to her for consolation after the failure of her brief first marriage. "Oh Dorothy, you are really very dear to me. . . . I care so much because you are suffering so. . . . It isn't the end; it's only the end of one of you, the close of a chapter," she replied.[32]

But when Dorothy Thompson's involvement with Sinclair Lewis produced a similar pattern of lengthy silences punctuated by renewed communication, her friend was not as patient. "Every woman has love affairs," Lane observed trenchantly. "It's the rarely fortunate one who has a sincere friend—I mean a *friend*. The time comes, eventually when one sees that a sterling silver friendship was really a rare thing, worth, perhaps, a little more than the other things one threw it away for." This caustic reaction articulates her annoyance over Thompson's inconsiderate behavior and her sense of rejection. However, Lane's comments also challenge the dominance of the heterosexual imperative, suggesting that some women questioned its validity in the context of their own friendship priorities.[33]

Their correspondence continued, and the friendship flourished for a few more years, but eventually conflict and misunderstanding damaged it irreparably. Lane resented the contrast between her own difficult circumstances during the Depression and the charmed life her friend appeared to enjoy. A combination of intellectual and political disagreements further complicated the situation, until Lane denounced Thompson in an angry, bitter letter that would have been inconceivable to most Victorian women: "My friendship for you has been genuine since 1920. It ends now, not because yours is a pretense, but because you are not the Dorothy I thought I knew. . . . Now you are coarse and stupid." Five days later in another letter, Lane declared, "You will hear nothing further from me." Thompson replied, "I have never had anything except a feeling of deep affection and gratitude for you, and that I shall continue to have. I regret that you have changed in your feeling toward me. . . . I still refuse to believe that a twenty-year friendship is over."[34]

A partial reconciliation ensued, and the correspondence resumed intermittently. "I wish our friendship were revived, but how can it be, after so many years," Lane asked. "We aren't what we used to be." Thompson disagreed: "I don't believe old friendships cannot be revived," she replied.

For a brief period, this more optimistic view prevailed, and they communicated energetically. "Look, Dorothy, Spengler and Toynbee and Social Science are cockeyed. A 'civilization' is not an organism, it is not biological, it is not an entity at all," Lane proclaimed. In her reply to this "delightful letter," Thompson wrote, "I agree with you wholly about the Socialist fallacy, but I don't think I do agree with you about 'civilization.' I wish you could come to Vermont next summer and stay with me for a little while. Conversation is much more pleasant than correspondence and more illuminating." Such a visit never occurred, however, as Thompson died several weeks after issuing this invitation.[35]

The saga of this friendship offers a graphic illustration of the intrusion and impact of the public world on a private relationship. As writers, these women paid more direct attention to social and cultural issues than many of their contemporaries. Eventually, conflicts—due to their divergent views on political and international issues, along with Thompson's recurrent neglect—created serious stress in the relationship.[36] Undoubtedly the failure of Lane's marriage and of several subsequent relationships intensified her reaction to her friend's blatant (though culturally acceptable) pattern of giving precedence to heterosexual relationships.

The intensity of the friendship between Georgia O'Keeffe and Anita Pollitzer also cooled in the post-1920 period. Although they stayed in touch and saw one another occasionally, O'Keeffe's marriage to Alfred Stieglitz and her subsequent rise to professional prominence created increasing distance between the women. Yet the artist continued to rely on her old friend in certain ways. "I made a will as I told you I was going to and gave you a job in it," she told Pollitzer, who was now married to a publicist for French performing artists. "Dont [*sic*] be worried though—I'll be about for a long time. . . . I hope to be seeing you in the fall. . . . Greetings to Elie—I so much enjoyed seeing you both last winter. Fondly Georgia." In 1950 Pollitzer published an article-length memoir titled "That's Georgia" and then embarked on a laudatory biography of her friend. O'Keeffe's rejection of the final draft of the book as too romantic and lacking objectivity effectively destroyed the remaining trust between them.[37]

These examples of tension and conflict between female friends reflect the influence of twentieth-century emotional culture. Victorian emotionology drew clear gender distinctions with regard to anger, thus constraining women's expression and possibly their experience of that emotion, as illustrated by the paucity of nineteenth-century evidence regarding conflict between female friends. In contrast, post-1920 emotional prescriptions did not differentiate between female and male anger. Despite the new emphasis on managing emotions, anger did not disappear from middle-class life after 1920, and women as well as men might express it.[38] Furthermore, conflict and disagreement, even between friends of long standing, may have actually increased as the parameters of women's lives moved beyond the home. Although such conflict did not necessarily end a relationship, explicit evidence of tension and anger between friends represents a change from traditional friendship patterns.

Female friendships increasingly played both an important personal role and a more utilitarian, untraditional, public role in a new context as more women entered the professional world. Their ranks included veterans of earlier Progressive reform movements, as well as their younger counterparts and other women from a variety of occupations. Although their concerns and activities extended beyond the domestic sphere in which women's friendships had flourished before 1900, the bonds between them resembled those of earlier women. Such individuals often drew vital emotional as well as practical support from female mentors and peers as they pursued career goals. For example, in 1921 seventy-year-old Ellen Sabin recruited Lucia Russell Briggs to succeed her as president of Milwaukee-Downer College. Their correspondence, which began with gracious, polite exchanges between "My dear Miss Briggs" and "My dear Miss Sabin," lasted until the latter's death in 1949. Sabin warmly supported and encouraged her successor, answered her questions, responded to requests for advice, and respected her decisions. "It has been a good two years for the College with accumulating understanding of the situation for the splendid helmswoman, solidifying cooperation and loyalty of the faculty, growing ideals and purpose of the students, but it is only a beginning of good things," she wrote to Briggs in 1923. As the latter told the student body after her friend's death, she valued their relationship highly: "She [Sabin] showed the greatest kindness and consideration, never criticizing, always encouraging. . . . I had the great privilege of her warm friendship."[39]

The network of women who played active roles in the New Deal offers a striking illustration of mutually supportive personal and professional relationships. Seasoned by their experiences in the suffrage movement and other efforts of the 1920s, this group included Eleanor Roosevelt as its most prominent member, along with leaders such as Molly Dewson, Frances Perkins, and Ellen Sullivan Woodward. Most of these women had been born around 1880, and they shared similar attitudes toward social reform and women's roles. Although they focused on issues of importance to women, they did not seek to be identified as feminists, preferring to emphasize humanitarian concerns rather than specifically female interests.[40]

As First Lady, Roosevelt not only provided access to her husband, but she also inspired loyalty and devotion in her own right. "I am sure, Eleanor dear, that millions of people voted with you in their minds also," wrote Rose Schneiderman, a friend from New York and the head of the National Trade Union League, in 1936. Molly Dewson, head of the Women's Division of the Democratic National Committee, derived some of her considerable political power from her friendship with Mrs. Roosevelt, through whom she developed a strong friendship with the president as well. The two women enjoyed a close relationship, and Eleanor Roosevelt looked forward to their weekly meetings: "The nicest thing about politics is lunching with you on Mondays," she told Dewson. A network of other close female friends also played a central role in Roosevelt's life.[41]

Frances Perkins gained strength from her friendships with both Eleanor Roosevelt and Molly Dewson as she coped with the demands of her position as secretary of labor. Dewson had proposed her to President Roosevelt for the job, and Perkins thought that if anything happened to her, he would want Dewson to "reset the labor department." Although her relationship with Mrs. Roosevelt cooled, Perkins remained close to other New Deal colleagues. "I can't tell you how much I miss you and the opportunity to have a good heart-to-heart talk with you once in a while. You are doing a grand job and everyone here thinks you are perfectly splendid," she wrote to Daisy Harriman, who was minister to Norway.[42]

Like those who held national political positions during the New Deal, other women benefited professionally and personally from their circles of female friends. Local and national women's reform networks, for example, provided important support for Miriam Van Waters as she embarked on a career in the juvenile justice system.[43] Ties between professional associates could be strong and lasting. "Beloved friend and coworker in the cause of working women," Rose Schneiderman wrote to her colleague, Mary Elizabeth Dreier, "It is with joy and pleasure I say to you that you have been my inspiration in the uphill fight to make industry a fit place for women to work in." A similarly affectionate tone pervades Dreier's correspondence with another colleague, Elizabeth Christman.[44]

Women clearly valued personal friendships that grew out of shared commitments in the public sphere, but such relationships could also complicate aspects of their work. During the years between the end of World War II and the resurgence of feminism in the 1960s, close friendships among members of the National Woman's Party enabled them to remain dedicated to their feminist goals in a hostile social and cultural climate. At the same time, however, such relationships contributed to a serious schism in the organization when personal and political conflict fused in a dispute in 1947. The closeness between existing members also hampered the recruitment process and the growth of the party.[45]

Personal and professional connections produced friendships among women in fields other than politics and public reform as well. Mutual medical interests often fostered the development of close relationships between physicians.[46] Not all physicians relied extensively on colleagues for friendship, however. Pediatrician Esther Clark's friends included "people whose children I took care of and their children."[47] Harriet Dustan intentionally pursued friendships outside the ranks of her profession in a conscious effort to "enrich my life with things other than medicine. God knows, it's rich enough—medicine is very rich; but there's the whole world besides medicine," she declared.[48] Nina Starr Braunwald and her husband enjoyed close friendships with their medical-school classmates and their colleagues after graduation. As a mature professional, though, Braunwald found herself so involved with her work, research, writing, and children that she had little time for cultivating new friends.[49]

Like many women in medicine, those in the intellectual and literary community found that shared professional interests could form the foundation of strong friendships. The relationship between Hannah Arendt and Mary McCarthy began inauspiciously when McCarthy's casual comment about Adolf Hitler infuriated Arendt, who was a refugee from Nazi Germany. Some three years later, the women made peace, and the loyal, affectionate friendship that developed between "Dearest Hannah" and "Dearest Mary" endured until Arendt's death in 1975. They relied on each other for both personal and professional encouragement and advice for twenty-five years, and eventually, as Arendt's literary executor, McCarthy set aside her own work to devote three years to editing and annotating her friend's last manuscript. In the course of this task, she felt as if she were engaged in an imaginary dialogue with Arendt: "I do not think I shall truly miss her, feel the pain in the amputated limb, till it is over," she wrote. "I am aware that she is dead, but I am simultaneously aware of her as a distinct presence in this room, listening to my words as I write, possibly assenting with her musing nod, possibly stifling a yawn."[50]

Shared intellectual and academic interests also linked Ayn Rand and Isabel Paterson. Rand, a novelist and philosopher, was delighted to have as a personal friend a writer with whom she could examine "important and abstract subjects." She was equally pleased that Paterson felt close to her as well as anxious to reassure Paterson that her feelings were reciprocated. "Thank you immensely for everything you said. Particularly for saying that I am your sister," Rand wrote, evoking earlier images of sororal friendship. A blend of lively philosophical debate and personal sentiments characterized Rand's letters. In one, for example, she expressed warm affection for her friend in terms reminiscent of the nineteenth century: "I suppose you will never believe how much Frank [Rand's husband] and I love you, so there." Yet shortly after this effusive declaration, the intensity of the bond between the women evaporated and the friendship ended, apparently because Paterson had insulted some of Rand's friends.[51]

Although the Rand-Paterson relationship did not endure, for many other women with common intellectual concerns, female friendships provided lasting reciprocal support and sustenance of the sort enjoyed by Hannah Arendt and Mary McCarthy. In key ways, these relationships also resembled the bonds between earlier women. Southern writers, to some extent relegated by their male colleagues to a "separate sphere" of the literary establishment, influenced and encouraged one another significantly. A brief but intense relationship between Ellen Glasgow and Marjorie Kinnan Rawlings had a major impact on both women's lives, and after Glasgow's death in November 1945, her literary executor asked Rawlings to write her biography, which the latter worked on until her own death in 1953. Similar bonds linked Katherine Anne Porter and Caroline Gordon, both of whom supported their younger colleague, Flannery O'Connor.[52]

Porter also promoted the career of Eudora Welty, proposing her work for publication and offering to sponsor her for a Guggenheim Fellowship. "She was to give encouragement to me from that time on in the ways that always applied to the serious meaning of a young writer's work—and life," Welty recalled. When they met, Welty was thirty, and Porter, nineteen years older, was a well-established writer; they differed in habits, style, and experience. As Welty matured professionally and personally, the gap between them narrowed, but the relationship remained essentially asymmetrical. Nevertheless, it endured for forty years, probably due primarily to the younger woman's uncritical acceptance of her friend's idiosyncrasies. Welty's memoir of the friendship alludes to her recognition of a "dark" side that contrasted with the "enchanting brightness" of Porter's presence, but it contains no explicitly judgmental comments. Thus, although Porter's procrastination over a 3300-word introduction delayed the publication of her protégée's first book, the latter effectively excused her mentor's cavalier disregard of the "unmentionable" deadline and of the publisher's repeated entreaties and reminders.

The dearth of critical comment in Welty's recollections of the friendship does not necessarily reflect the absence of conflict in the relationship. Other sources suggest that the episode of the introduction upset Welty, and that periods of strain and tension disrupted and altered the friendship over the years. Porter may have resented Welty's growing success, and the younger writer apparently found her former mentor difficult. Yet the connection between them endured, at least in their perceptions and memories, as they aged.[53]

Another complex literary friendship began in 1934, when the college librarian arranged for Elizabeth Bishop, a senior at Vassar, to meet Marianne Moore. The older poet quickly became Bishop's mentor and friend, although two years passed before they addressed one another by their first names. "It seems to me that Marianne talked to me steadily for the next thirty-five years, but of course that is nonsensical," Bishop remembered. Visits to the Brooklyn apartment Moore shared with her mother reminded Bishop of "being in a diving bell from a different world, let down through the crass atmosphere of the twentieth century." Yet those visits made her feel happy, "uplifted, even inspired, determined to be good, to work harder." The eccentric, accomplished Moore encouraged her, reassured her of the value of her work, and sometimes provided concrete editorial suggestions. "It was because of Marianne that in 1935 my poems first appeared in a book," Bishop recalled.[54]

Marianne Moore seems to have functioned as a quirky surrogate mother as well as a professional mentor for Bishop, whose own mother had been confined to a mental hospital since her daughter was five years old. Bishop wrote detailed letters and sent gifts to Marianne and Mrs. Moore when she traveled; in turn, they always commented at length on what she said.[55] Nevertheless, disagreements occasionally disrupted the friendship. Moore disapproved of her friend's decision to consult a psychoanalyst on the grounds that such people teach that "[e]vil is not *evil.*

But we know it *is*." The younger woman did not argue with her, and they never discussed the issue again. Nor did they discuss religion, about which they also disagreed.[56] A major rift occurred when Moore and her mother urged significant revisions in one of Bishop's poems and she rejected some of their suggestions, but eventually this issue was fully resolved. Bishop confessed openly to "one very slight grudge" regarding her friend: She never understood why an original phrase of hers appeared in one of Moore's poems. Yet, like Eudora Welty, she was reluctant to blame her mentor and wondered instead "how much" she herself had "unconsciously stolen" from Moore.[57]

As Bishop's poetry matured, the friendship lost some of its master-apprentice quality and moved toward a more equal relationship. The younger poet resented critics' suggestions that her friend was insufficiently feminist. "Have they really read 'Marriage,' a poem that says everything they are saying and everything Virginia Woolf has said?" she asked indignantly. Moore found her friend's support particularly comforting when she lost her mother, and she was overwhelmed by Bishop's contribution of a poem and three laudatory essays to an issue of the *Quarterly Review of Literature* that honored her sixtieth birthday: "Words fail me, Elizabeth," she declared.[58]

One final literary example reveals a more symmetrical friendship. Sally Wood and Caroline Gordon met when the latter, like many of her Southern colleagues, migrated to the New York area in 1924. Wood, who was not a southerner, recalled that after their first visit, "it was as if we had known each other for years. I can't remember anything preliminary. We talked about what interested us most—writing." She believed that the friendship filled a special and very particular need for both of them: "Yet although, as Virginia Woolf said, a woman writer needs a room of her own, she needs something else as well. Men who write often congregate in groups. Women do not, or they did not then. . . . And though our backgrounds were different, our foregrounds were the same," she observed.

After an initial period during which they both lived in Greenwich Village and visited almost daily, talking "from lunch until dinnertime," Gordon and Wood saw each other infrequently but maintained a lively correspondence. Their letters addressed both personal issues and professional concerns, and they read and critiqued each other's manuscripts: "My novel is turning out a mess. And this is no mock modesty. Too much stuff and not organized. I am sick over it. Nothing to do but stagger on," Gordon confided to her friend. Gordon was "quite overwhelmed" by

Wood's gifts of a ring and a "lovely velvet coat," and very grateful for the latter's financial assistance when she experienced serious health problems. The lifestyles of these women and most of their literary colleagues would have seemed strange to their nineteenth-century predecessors, even to those "scribbling women" who managed to practice their craft within the confines of Victorian domesticity. Yet strong bonds between two friends who found it difficult "to get along without" one another and rejoiced that they could communicate "safely. . . . without rounding off the corners" would have seemed completely familiar, as would personal gifts and financial help.[59]

Female friendship played an especially important role in the lives of aging women. Single women in particular relied on friends as they confronted the difficulties and infirmities of advancing years. As one stated poignantly in 1945, "The road seems long as one draws near the end, long and a bit lonely. It is good to have footsteps chiming with one's own, and to know that a friend in whom one has a deep and abiding trust is on the same track, moving toward the same goal." Another woman's description of a visit with elderly friends, one of whom was "exceedingly lame and also deaf," conveyed a similar tone. "I wish you could have seen the meeting—with our friends sitting up together on the sofa very much themselves in spite of Time," she wrote.[60]

But friendship between women who had reached "senior citizenship" could also manifest a more cheerful tone. Sarah Cleghorn was delighted to share the major achievement of her mature years with Elizabeth Kent. Enclosing copies of some of the galley proofs for her book, *The Seamless Robe—The Religion of Loving Kindness,* she confided proudly, "It's the top cream of my 69 years' little wisdom and very burning faith." And Alice Shoemaker wrote enthusiastically to Eleanor Coit, "You look *wonderful.* Better than I've seen you for years and years. Do take care of yourself all you can. . . . I thought your hat was stunning." Attributing her friend's "special kind of beauty" to her "devoted years of professional effort," she exclaimed, "No wonder all the organizations want you on their boards. Not fair for you to have this *and* brains *and* skill!" A light and casual twentieth-century tone marks these compliments, but a few years later, when arthritis forced her friend to use crutches, Shoemaker too spoke soberly of the infirmities of age, offering empathetic support as well as the practical suggestion that a change of climate might be useful: "For you who have always been so active it must be harder than for most.

I hate to think of you suffering so much, and of your bright spirit being so held down by a recalcitrant body."[61]

For aging married women as well, friends served as confidantes and sources of support. Rose Abramson confided her anxiety about her husband's illness and the difficulty of getting him to eat enough to rebuild his strength to Mary Elizabeth Dreier. "The doctors think that if he can be built up physically he will be able to live a sort of half active life for whatever time is allotted to him," she wrote. "All my waking and even night hours are devoted to my poor suffering husband. And all my conscious moments are just full of him," she confessed. "It is a very selfish way to live but I just can't seem to throw it off."[62]

Janet Brown, Dreier's summer neighbor in Maine, shared her concern about her physical weakness: "It makes me feel so ashamed to be so limited. I know you know dear Mary that the spirit is more than willing. . . ." Brown's letters often reiterated her gratitude for Dreier's friendship and support, her admiration of the latter's "valiant" and "gallant" spirit, and her concerns about her friend's health. Dreier replied philosophically to one of Brown's solicitous inquiries, "I am getting along as well as I can be I presume. After all when one is nearer 100 than 50, and has no long lived ancestry behind, as you have darling, one has a different point of view." Like Esther Burr, who had related news about the movements of local Indian tribes to her friend Sarah Prince two centuries earlier, she then proceeded to discuss current events, observing that "the excitement over Cuba is just too bad" and that Castro "is a very touchy young man apparantly [*sic*] and needs careful handling."[63] Undoubtedly many aging women would have agreed with Janet Brown's summary of the significance of their relationship: "Nothing is so dear as a friend of many, many years. They understand the pattern of each others [*sic*] lives. . . . Perhaps this is why you and I can so poignantly feel for each other. We have seen the warp and the woof in its making."[64]

The friendship experiences of middle-class adult women in the first half of the twentieth century link them with their eighteenth- and nineteenth-century predecessors in various ways. Yet those experiences also mirror the specific social and cultural context of the period. The history of Heterodoxy, a Greenwich Village club for "unorthodox women," recapitulates the interplay between continuity and change that defined the friendship styles of adult women between 1900 and 1960. Founded in 1912,

Heterodoxy existed until the early 1940s. Many of its approximately 103 members had active professional careers. They represented a wide range of views and backgrounds, but they shared a general commitment to feminist concerns. The roster, which included Mabel Dodge Luhan, incorporated married and divorced women, free-love advocates, and single women, some of whom shared their lives with female partners. Only one nonwhite woman belonged to Heterodoxy. During the organization's most active years, the group met biweekly for lunchtime discussions of a wide range of issues. Despite increasing cultural antipathy toward closeness between women, this setting fostered the development of warm friendships that lasted throughout the lives of club members. Yet few new members joined Heterodoxy after the mid-1920s, suggesting that in the context of the dominant cultural ambiance, younger women may have found both the idea of community among women and the concept of "heterodoxy" less appealing than their early twentieth-century predecessors had.[65]

Like the growth and decline of Heterodoxy, the patterns of adult women's relationships in the first half of the twentieth century reflect both change and continuity, but they primarily exemplify the abiding strength of female friendship. The friendship styles of mature women highlight the blend of personal factors that structured female friendships in the emerging modern American social context. Age, marital and parenting status, public and professional commitments, and individual idiosyncrasies determined the impact of social and cultural influences on adult women's relationships. Thus, while the heterosexual imperative clearly altered younger women's friendship styles, it affected those of mature women in a more nuanced fashion. The cultural stress on emotional management and consumerism similarly impinged on adult friendships but did not transform them fundamentally. Shades of difference distinguish the friendships of the generations of twentieth-century adult women from one another, as well as from those of their mothers, grandmothers, and great-grandmothers. Yet the "staunchness of female friendship" connects their experiences.

5

"Partner and I"
Twentieth-Century Romantic Friendships

Janet Flanner and Natalia Danesi Murray met at a cocktail party in January 1940. Flanner, the renowned Paris correspondent for the *New Yorker,* was forty-eight years old and divorced. Murray, an Italian-born broadcaster and publishing executive whose marriage had also ended, was ten years younger. Five months later they encountered each other again. This time, as Murray recalled, the meeting was more significant: "Something struck us, a *coup de foudre.* Janet and I knew that night that we were to become great friends."

Shortly thereafter, Flanner sublet a small apartment in Murray's house, and for the next four years, they "shared [their] lives . . . hopes . . . and the war drama." Eventually the demands of their respective jobs intervened, and the women found themselves on opposite sides of the Atlantic for extended periods. But their relationship—punctuated by long separations, joyous reunions, and occasional conflicts—endured until Flanner's death at the age of eighty-six on November 7, 1978. "Janet entered my life unexpectedly on a lively New York afternoon," Murray observed, "and there she remained until . . . that sad November day."[1]

In its constancy and emotional warmth, this friendship closely resembles the romantic friendships experienced by many nineteenth-century women. Janet Flanner's letters to Natalia Murray clearly document what Murray characterized as "a passionate friendship. . . . framed by two continents." Flanner's use of affectionate salutations—including Darlinghissima, My beloved one, Dearest darling, My darling love, and Darling one—and her fervent expressions of love mirror the sentiments expressed by women like Sarah Orne Jewett and Annie Fields in earlier generations. As the relationship between Flanner and Murray entered its nineteenth year, Janet Flanner revealed the depth of her feelings: "Thank you for the most beautiful and complete love letter I have ever known in my life. . . . I shall never forget this letter or lose it," she wrote to Murray. "It is the major apogee of the reception of the gift of emotion in my long life. I cannot in any way express my love for you in an equality of discovery and appreciation. . . . I adore and love and appreciate you, the first two as since the day I first met you, the last in a fête of special identification." Murray's comments about Flanner's reaction to her letter offer a simple but eloquent explanation of the connection between them: "We complemented each other. We were so completely in unison in our way of thinking, of understanding, that we simply could not do without each other, despite distances, loneliness, difficulties."[2]

As the allusion to difficulties suggests, a current of tension periodically disturbed this relationship. Janet Flanner could not bring herself to leave Paris, but she was unhappy about living so far from her friend and blamed herself for their long separations. Although Murray never really expected Flanner to give up her work and life abroad, she often felt lonely and discontented. By the 1960s, their lives had developed a pattern, usually consisting of two visits a year, and the relationship had achieved an equilibrium. Natalia Murray's earlier concerns about "challenging the accepted social tenets of the day by living openly according to my beliefs, in honesty and truthfulness" no longer troubled her, and the passage of time had not altered their affection. "We did not *feel* older," Murray observed. "Our loving[,] tender feelings for each other had not grown dim with time; if anything, they had evolved, increased, deepened. For me, Janet was immutable, unique and eternal."[3]

Natalia Murray's evaluation of the enduring quality of her relationship with Janet Flanner links these individuals to past generations of American women who maintained similar affiliations over long periods. At the same time, her subtle reference to the problem of challenging "accepted social tenets" introduces an issue that was not integral to the frame of reference of most pre-twentieth-century romantic friends. The blend of continuity and change that characterized the Flanner-Murray friendship raises a series of more general historical questions about romantic friendship: How closely did the adult relationships of twentieth-century romantic friends resemble those of their predecessors? Did adult romantic friendships change more or less than friendships that did not involve a romantic component? Were similar or different social and cultural factors responsible for the changes? To what degree does the pre- and post-1920 periodization posited in the previous chapters apply to romantic friendship? Finally, what connections can be drawn between the structure of mature romantic friendship and the evolution of adolescent friendship over the first half of the twentieth century?

Like the relationship of Janet Flanner and Natalia Murray, other devoted, emotionally intense affiliations between female friends document the persistence of romantic friendship throughout the twentieth century, despite increasingly prevalent cultural criticism of intimacy between women. As in the case of nineteenth-century romantic friendships, at least some, if not most, of these relationships encompassed a physical dimension as well as a strong emotional connection. The persistence of ardently affectionate language also links many twentieth-century romantic friends with their predecessors, both before and after 1920.

Yet despite the resemblance between earlier romantic friendships and those that developed in the period after 1900, one particularly significant factor differentiates them. As Natalia Murray's allusion to contemporary social norms indicates, increasing cultural condemnation of same-sex liaisons and the concomitant privileging of heterosexual relationships introduced a new and perplexing source of strain into twentieth-century romantic friendship.[4] The contrast between Murray's circumspect reference and the absence of similar expressions of concern on the part of nineteenth-century women underscores this change. Recent studies highlight an additional dimension that complicates the issue of change. While a number of historians have concluded that intimate female friendships were socially acceptable and even encouraged prior to the twentieth century, some research suggests that this image of a golden age of romantic friendship fails to recognize the complexity of the sexual culture of nineteenth-century America. Strong ties between female friends were not universally denounced, but the popular fiction, advice literature, and scientific discourse of the period document the existence of cultural ambivalence about female intimacy as well as a developing tendency toward pathologizing such relationships. Thus, although William Alger could describe women's "enthusiastic and steadfast friendships" in glowing terms in 1868, other authors warned against these ties. When the research of several prominent physicians, often referred to as sexologists, medicalized the issue of erotic relationships between women, the conflict and uncertainty evolved into a cultural consensus on female intimacy: It was defined as unfortunate, unhealthy, and harmful.[5]

Although such evidence suggests that nineteenth-century American society did not fully support close female friendships, other data demonstrate that many individuals did not feel constrained by the existence of cultural ambivalence toward passionate relationships between women. Whether they remained unaware of any cultural stigma attached to such relationships, failed to understand the implications of contemporary discussions of this topic or their relevance to their own experiences, or simply did not care about cultural censure, many women expressed their feelings for one another freely in letters and diaries that document both the emotional and physical dimensions of their friendships.[6]

But this situation changed as the twentieth century unfolded. Articles complaining about lesbianism in women's colleges, clubs, prisons, and reformatories appeared frequently in the years before World War I as female reformers increased their power and the suffrage movement grew more vocal and active. During the same period, college administrators adopted restrictive dormitory policies and warned young women of the dangers of intense female friendships. By the post–World War I era, when opportunities for education and employment permitted middle-class women to support themselves, close female friendships had become socially threatening as symbols of women's growing autonomy. In addition to manifesting excessive emotion, which the new, post-Victorian emotional culture strongly discouraged, romantic friendships between independent women challenged male prerogatives in several areas—sexual, economic, and even political.[7]

In response to the unmistakably negative evaluation of romantic friendship in the twentieth century, editors and biographers began to exhibit a tendency to edit sources expressly to protect the reputations of nineteenth-century subjects. Thus, for example, when Martha Dickinson Bianchi compiled Emily Dickinson's letters to Sue Gilbert, who eventually became Dickinson's sister-in-law, she carefully deleted passages that revealed the intensity of the friendship between the two women. As the poet's niece and Gilbert's daughter, Bianchi probably wanted to document her mother's influence on Dickinson's poems and the closeness of the relationship. At the same time, however, she recognized that even if fervent expressions of affection for a female friend were not necessarily suspect in the 1850s, they would be unacceptable in letters published in 1924 and 1932.

When Annie Fields decided to publish a volume of Sarah Orne Jewett's letters after the latter's death, she faced a similar situation. Mark Antony DeWolfe Howe, Jewett's editor and friend, strongly advised Fields to delete the nicknames she and Jewett had used, "especially where an assumed childish diction is coupled with them." He explained this suggestion pragmatically: "For the mere sake of the impression we want the book to make on readers who have no personal association with Miss Jewett. . . . I doubt . . . whether you will like to have all sorts of people reading them wrong."[8]

At the same time as this sort of protective literary stewardship emerged, women also began to behave more circumspectly with regard to their relationships with one another. Natalia Murray's oblique reference to her anxiety about a lifestyle that challenged the heterosexual norm suggests that she and other twentieth-century romantic friends clearly recognized the implications and the personal relevance of the cultural antipathy toward affection between women, and that they felt uncomfortable about their personal choices and emotional commitments. Murray's rationale for her decision to publish Janet Flanner's letters documents a conscious effort to address this issue:

I hope that my grandchildren, and other young men and women like them, born in a freer, more liberated society, more knowledgeable about the relationships between the sexes and without the inhibitions or taboos of an earlier era, will understand and value our experience and efforts to be above all, decent human beings. That is the intention of this book.

Although she and Janet Flanner overcame the social and cultural impediments to their relationship, Murray's comments reveal that even sophisticated, cosmopolitan, and financially independent individuals who inherited the legacy of the turn-of-the-century "new woman" could find the societal disapproval of intimacy between women intimidating. This reaction reflects their exposure to the mandate of the heterosexual imperative in adolescence as well as their reluctance to challenge cultural norms openly as adults. Natalia Murray chose to share the story of her relationship with Flanner "as a demonstration of how two women surmounted obstacles, trying to lead their personal and professional lives with dignity and feeling."[9] Nevertheless, the threat of censure and condemnation prompted extra caution and discretion on the part of many women and generated ambivalence and even self-hatred in some cases. Moreover, such responses to the growing bias against female intimacy affected the nature and quantity of the available historical evidence regarding romantic friendships—a situation that graphically illustrates the problems faced by the historian who seeks to analyze and understand the nature of an experience deemed unacceptable by the society in which it occurred.

The task of the historian is further complicated by the articulation of the concept of lesbianism, which did not exist in its current form prior to the twentieth century. By the 1920s, a few communities of women who identified themselves publicly as lesbians existed in the United States. An active black lesbian subculture in Harlem and a lesbian subculture centered in working-class bars in other communities became increasingly visible. Although a small number of middle-class women consciously claimed a lesbian identity in the decades after 1920, most of those who chose female partners kept their personal lives private rather than risk their professional reputations and perhaps their livelihoods.[10]

In this context, contemporary scholars disagree about the appropriate way to characterize women's relationships in the past, and particularly in the post-1920 period, when the modern concept of lesbianism did exist. Some reject the notion of separate, chronologically determined categories, maintaining that women whose primary commitments were to other women in any historical period should be labeled lesbians. Thus, for example, Blanche Wiesen Cook has argued that "women who love women, women who choose women to nurture and support and to create a living environment in which to work creatively and independently, are lesbians." Other scholars contend that the term "romantic friendship" represents an effort to desexualize women's relationships; hence they consider this phrase inappropriate in relation to women's experiences both before and after the emergence of the concept of lesbianism. From still another perspective, the notion of classifying intimate friendships as lesbian when they existed in eras prior to the definition and recognition of that concept can be viewed as anachronistic.

Two additional, contrasting factors further complicate this classification issue. First, even after woman-committed women had access to the concept of lesbian identity, they did not always choose this option; hence it appears both presumptuous and inaccurate to describe such women this way. However, other evidence indicates that some women experienced themselves as "different" even before theoretical ideas were imposed on them by male researchers. Finally, confusion also arises as a result of the historical suppression of female sexuality, the influences of late twentieth-century identity politics, and the current debate about essentialism and social construction in relation to sexual preference.[11]

This study acknowledges the linguistic and conceptual complexity that is integral to the historical investigation of intimate female friendships. It also recognizes that both emotional and erotic intimacy between women have held different meanings in different times. While no one term can adequately capture all the nuances of close female friendships, the term romantic friendship is employed here to discuss both earlier and twentieth-century relationships for several reasons. This term acknowledges the importance of these relationships in women's lives, while it avoids the possibility of disregarding their voices by assigning to them an identity that they did not choose for themselves. Although the concept of romantic friendship may have been used to deny the sexual component of women's relationships in the past, it does not necessarily imply the absence of an erotic dimension in female friendship. Furthermore, it encompasses the discussion of sexual identity as socially constructed and historical, and it acknowledges that identity and sexual behavior are two separate entities. Finally, the concept is compatible with the effort to historicize women's relationships, but it can also support the fact that the existence of same-sex erotic attraction appears to be transhistorical.[12]

Despite the conceptual intricacy surrounding the discussion of romantic friendship, it is clear that during the first half of the twentieth century, both individuals who identified as lesbians and those who did not choose this identity enjoyed strong, devoted, supportive friendships, often with the women they loved (occasionally while married to men), and also with female friends who were not their intimate partners. Like Janet Flanner and Natalia Danesi Murray, couples frequently expressed their attachments in terms reminiscent of the emotional intensity of the Victorian period. At the same time, they established and valued congenial friendships with colleagues and other single and married women. While they might express warm regard for these friends, however, they reserved ardently affectionate language for situations in which romantic attachment and friendship were combined.

Long-term partnerships, often described as Boston or sometimes Wellesley marriages, provided companionship, intimacy, and mutual support for many women at the turn of the century and beyond. The community of women at Hull House included several such relationships, among them the forty-year tie between Jane Addams and Mary Rozet Smith.[13] Because colleges and universities often did not employ married female faculty members, these partnerships were common among women in the academic world. During this period, the close female community at Wellesley College included a number of Wellesley marriages. Women like Vida Scudder and Florence Converse and Katharine Lee Bates and Katharine Coman shared their lives until death separated them. These partnerships did not preclude close friendships with other women, such as that of Bates and Caroline Hazard.[14]

Not all romantic friendships formed in the academic setting endured as partnerships. Ludella Peck's correspondence with Mary Frances Willard, her former student at Smith, documents a relationship that declined in intensity over a period of about ten years. Early letters reveal Peck's affection for her younger friend, who had graduated in 1890: "I do miss you very much and I never expect another such pleasant circle of friends among the students," she wrote. After a visit to Willard, her tone grew more expressive and explicitly romantic. "I have longed unspeakably for you and the blue world—the drop of dew in which I have lived for the last month. . . . I love to think of you in that luminous blue world; I am not sure that I am not there myself. . . . Lovingly yours, Ludella L. Peck." Although the correspondence continued until 1912, Peck's letters eventually became less fervently affectionate, reflecting unhappiness and dissatisfaction with her own situation generally and with the state of their relationship. "I mean a little to everybody and not much to anybody," she lamented bitterly. "It is human that one should love with a great passion, and be loved, instead of which we meander along throwing sops to ourselves and making believe we have the real thing."[15]

No such bitterness intruded into the relationship of Mary Woolley and Jeannette Marks, who were, respectively, teacher and student when they met at Wellesley. Eventually Woolley served as president of Mount Holyoke College and Marks taught English there. Their fifty-two-year relationship, which endured until Woolley's death in 1947, offers a classic example of a devoted Boston marriage. It also illustrates the extent to which the growing cultural condemnation of affection between women could influence even those for whom such affection defined the central relationships of their lives. In an unpublished 1908 essay entitled "Unwise College Friendships," Jeannette Marks criticized sentimental female friendship and characterized love between women as abnormal. She also discussed the dangers of romantic friendship in 1911 in *A Girl's Student Days and After,* and she considered writing a book about homosexuality in literature with an emphasis on insanity and suicide. The incongruity of these endeavors on the part of a woman whose own lifestyle incorporated the type of commitment she denounced underscores the stress generated by twentieth-century views of romantic friendship for women like Jeannette Marks. Whether her discussions of these topics reflect a pragmatic effort to camouflage her own preferences or an unconscious expression of self-alienation, they highlight the difficulties created for individuals when their strongest emotions conflict with the dominant emotionology in their culture.[16]

The power of cultural prescriptions regarding romantic friendship also emerges in the diaries of Louise Marion Bosworth, particularly in entries written in 1943, when she was being treated for psychological difficulties. These documents reveal a troubled individual's thoughts and recollections about an earlier college friendship and about close relationships between women more generally. Recalling her attachment to and dependence on her friend Ethel Sturtevant at Wellesley in the first few years of the twentieth century, Bosworth noted that their mutual friends had disapproved of this relationship. "I never saw then why 'crushes' were disapproved. I thought them natural enough—they were for me," she wrote. "I know now that it was the sex element everyone disapproved."

Bosworth's correspondence with Sturtevant contains intense mutual expressions of affection as well as indications of some ambivalence about the physical side of their friendship on Bosworth's part. One letter from Sturtevant declares, "My dear, you are mine and I want you . . . I know I'm selfish to want you to myself, but I love you." Bosworth's letters, some of which extend to sixteen and even twenty-two handwritten pages, express similar sentiments. They also include direct references to the subject of physical affection, as in comments about the "animalism" of other young women and an assurance that although "it" repelled her when Ethel demonstrated this sort of behavior, "I knew that I loved the rest of you more than I dislike that. . . . And you know that I love you now."[17]

Bosworth's reflections in 1943 suggest that this ambivalence about her feelings for women distressed her long after her college years, playing a significant role in the emotional difficulties she suffered as a mature adult. Recalling other close friendships that "fully satisfied me," she noted she had only desired marriage, "the more normal way of life," when she did not have an intimate friend. "Of course Ethel was my answer if I had understood better my self," she observed, "my re-actions [*sic*] and my relation to her." Yet she still found it painful and frightening to think and write about Ethel and wondered whether she might avoid seeing her again "if there were a likelihood." "I dont [sic] know exactly what this fear is. . . . perhaps it really was sex fear, or disapproval of a sex element in friendship," she wrote. "Now, if I think differently about that, believe it to be permissable [sic], allowable, not perverted or unusual, I could lose my fear." The preceding comments and Bosworth's equation of "emotion" with "uncontrolled feeling" reveal the degree to which cultural prescriptions regarding heterosexuality and emotional expression affected her in adolescence and adulthood.[18]

The confusion displayed by Jeannette Marks and Louise Bosworth appears to reflect what Carroll Smith-Rosenberg has described as an inability on the part of the first generation of "new women" to conceive of themselves as sexual subjects as well as the absence of a language to understand their erotic relationships with other women as sexual. It also reflects the dissemination of early twentieth-century medical representations of the specter of the lesbian as deviant and degenerate. While these women did not question mainstream sexual conventions, the next generation did, which enabled them to view sexual experimentation as a right and a form of self-expression. By resisting the dominant discourse of heterosexuality, however, such women risked marginalization, as Natalia Murray recognized.[19]

Even a woman as unconventional and independent as Margaret Mead never acknowledged publicly that her twenty-five-year relationship with Ruth Benedict involved physical love as well as friendship and shared professional interests and commitments. Mead and Benedict met at Columbia University in 1923. Although a fifteen-year age difference separated them, they soon developed a close friendship that had elements of a mentor-protégée relationship, as Benedict encouraged her younger friend to pursue a career in anthropology. A complicated, long-term love affair as well as a strong friendship linked the women until Benedict's death in 1948. During the same period, Mead married three times, became a mother, and had a love affair with Edward Sapir, a fellow anthropologist and also a close friend of Ruth Benedict.

Although the women only lived together once, for a month, the bond between them was permanent. In her autobiography, Mead summarized their connection as one of complete mutual trust in intellectual, professional terms: "When she died, I had read everything she had ever written and she had read everything I had ever written. No one else had, and no one else has." But she never revealed their personal intimacy. Ruth Benedict insisted on similar secrecy in relation to her own life, as did Natalie

Raymond, with whom Benedict lived for seven years after she separated from her husband, and Ruth Valentine, who shared Benedict's home later and was the chief beneficiary of her will.[20]

Discretion of this sort contrasts sharply with the openness of the unconventional women who lived in the artistic and intellectual Greenwich Village community and experimented with lesbianism and bisexuality during the 1920s. A similar frankness characterized the attitudes and behavior of a very small subset of American women who lived in the expatriate community in Paris before World War II. This group included Gertrude Stein and her partner, Alice B. Toklas, as well as Natalie Barney, whose homes became centers of literary life during the ten or fifteen years following World War I.[21] But most middle-class women whose lives were structured around romantic friendships chose more private and conservative lifestyles, particularly as the social and cultural censure of love between women increased in the twenties and thirties.

Nevertheless, despite the constraints imposed by the threat of condemnation, many women found contentment and happiness in relationships with one another, often embedded in a larger women's community. Molly Dewson and Polly Porter, who met in 1910, shared a home for fifty years. Dewson was thirty-eight and Porter was twenty-eight when they decided to live together in 1912. During the first years of their relationship, they both maintained active professional interests in social work, suffrage, and war work in France during World War I. Eventually, Porter gave up her career, while Dewson moved into a busy political career at the invitation of her friend, Eleanor Roosevelt.

Molly Dewson played a prominent part in national politics as head of the women's division of the Democratic National Committee, but she never permitted her political and professional responsibilities to take precedence over her partnership with Polly Porter. As a result, the women were rarely separated. After Dewson's retirement in 1938, they devoted their time to each other and to a wide circle of friends, who had viewed them as an inseparable couple from the earliest days of their relationship. And this was the way they saw themselves. Thus in 1920 Dewson could begin a congratulatory letter to a suffrage colleague with the sentence, "Partner and I have been bursting with pride and satisfaction ever since you were elected chairman of the League of Women Voters."[22]

Because they spent little time apart, they seldom corresponded. Hence it is difficult to document the nature of their feelings with any precision. Yet various examples demonstrate the strength of the bond between them—the common library of books stamped "Porter-Dewson," their shared bedroom, the pet names they used, the acceptance and acknowledgment of their relationship by family and friends, their observances of anniversaries, and the durability of their lifelong partnership. A letter from Polly Porter to her godchild offers a glimpse of her vision of the relationship as she reflected on it late in life: Porter refers to the existence of two kinds of love, one based on temporary passion of the sort that "must seek, on and on for fulfillment," and another "that settles down into complete companionship, this time not only of the pulsating womb but of the spirit itself."[23]

The same kind of complete companionship linked Mary Elisabeth Dreier and Frances Kellor for almost fifty years, until Kellor's death in 1952 plunged her partner into "the deep waters of grief." Frances Kellor's letters to Dreier document an intensely romantic relationship. "My own dear beautiful Sweetheart," she wrote about a year after they became partners, "My heart is full of love and longing to gather you up . . . and tell you how wonderfully beautiful you have been in all these months. . . . Dear dear heart I love you even more tenderly than in those beautiful days when I first found you." Another letter from the same time period commented on the need to be discreet about her feelings for Dreier: "I have to be very circumspect in my looks and not look all I want to," Kellor wrote. "Seems to me I never can look into those eyes all that I want to. Well, perhaps its [sic] best not to."[24]

Although the tone of their correspondence grew slightly less intense over the years, it did not change appreciably. Kellor continued to use pet names for Dreier, send valentine cards to her, and reiterate her love. These women discussed many other matters in addition to their feelings for each other, but they clearly cherished their relationship over the years. As late as 1951, Kellor threatened to write "a 6 line letter" to say nothing but "I love You!" After she died, Dreier apparently found comfort in sharing the story of their friendship without revealing the romantic side of it. "Miss Kellor and I had become very close friends and she moved into my home with the consent of the other members of the family and became one of our family," she wrote to an acquaintance. She also worked to preserve the memory of Kellor's professional accomplishments, as in a letter to the librarian in her friend's hometown: "Her creative achievements have never received the recognition to which they are entitled," Dreier wrote.[25]

Like Frances Kellor and Mary Elisabeth Dreier, Frieda Segelke Miller and Pauline Newman formed a long-term partnership. They shared a home most of the time after 1924, and they raised Miller's adopted daughter, Elisabeth, together. Unlike Polly Porter and Molly Dewson, both Miller and Newman maintained active careers that often involved traveling. This resulted in a voluminous, frequent, and detailed correspondence that documents their daily activities as well as their devotion to one another and to Elisabeth. At one point, Miller air-mailed Newman's favorite sections of the *New York Times* to her in Europe. When professional obligations took Miller to London during World War II, Newman worried about her safety. "You know my disposition and you know that my imagination is never asleep . . . when it concerns you or Elisabeth," she wrote.[26]

Their letters contain salutations such as "Paul dear" and "Paul darling" and closings such as "Lots of love, Fried" and "Much love to you, Fried," but their language exhibits a less extravagant tone than that of many other romantic friends. While these individuals may have been particularly susceptible to the influence of post-1920 emotionology, they may also have been less satisfied with their partnership. Occasional hints of tension characterize this relationship: For example, Newman objected to Miller's absence during the Christmas season and urged her speedy return. "It cannot be too soon for me," she observed. Other strains also intruded, including domestic and financial conflicts, and a major crisis occurred over the appearance of a man in Miller's life when she was nearly seventy. It appears that their relationship may have disintegrated as a result of this, but after Frieda Miller suffered a stroke in 1969, Newman and Elisabeth cared for her until her death in 1973.[27]

Despite the upheaval in the later years of the relationship, letters of condolence to Pauline Newman attest to the recognition and acceptance of their partnership by both professional and personal friends. Newman saved these documents, along with a handwritten list of fifty-one names headed "Letters I received" and two other lists, headed "Notified of FSM's Death" and "People Who Cald [*sic*] me." The letters consistently mention the long friendship and shared companionship enjoyed by Newman and Miller and the suffering endured by the latter. One particularly interesting and revealing letter compared Newman's feelings of loss to the writer's grief over her husband's death. "I know how you must feel, Pauline," Frances Doyle wrote. "Indeed 55 years of close association cannot be thrown out the window. I know. I had 56 years—from 1917 when I went to high school—lopped off my life when Bill died. . . . The only consolation [*sic*] either one of us has is that it is the best for them."[28]

As the preceding examples suggest, twentieth-century romantic friends frequently established lasting partnerships that were recognized and acknowledged by family members and other friends, who typically included regards to "both of you" in letters to one member of a couple.[29] Leila Rupp has described a number of such relationships between active participants in the women's rights movement during the 1940s and 1950s. For example, Lena Madesin Phillips lived with Marjory Lacey-Baker, whom she described as "my best friend," for three decades, and Alma Lutz and Marguerite Smith shared their lives from 1918 until the latter's death in 1959. The sources offer few details of these women's interactions, often providing only oblique references like that of Agnes Wells, who alluded to the death of her "friend of forty-one years and house-companion for twenty-eight years."

Rupp also describes two other types of romantic friendship: lasting connections between women who did not live together but traveled together and cared for one another as they aged, and devoted love and affection on the part of individuals for prominent female leaders like Alice Paul and Anna Lord Strauss. Because these women had professional jobs, financial independence, and the protection of class privilege that accompanied their middle-class status, they became targets of homophobic suspicion only infrequently. The conscious and deliberate practice of discretion concerning their personal lives also protected them. Occasionally, though, accusations of sexual deviance blocked the appointments of women to prestigious public or political positions. Such incidents imply that when romantic friendship appeared to pose a threat to patriarchal hegemony, it was unequivocally defined as unacceptable.[30]

In addition to provoking social and cultural censure, some twentieth-century romantic friendships were fraught with interpersonal tension that could result in the painful termination of a relationship. Winnifred Wygal, who worked for the Y.W.C.A. from 1919 to 1944, recorded several intense female friendships and a long-term connection with Frances Perry in the diaries she kept from 1916 to 1942. Diary entries document the happiness she experienced in Perry's company, her anxiety and distress over the periodic conflicts that plagued their relationship, and her sense of relief when these difficulties were resolved. On one occasion, she noted with regard to Frances Perry, "We are in a friendship deeper than any we have ever had." Perry expressed similar feelings in a telegram to Wygal that stated, "Loving you constantly in new completely free profound way." Both women reiterated the importance of the relationship to them, often with an emotional intensity reminiscent of the Victorian era. "O Winnifred Wygal this friendship of ours is something made beautiful by being in a crucible of fire, of pain, or agony," Perry wrote in 1932. "Tell me you understand. . . . I am filled with joy, filled with joy. . . . and I love you and love you and love you, my own other soul," she proclaimed.[31]

Wygal struggled to understand and respond to her friend's needs. She feared losing her and tried "to reckon with the sickening sense that I could not get on without her." At the same time, Wygal cultivated and valued a wide circle of other female friends, rejoicing, for example, when she received 150 Christmas letters from loyal and appreciative friends. These friendships apparently made Frances Perry uncomfortable; she objected to her friend's habit of saving correspondence, and she disapproved of her journal-keeping as well. Eventually, Wygal destroyed many letters from Perry and from Helen Price, another friend of whom she was particularly fond. She recorded this action in her diary as a "*sad* ceremonial," adding that Perry had urged her to do it "because of my small closet space and because of my possibly leaving suddenly and saddling others with the private and sorry job of examining them [the letters]."[32] Yet more serious concerns than closet space dictated this "sad ceremonial." The destruction of personal letters was a direct response to social and cultural attitudes toward intimacy between women, and Wygal and Perry were not unique in their decision to protect their privacy in this manner.

Despite their difficulties, Frances Perry occupied a central place in Winnifred Wygal's life for at least three decades and possibly more. "Frances knows I've never been untrue to her. She's unique and no one ever replaces another. . . . I adore her," Wygal confided to her diary in 1932. She tried to explain these sentiments in a letter to Perry:

You *are* the lamb of my bosom. You have been since 1918 and will be till we die. . . . You are my precious precious child . . . but I have other sheep not of this fold and there are times when the precious lamb must wait while one goes among the ninety and nine.

Ten years later, their relationship had lost some of its intensity, but a combination of lingering affection and nostalgia still characterized Wygal's feelings for Frances Perry. Her diary records "a nice talk" with Perry on New Year's Eve (on the telephone). It also documents her disappointment over the fact that her previous invitation to another houseguest made it impossible to accommodate Perry's request to stay overnight after a meeting she planned to attend. "She has not slept here in two or three years. . . . I am *very* sad," Wygal confessed to her diary.[33]

Elizabeth Bishop experienced sadness of another sort at the end of a fifteen-year relationship with Maria Carlota Costellat de Macedo Soares, a Brazilian woman with whom she lived from 1951 to 1966. The relationship had been a happy and compatible one, but as Lota's health declined, she grew impatient and angry with Bishop. Her suicide in 1967 devastated Bishop, who described the time she spent with Lota as the happiest years of her life and expressed the grief and anguish she suffered as she tried to understand her friend's choice. "It is awful—to love someone so much and not be able to do the right thing or say the right thing, apparently," she wrote during the days before Lota's death. "I can't help thinking I might have saved her somehow . . . ," she lamented later, "but honestly can't think of anything I did especially wrong."[34]

While the circumstances surrounding Bishop's loss were particularly tragic, stressful and troubling situations and painful disappointments marked other romantic friendships. An intense relationship between Barbara Deming and Vida Ginsberg grew very complicated when Ginsberg married her friend's brother. The affair apparently continued after the marriage, but their relationship eventually evolved into a friendship between sisters-in-law. This situation was especially difficult for Deming, who believed she would always love Vida; she realized she could never marry a man, but she also thought she would be able to fall in love again. When she did, she found herself attracted to an old friend, Annie Poor, who could not reciprocate her romantic feelings. Barbara Deming's papers document other romantic relationships and indicate that, unlike many earlier woman-committed women, she eventually identified publicly as a lesbian when she was in her fifties.[35]

Deming's relationship with her sister-in-law raises the issue of women's experiences of romantic friendship after marriage. Although studies of nineteenth-century friendships suggest that it was not remarkable for a married woman to maintain this sort of relationship, this was not necessarily the case in the twentieth century. In a social and cultural climate that devalued women's friendships generally, condemned romantic friendships specifically, and directed women to find fulfillment, romance, and companionship in heterosexual marriage, the concept of romantic friendship after marriage became culturally unacceptable. Despite the proscription of such relationships, however, a married woman might still establish and maintain a relationship of this type. Moreover, in certain cases, such friendships played central roles in women's lives.

Geraldine Thompson and Miriam Van Waters met in the late 1920s. Thompson, a wealthy philanthropist with a husband and four grown children, was fifteen years older than her friend and supported the latter's work in prison reform. Van Waters had previously shied away from intimacy with another female colleague, and she insisted on maintaining an extended spiritual rather than sensual relationship with Hans Weiss, a male admirer who wanted to marry her. Nevertheless, she became deeply involved with Thompson in a romantic friendship that would last for forty years. Publicly, they remained colleagues, but the relationship assumed major importance in both of their private lives. Although they never lived together, they visited frequently, spent annual vacations together, wrote and/or phoned daily, and developed warm relationships with each other's families. Thompson expressed her feelings for Van Waters in emotionally intense, fervently romantic terms. "All of me answers you 'yes' to all you say—all the cherishing thoughts and tenderness of your love. . . . I love you with all my heart," she proclaimed in one letter.[36]

These women examined their relationship self-consciously, considering how they might retain their independent identities while in love. Thompson wondered whether and what to tell her husband about the relationship. Van Waters wondered if she would now relate to her male friend in a different way. Jealous and possessive, Thompson feared that she would lose her friend to one of the other people in the latter's life—the female colleague with whom she had been involved before; Hans Weiss, who remained devoted to her; or even another benefactor who supported her work. "I am haunted constantly by Mrs. Dummer—She is a symbol—and a challenge," she confessed. "Don't you love me *at least ten* times more than you do Mrs. Dummer?"[37]

Like most other white, middle-class romantic friends in the first half of the twentieth century, Thompson and Van Waters did not claim a lesbian identity, whether or not they experienced or acted on erotic feelings for one another. They continued to present themselves as colleagues, preferring not to be categorized as a couple or viewed as abnormal in any way. At one point, Van Waters was pleased to learn that a Rorschach test had not identified her as homosexual.

Thompson may have felt less restricted after her husband's death, but Van Waters faced constraints of another sort. As a professional in the field of prison reform and as superintendent of the Reformatory for Women in Framingham, Massachusetts, she was fully aware of the contemporary identification of homosexuality with criminality, pathology, and even subversion in the emerging context of McCarthyism. Both she and the reformatory were investigated on charges that included homosexual behavior in the institution. Although she was dismissed in 1949, she was eventually reinstated and retired in 1957.

Throughout the investigation, Van Waters denied the charges and refused to label the reformatory inmates as homosexual. She drew a clear distinction between nurturing, loving female relationships and destructive, harmful perversions, and she believed that the charges did not apply to her experiences. At the same time, however, she deemed it prudent to burn most of Geraldine Thompson's letters. "One can have no personal 'life' in this battle," she wrote in her journal. Van Waters eventually developed a close relationship with another woman, but she continued to visit the aging Geraldine Thompson, who died in 1967 at the age of ninety-three.[38]

Dorothy Thompson, living in Vienna in 1932, was surprised to find herself romantically interested in Christa Winsloe, the divorced wife of a Hungarian baron. Thompson's ambivalent response to her emotions when she first realized how she felt about Winsloe reflects the influence of twentieth-century culture. "So it has happened to me again, after all these years," she observed, remembering two earlier occasions when she had been attracted to women. These recollections and her present feelings made her uncomfortable: "There's something weak in it and, even, ridiculous. To love a woman is somehow ridiculous," she declared. She saw herself as heterosexual and wondered how to explain that once again she felt "the strange, soft feeling . . . of being at home, and at rest; an enveloping warmth and sweetness." Yet, she wrote, "I love this woman."[39]

During the next two years, the women corresponded and visited, becoming inseparable companions for a short period. Like the letters of Frances Kellor, Winnifred Wygal, Frances Perry, and Geraldine Thompson, Winsloe's letters resemble those of nineteenth-century romantic friends in their use of ardent and impassioned language. Although Dorothy Thompson's volatile marriage to Sinclair Lewis continued during this relationship, various friends viewed the two women as a couple: "If you asked Dorothy to dinner, you asked Christa, too," one recalled. Thompson was devastated when the romance waned: "I feel that something between us has broken, and like all that love I wonder now if it was ever there," she wrote to Winsloe. "I write with my eyes full of tears, and my heart full of tears, and I wish they flowed because of someone else, because then perhaps you would comfort me."[40]

Despite the brevity of Dorothy Thompson's relationship with Christa Winsloe, its importance lingered. Winsloe's letters remained in her files for the rest of her life. Unlike Miriam Van Waters, she made no attempt to censor or explain them. Apparently she never again experienced a romantic friendship with another woman; nor, according to one biographer, did she ever love anyone else the way she had loved Winsloe, although she eventually enjoyed a happy and compatible third marriage.[41]

Eleanor Roosevelt was the wife of the Democratic candidate for president of the United States, a woman who had borne six children, and an active public figure in her own right when she met Lorena Hickok, a political reporter for the Associated Press assigned to cover the activities of the future First Lady near the end of the presidential campaign. Their relationship soon evolved into an intimate friendship. As Lorena Hickok traveled with her in 1932 and followed her activities in the succeeding months, Roosevelt began to rely on her advice and judgment. While Hickok's newspaper columns played a major role in shaping Eleanor Roosevelt's public image, the reporter's friendship and affection held an equally important place in Roosevelt's private life. Despite the public nature of life in the White House, the two women experienced a romantic and passionate friendship for about six years and an enduring affection for thirty years.

During the intense phase of their relationship, Roosevelt and Hickok spoke on the telephone and wrote daily letters that provide unambiguous documentation of their feelings for one another. After one separation, Roosevelt wrote, "I wish I could lie down beside you tonight and take you in my arms." In a letter to her, Hickok referred to "the feeling of that soft spot just north-east of the corner of your mouth against my lips." Although she was present at family gatherings and at gatherings of Roosevelt's strong network of female friends (some of whom found her less polished and genteel than they would have liked), Lorena Hickok's status as the First Lady's closest female friend was concealed for many years. However, the recollections of a White House employee indicate that staff members realized how close the two women were as early as Inauguration Day in 1933. Lillian Rogers Parks remembered that on that day, "Eleanor and Hicky, as we were soon calling her, spent a lengthy time together in Eleanor's bathroom and came out claiming that was the only place they could find privacy for a press interview." Furthermore, she observed that the staff did not consider this "the kind of thing one would do with a reporter. Or even with an adult friend." But Lorena Hickok clearly represented more than "a reporter" or "an adult friend" to the First Lady, as Roosevelt's letter after the inauguration confirms: "Hick my dearest— I cannot go to bed tonight without a word to you. I felt a little as though a part of me was leaving tonight."[42]

It is hardly surprising that Eleanor Roosevelt never published anything about her feelings for Lorena Hickok. While Dorothy Thompson's cosmopolitan circle of friends could regard romantic friendship between women with equanimity and invite the couple to dinner, even in the thirties when such relationships were clearly and unambiguously stigmatized in middle-class American culture, the president's wife could expect no such acceptance of her bond with Hickok. Moreover, even the urbane Thompson expressed ambivalent feelings about her affection for other women, and the First Lady might have experienced similarly mixed emotions. Nevertheless, she saved her correspondence with Lorena Hickok for the rest of her life. After her death, however, Hickok and another friend burned a large segment of it, and eventually Hickok's sister burned an additional group of letters.[43]

The destruction of these documents reflects the power of twentieth-century cultural norms regarding female friendship. Hickok's decision to burn letters that obviously meant a great deal to her and Roosevelt's silence about their relationship illustrate the pragmatic reticence with which most middle-class women who maintained romantic friendships responded to that power. The conscious choices of Roosevelt and Hickok, along with those of other romantic friends who practiced similar discretion, effectively limit the historian's effort to reconstruct and understand the nature of their friendships. At the same time, however, their choices, and those of other women who preferred to leave no evidence of their closeness with one another, provide compelling evidence of the impact of twentieth-century prescriptions for female friendship.

That impact is also reflected in a contemporary phenomenon that Blanche Wiesen Cook has termed "the historical denial of lesbianism." When the surviving correspondence between Roosevelt and Hickok was made public in 1978 and various journalists reported evidence of a same-sex love affair between the women, their assessments were rejected. Thus, for example, a biographical study of Lorena Hickok published in 1980 categorically denies the possibility that someone of Eleanor Roosevelt's stature could have actually acted on the romantic feelings she expressed to Hickok. On the other hand, the book argues that the unattractive, unfeminine reporter may have had a tendency toward homosexuality, but it also contends that even she cannot be classified as "gay." The editor of the letters and journals of M. Carey Thomas, a prominent educator and president of Bryn Mawr College, reflects a similar viewpoint in her insistence that although Thomas's relationships with other women included physical contact, sexuality was definitely not involved.[44]

These interpretations reveal more about the influences of particular cultural prescriptions on their authors than about the women whose lives they address. Yet they also relate to the question of whether or not it is appropriate for historians to classify as lesbians women who, for whatever reason, did not identify as such during their lives. The concept of romantic friends, construed broadly to encompass a continuum of experiences, offers a viable, appropriate, and accurate designation for individuals in this category. This concept respects the bond between two women, acknowledges their love for each other, admits that they may have acted physically on that love, and respects their self-perceptions.

One final example illustrates the pattern of mid-twentieth-century romantic friendship. Dorothy Freeman and her husband and son were summer residents of Southport Island, Maine, when Rachel Carson decided to build a cottage near their home. Freeman's 1952 letter of welcome to her new neighbor initiated a twelve-year friendship that quickly evolved from excursions to explore tidal pools, observe the habits of local birds, and watch the rugged surf, to a close relationship between two individuals who regarded themselves, in Carson's words, "to an incredible degree 'kindred spirits.'"[45]

Their summer conversations continued throughout the seasons in occasional short, intense visits and frequent letters and phone calls between Freeman's winter home in Massachusetts and Carson's in Maryland. Their correspondence often consisted of two sections: a "public" letter, intended to be read by Freeman's husband and mother or by Carson's mother and niece, and a private one to be read only by the recipient. The latter category in particular reveals an ardently romantic and loving friendship of vital importance to both women. Some early letters suggest that they were concerned about the romantic tone and language that characterized the correspondence. Like Winnifred Wygal, Miriam Van Waters, and Lorena Hickok, on at least two occasions they addressed that concern by destroying selected letters. Near the end of Rachel Carson's life, she apparently offered to return her friend's correspondence to her, but Freeman urged her to "just let Ida take them into the study and burn them quietly" on the grounds that she would never find time to read the letters. Furthermore, she confessed to feeling "uneasy" about them. "In the *Sat. Review* I read about Dorothy Thompson's correspondence that went to Syracuse and there was one statement that really frightened me," she told Carson. "I don't want to put it in writing but I'll just say that the same implication could be implied about our correspondence. . . . We know even such volume could have its meanings to people who were looking for ideas."[46]

Freeman's apprehension represents a self-conscious response to the cultural proscription of intimacy between women as it had evolved in the increasingly homophobic climate of the 1950s. Despite her anxiety about the potential for what she obviously viewed as misinterpretation of their closeness, the bulk of the correspondence was preserved, and it clearly conveys the intensity of the love and affection that linked these two women. In what they subsequently referred to as the "hyacinth letter," written in February 1954, Carson quoted a writer who had envisioned having two pennies and using one to buy bread and the other to buy "a white hyacinth for his soul." She told Freeman, "You, dearest, are the 'white hyacinth' in which I invest part of my time." During the next year, Dorothy Freeman reread the letter "literally a thousand times," and it became the emblem of their relationship.[47]

This friendship coexisted with Freeman's apparently happy and companionable marriage. While the letters offer no direct evidence of Stanley Freeman's feelings about the attachment between his wife and Rachel Carson, it appears that he and Carson had a warm, cordial relationship. The latter's decision to dedicate *The Edge of the Sea* to "Dorothy and Stanley Freeman" seems to reflect that relationship as well as to acknowledge Dorothy's importance to her discreetly. As in the case of most romantic friendships, it is impossible to determine whether this friendship involved a physical dimension as well as an emotional connection between soulmates. But no such ambiguity obscures its significance in the lives of the participants.[48]

As Carson's health declined, Dorothy Freeman's love and concern supported her. Freeman's letters during this period reiterate her devotion with sentiments such as "You are never out of my mind dear" and "Dear, you know how much I love you. I'm sure, but do you mind my telling you once more?"[49] After Carson's death on April 14, 1964, Freeman received an envelope containing three letters her friend had written in 1963 as she confronted the gravity of her illness. "What I want to write of is the joy and fun and gladness we have shared—for these are the things I want you to remember—I want to live on in your memories of happiness," Carson told her in the first of these letters. "Never forget, dear one, how deeply I have loved you all these years," she instructed her in the last one.[50] Many nineteenth-century romantic friends would have been puzzled by Dorothy Freeman's fear of the "implication" that could be drawn from her letters to Rachel Carson. This conscious articulation of the need for discretion clearly locates their relationship in the specific historical context of the twentieth century. But earlier women would have completely understood both the frequency and the content of Freeman's letters, just as they would have recognized every other aspect of this mid-twentieth century romantic friendship—a relationship that clearly illustrates a continuity in female friendship across the centuries.

Although the displacement of Victorian emotional culture and values, along with other social and cultural changes, produced a new adolescent friendship model in the twentieth century and also altered mature women's friendships to some degree, the relationships of woman-committed women and their partners closely paralleled nineteenth-century female friendships in their ardor and endurance. Despite the challenges of a new emotionology that stressed emotional management, discouraged emotional intensity, and produced new conventions regarding the expression of love, romantic friends continued to voice fervent affection for one another through the middle of the century. Unlike other female friends and heterosexual couples whose interactions reflect the impact of the revised emotional culture, these women's exchanges preserved the spiritual intensity of Victorian relationships.[51] For the most part, neither their personal expressions of emotion nor their actual experiences of emotion seem to have been altered by the dominant emotionology.

For many of their contemporaries, the ideal of romantic marriage seems to have supplanted romantic friendship in the twentieth century, although female friends continued to be important in women's lives. Thus while intimate relationships between both young and adult women were common in earlier periods, now only a subset of middle-class American women exhibited this friendship style. This group of woman-committed women responded to the powerful social and cultural norms that proscribed female intimacy and valorized heterosexual relationships in a unique manner. They continued to maintain cherished, often lifelong relationships as romantic friends. Yet they carefully guarded the privacy of their personal lives, a practice that represented a conspicuously new twentieth-century behavior as well as a pragmatic acknowledgment of the contemporary social and cultural climate. While the necessity for reticence and discretion dictated certain patterns of public conduct for these individuals, it also strengthened the bonds of community among them. This circumstance contrasted sharply with the disintegration of the larger female community in the post-suffrage era, a development that contributed to diminished intensity in women's friendships more generally.

The patterns of twentieth-century romantic friendship, then, did not change as clearly after 1920 as those of other female friendship styles. New priorities in adolescent friendship and more subtle alterations in adult friendship mark the post-1920 decades as a distinctive period in the history of female friendship. Romantic friends definitely became more reticent as social condemnation of female intimacy grew more pervasive, and specific behaviors such as the burning of letters and expressions of concern and/or confusion regarding the nature of their relationships increased. Yet even as the tradition of romantic friendship confronted an emerging new concept of lesbian love in the twentieth century, woman-committed women preserved the earlier tradition in their lives and self-images. They chose female partners, but for the most part they did not choose a new category of identity for themselves. Despite twentieth-century influences that were conducive to change, then, the friendships of these women mirror those of their predecessors in a very specific manner that distinguishes them from their post-1920 peers.

6

"The Most Straining of All Experiences"

Friendships with Men after 1900

"A straight friendship between a man and a woman is, as you know, a happy, helpful and beautiful thing; but a friendship of which one side is passionate love is, I suppose, almost the most straining of all experiences," Mary Pratt Sears wrote to a friend around the turn of the century. "I should dread unspeakably for a nature as emotional as yours any long continuation of such an experience. The nobleness of the love you described will make the strain less, yet even so you will find it a subtle and terrible one."[1]

These sober thoughts underline the special complexity that has permeated the concept and the experience of cross-sex friendship throughout the twentieth century, as well as in earlier American society. The enduring question of whether women and men can ever be "just friends" centers primarily on a fundamental issue, the problem of sexual tension: Does the "sex part" always get in the way, as one of the main characters in a popular contemporary film insists—and as Sears's observations seem to suggest?[2] Does "platonic" friendship exist? Or does it represent an abstract idea with no basis in either past or present human experience?

At one level, the eternal problems of this kind of friendship place it in a different category from women's relationships with one another. But the assumption that the sexual dimension negates all other influences on cross-sex friendships denies the historicity of such relationships. Like female friendships, friendships between women and men are socially constructed, and the same historical questions relate to both genres. Thus it is essential to consider how the social and cultural factors that have shaped female friendship since 1900 have affected friendship between women and men, as well as to examine the issues of change over time and periodization in this context.

No focused historical research exists on cross-sex friendship in the first half of the twentieth century, although the subject has provoked some interest on the part of contemporary scholars, as opportunities for the formation of such relationships have become an integral part of the current social milieu. The observations of Mary Pratt Sears and others imply that the intricacies of female-male friendship could trouble middle-class American women even before changes in educational settings and work and leisure environments placed increasing numbers of individuals in situations conducive to such relationships. Thus, for example, at the end of the nineteenth century, Ida Sophia Scudder described the stress she felt when she found herself unable to reciprocate the affectionate feelings of two male friends. "A good friend is a sad one to lose," Scudder lamented.[3]

The notion of cross-sex friendship inevitably invokes images of sexual tension. It also contradicts the dominant emotional culture of virtually every period of American history until the late twentieth century, when an emphasis on the centrality of friendship generally and a debate over gender equity began to alter societal views on this subject. Although heterosexual interaction between young people increased in the twentieth century, the explicit articulation of the heterosexual imperative dictated that young women's encounters with the opposite sex would focus primarily on courtship and marriage rather than on platonic friendship. Concurrently, the ideal of companionate marriage, in which love and friendship blended, implied that women's emotional needs could and should be filled by their husbands. This scenario not only downplayed the importance of female friendship, but it also specifically confined cross-sex friendship between mature adults within the particular context of marriage. Mid-twentieth-century images of women's domestic, maternal, and sexual roles emphatically reinforced the implicit cultural rejection of female-male friendship. As in earlier periods, then, the social and cultural climate of post-1900 America essentially inhibited the development of this type of relationship.

Although—or perhaps because—the dominant cultural ideology conflicted with the notion of friendship between women and men, discussions in popular periodicals suggest that the subject interested middle-class readers in the early twentieth century and beyond. In response to a query about why the world does not allow women to have friendships with men, one male author opined that the average "girl" is "too silly" to be a worthwhile friend for a man, to inspire and stimulate him to higher thoughts. Nevertheless, he noted, the few independent-minded women who realize the positive effect they can have on men make invaluable friends. A female writer's pointed reply to these comments questioned whether the "average man" was actually worthy of friendship. Interestingly, she noted that her own "most deep, lasting, and *romantic* friendships" were with other women. However, she believed that platonic friendship was also possible, although sex was undeniably a factor in friendships between women and men. Furthermore, she argued that such relationships could be invaluable, whether or not they led to marriage.

A less optimistic author maintained that since friendship would ultimately lead to love, platonic relationships could not exist. In contrast, another commentator, who regarded real friendship between women as a rare occurrence, referred to examples of "noble" cross-gender friendships. Similarly, an article about the seventeenth-century friendship between John Evelyn and Margaret Godolphin, aged fifty-one and nineteen respectively, pronounced their relationship "as near perfect as human relationships can be." Other writers argued that cross-sex friendship could be particularly valuable in enabling "boys" and "girls" to develop mutual understanding by overcoming their self-consciousness, and even proposed that girls initiate activities like "dutch treat" trips to the theater.[4]

One interesting discussion, published in 1924 as part of a series of articles focusing on "New Morals for Old," reflects both the social freedom of the 1920s and the strong influence of the heterosexual imperative. The author described friendship between women and men as "rather a new thing in the history of the world." He observed that neither equality nor choice, the factors upon which friendship depends, had characterized "the relations of the sexes, up to the present," although he believed that this situation had changed. More relaxed family bonds and more freedom in choosing marriage partners made friendships between women and their fathers, brothers, and husbands more likely. At the same time, the intensity of same-sex friendships, which he characterized as "an artificial product, the result of the segregation of the sexes and the low social position of women," was diminishing, as "such a romantic intensity of emotion finds a more biologically appropriate expression." Thus he predicted that friendship's place in marriage would become more important, and new conventions would develop "to give social protection and dignity to extra-marital friendships." This writer acknowledged the presence of "some degree of sexual attraction" between female and male friends and suggested that extramarital romance should be accepted "with a tender and humorous courtesy" in order to defuse its social consequences. Then individuals might recognize that romance would spoil their friendship and decide that they "prefer talk to kisses."[5]

This unorthodox proposal contrasted strongly with mainstream opinions about cross-sex friendship. Moreover, as the century advanced, popular periodicals discussed this topic—and friendship in general—less frequently. A 1950 article in the *Ladies Home Journal* conveyed the prevailing view at mid-century. Friendships between men and women were not socially acceptable, the writer noted. Most men were reluctant to admit that they liked women, but he liked them for a number of reasons, particularly for their femininity, which incorporated "all the aspects of sexuality which permeate the female personality." However, their most "endearing" trait was "their love for men."[6] Such sentiments clearly reflect the post–World War II domestic ideology and the feminine mystique of the 1950s, and they were undoubtedly shared by many contemporaries of the author. These ideas also suggest that in the middle of the twentieth century, most conventional middle-class American women, like their predecessors, did not expect or aspire to be "just friends" with their male contemporaries.

Despite cultural constraints and contradictory messages regarding the possibility and significance of such relationships, a range of evidence indicates that some women between 1900 and 1960, as in earlier periods, experienced friendship with men outside their own families. Like their eighteenth- and nineteenth-century predecessors, these individuals represent a small segment of middle-class American women. And female-male friendships continued to evolve primarily out of mutual interests in the public realm and to constitute exceptional rather than typical experiences.

Married women whose primary commitments centered on the domestic realm had little opportunity or impetus to develop close relationships with unrelated men. The same expectations and responsibilities that constrained their friendships with one another restricted the possibility of cross-sex friendships even more stringently. Those whose lives followed less traditional paths, including literary or professional women, often unmarried, were more likely to establish such friendships. The bonds between these individuals and their male friends and the patterns of their interactions with those friends illustrate several historical models of the elusive and "straining" experience of cross-sex friendship. Although subtle differences distinguish these models, it is more difficult to discern the sort of clear periodization that is evident in other genres of female friendship. Some examples hint at the impact of new social phenomena and cultural trends. While most reflect the lasting presence of the "sex part" as an issue between female and male friends, others suggest that platonic friendship could occur under certain circumstances.

The volatile relationship between Gertrude Atherton and Ambrose Bierce resembles earlier cross-sex literary friendships in its emphasis on shared intellectual interests. Yet it also projects a distinctly modern tone, as in the participants' lack of reticence regarding their reactions to one another. The friendship developed after Bierce wrote critically to Atherton about her second novel. Although she was offended by his harsh words, she eventually invited him to call on her: "I hate you generally, but I think you would be interesting," she remarked. This curious observation, which would have been unimaginable to any conventional Victorian woman, set the pattern for a complex relationship that endured for seventeen years. Their first meeting, which actually took place in his home in 1891, culminated in Bierce's attempt to seduce the attractive young widow, who was fifteen years his junior. Atherton rebuffed his advances, but she made him both a confidant to whom she revealed her feelings of self-doubt and a colleague whose professional guidance she sought. "I would rather have your opinion than that of all the critics of America put together," she declared in one letter.[7]

This friendship flourished at long distance. Atherton teased Bierce and flirted with him in letters. He complained about the length of her letters and her handwriting, but he published positive evaluations of her work and, for a time, carried her photograph, which he showed to other friends. Yet when they met, trouble inevitably followed. "I like you tremendously on paper—in correspondence and in the abstract—I do not like you at all when I am with you," Atherton complained. After she moved to England in 1895, their correspondence dwindled, but Atherton continued to regard Bierce as a sort of icon: "Your picture hangs in my salon," she reported from across the Atlantic.[8] For six years prior to his mysterious disappearance in Mexico in 1914, they had no communication. The enigmatic conclusion of this relationship seems to match the intricacy and ambivalence that characterized the interactions of two individuals who might well have been more than "just friends" but who apparently resisted any conscious definition, recognition, or acknowledgment of the nature of their feelings.

Given the absence of cultural support for friendship between women and men at the turn of the century and the perpetual possibility of sexual attraction, ambivalence would not be surprising in any relationship of this type. But Atherton's flippancy and Bierce's aggressiveness, along with their evident unwillingness to examine their feelings for one another, may also reflect the combined impact of two new influences: the increasing freedom enjoyed by "new women" as Victorian sexual norms declined and the emerging early twentieth-century cultural trend toward emotional management.

The experiences of another woman of Atherton's generation offer an interesting contrast to the latter's interactions with Ambrose Bierce. Ellen Gates Starr found a comfortable and distinctly traditional way to categorize her feelings for Charles Wager, a married male friend with whom she exchanged over three hundred letters during more than four decades of friendship. By addressing him in familial terms, for example, as "Dear Cousin Charles," and by referring to herself as "an adopted relative," Starr conferred legitimacy on their relationship.[9] No romantic feelings seem to have complicated their interactions, undoubtedly in part because Starr's primary commitments were to other women.[10] Despite lapses in communication, this relationship lasted more than forty years. A poignant letter in which Starr apologized for the shaky condition of her handwriting after she had suffered a stroke attests to the enduring importance she placed on her friendship with Wager.[11]

Perhaps the consummate illustration of the possibilities of cross-sex friendship in the transitional period before 1920 is offered by the experiences of Edith Wharton, a contemporary of both Atherton and Starr. For Wharton, who was the product of a lonely and isolated childhood, friends defined the essence of existence. "What is one's personality, detached from that of the friends with whom fate happens to have linked one?" she observed in her autobiography. Probably as a result of her unhappy marriage, Wharton surrounded herself with many male friends, often single or widowed men whose attentions she could claim. She regarded Henry James as "perhaps the most intimate friend I ever had" because they could laugh at the same things. "The real marriage of true minds is for any two people to possess a sense of humor or irony pitched in exactly the same key, so that their joint glances at any subject cross like interarching search-lights," she observed in her memoirs.[12] Both lived as expatriates in Europe, where their paths intersected several times, but neither remembered exactly how their relationship developed: "All we knew was that suddenly it was as if we had always been friends," Wharton recalled, "and were to go on being (as he wrote to me in February 1910) 'more and more never apart.'"[13]

Although in many ways these two writers were incompatible, they remained close friends for thirteen years. Wharton confided the details of her unhappy marriage and her difficult love affair with Morton Fullerton to James, and he gave her advice. She worried about his failing health and precarious fiscal situation and organized secret plans to help him financially. Wharton's willingness to risk a wartime crossing of the English Channel to visit her ailing friend in 1915 highlights the friendship's importance to her. The following year, as James lay dying in England, Wharton summarized her feelings about their relationship: "His friendship has been the pride and honour of my life," she wrote to another friend. "*Plus ne m'est rien* after such a gift as that—except the memory of it."[14] Edith Wharton guarded and cherished that memory for the next twenty-one years, until her own death at the age of seventy-five.

James may have been her most intimate friend, male or female, but Wharton's wide and diverse circle included a number of other men.[15] While she expressed great affection for all of these individuals, she felt a unique connection with Walter Berry, whom she described as the "one friend in the life of each of us who seems not a separate person, however dear and beloved, but an expansion, an interpretation of one's self, the very meaning of one's soul"—in other words, another self. In the early weeks of their acquaintance, Berry introduced Wharton to "what the communion of kindred intelligences might be." Unlike Henry James, whose sexual orientation apparently was predominantly homosexual, Berry also inspired Wharton's romantic interest, and they eventually had an affair. Walter Berry's death in 1927 left Wharton desolate. "The stone closed over all my life," she wrote in her diary. "He had been to me in turn all that one being can be to another, in love, in friendship, in understanding," she told her friend Gaillard Lapsley.[16]

Wharton's personal style and circumstances, along with those of her male friends, shaped the nature of their affiliations and determined the quality and quantity of the evidence that exists to document their relationships. American women whose lives followed more traditional paths rarely had opportunities to develop cross-sex friendships, and even those who moved in literary circles seldom established so many and such varied close friendships with men. Nevertheless, some of the substance of Wharton's experiences was mirrored in the experiences of other women of her era and those of later generations.

Ella Lyman Cabot probably would have agreed with Wharton's views about the centrality of friendship. Although the more conventional Cabot enjoyed a long, happy marriage, friends of both genders played a major role in her life, no doubt partially because she and her husband never had children.[17] Untraditional "new women" who espoused heterosexual intimacy and sexual freedom in the years before World War I and during the 1920s also developed strong friendships with men who shared their creative, social, and political interests. While their relationships might involve a romantic element, this was not necessarily the case.[18]

Still, romantic feelings did complicate the interactions of other friends, such as Miriam Van Waters and her colleague, Hans Weiss, whose relationship vividly illustrates the "straining" experience of unrequited passionate love. Weiss shared her commitment to social justice, but he also wrote Van Waters romantic letters expressing his desire for intimacy. Although she saw him as a sort of soulmate, she told him that she preferred an active career to a home and children and a more spiritual union to the emotional and physical commitment of marriage. Eventually their relationship evolved into a lasting friendship. Van Waters told him about her attraction to "someone else," probably Geraldine Thompson, and Weiss sought her advice in his search for a wife.[19]

Like Miriam Van Waters, Ada Comstock had embarked on a successful career that would culminate in her appointment as president of Radcliffe College in 1923 when her relationship with a colleague threatened her professional equilibrium. Comstock's friendship with Wallace Notestein grew out of shared intellectual and academic interests. Although he was in love with her, she could not imagine herself as a wife and thought that a "swift and almost complete estrangement" might be the best solution to this dilemma. Yet no such estrangement followed. Instead, a warm friendship linked Comstock and Notestein for more than thirty years. Eventually their meetings became increasingly important to both of them: "Whatever the gods may originally have intended," she observed after a weekend visit in 1935, "there is a compatibility between us which is unusual, and which I should like to believe indestructible."

This declaration foreshadowed the final stage in the evolution of their friendship, which ended very differently from the Van Waters–Weiss relationship. Eight years later, though Ada Comstock found it hard to believe that "anyone should love so old a woman," the sixty-six-year-old, retiring college president and her long-term friend, who was three years younger, were married. As she anticipated their wedding, she told Notestein that their relationship "was always strongest in spirit and mind. . . . At moments I have a glimpse of a harmony so close and sweet that it might be a revelation to both of us."[20] These sentiments offer a testament to friendship as well as a clue to the pattern of their interactions over the decades.

Josephine Peabody experienced a different sort of harmony, an undefinable sense of connection, in her friendship with Kahlil Gibran. The expressive young Syrian poet developed a romantic attachment to the woman he called "the Mother of my soul," "divine Mother of my heart," and eventually "my dear God mother."[21] Peabody, herself a poet, was drawn to him, but she was troubled by the fervor of his feelings for her. Although she believed she had no romantic interest in him, her detailed notes about their conversations, written in the third person, suggest the sort of mysterious tie that links Catherine Earnshaw to Heathcliff in Emily Brontë's *Wuthering Heights*. On more than one occasion, just before she fell asleep, Peabody "felt as if *she were* housed in his *own personality* for the time;—she felt as if she had changed consciousness with him and she seemed literally to be wearing his features, to be changed into him; to be looking out of his eyes and over his own very different nose, at the ray of moonlight on the wall." In the same vein, Gibran told her that even before they had met, he had felt someone or something *"with"* him, which he had regarded as his other self; now he understood that she was that presence. Despite their mutual feelings of connection, their expectations about the relationship differed drastically, and they quarreled when she realized that Gibran was in love with her.[22] Peabody's notes indicate that the relationship continued at a diminished level of intensity after this quarrel, but they do not explain how she interpreted her own feelings for Gibran.

In a sense, Josephine Peabody and Kahlil Gibran represent the far end of a spectrum of turn-of-the-century cross-sex friendships. The dilemma of coping with a male acquaintance whose romantic feelings were not reciprocated was familiar to other middle-class women of Peabody's generation. However, several exceptional aspects, including the significant cultural differences between the participants and their powerful shared sense of a mysterious link between them, distinguish this relationship. While

Peabody's evident surprise about the nature of her friend's feelings may reflect naivete on her part, more likely it indicates that she resisted the culturally unsuitable possibility of a romantic relationship between a proper middle-class woman and a young man of such exotic origins, even though she felt a strong emotional connection to him. While friendship with Gibran might have been acceptable, the idea of any other affiliation must have been too difficult for her to confront consciously.

At the other end of the spectrum, a very traditional and far more conventional model of cross-sex friendship linked Mark Antony DeWolfe Howe with several women, married as well as single, who shared his interests in books, politics, and Harvard and his social status as a member of a prominent Boston family. Ties of this sort between female and male members of an established social circle were compatible with the nineteenth-century patterns of socialization to which Howe and his friends had been exposed. His daughter's observation that "those affectionate friendships with a member of the opposite sex . . . enriched the lives of my parents' generation in Boston" underlines the historicity of cross-sex friendship. Like Josephine Peabody's guarded observations about her relationship with Kahlil Gibran, this comment also alludes to the relevance of social class as a factor in shaping the experience of friendship more generally.[23]

Occasional references reveal that after 1920, some younger women began to view platonic friendships as both feasible and desirable, particularly as forums for advice and support when they had romantic problems with other male peers. In 1924, Gladys Bell rejoiced that she had "so wise a confident [sic]" as Boyd Henry, with whom she could discuss her doubts and fears about her impending marriage. Several years later, in 1931, Yvonne Blue found living proof "that friendship *is* possible between men and women" in her friend Herbert, "the finest fellow in Flossmoor." At the same time, however, her observation that he was the only "boy" to whom she could speak frankly marks their relationship as unusual rather than common. Nonetheless, in 1959 June Calender was grateful to have a male friend after she broke her engagement: "Thank heaven I have a friend like Keith," she wrote in her diary. "I have needed him so much at times."[24]

These examples of ordinary young women's friendships with male contemporaries suggest the advent of change in the history of this type of relationship. They also highlight the altered character of post-1920 adolescent and young adult friendship styles. But the bulk of the available evidence indicates that among adult women, cross-sex friendship remained the province of a subset of atypical individuals with intellectual and literary interests, as it had been prior to 1920. Thus, Hannah Arendt's close friends, like those of Edith Wharton, were all men, with the exception of Mary McCarthy and a childhood friend from Germany.[25] Gertrude Stein also established warm relationships with male friends, among them Samuel Steward and Thornton Wilder, two younger writers whose work interested her.[26] Hilda Doolittle, the poet known as H. D., exchanged more than a thousand letters with Norman Holmes Pearson, who served as her literary adviser and agent, her confidant and close friend, and finally as the executor who worked to protect and enhance her reputation after her death in 1961.[27] Elizabeth Nowell, Thomas Wolfe's literary agent, conscientiously promoted his professional interests and also provided support and encouragement as a close friend.[28] And although Ruth Benedict and Edward Sapir met professionally as anthropologists, their mutual interest in writing poetry fostered a close friendship between them for almost a decade.[29]

Poetry forged a more lasting link between Elizabeth Bishop and Robert Lowell. (See figure 10.) Their thirty-year friendship began in 1947, soon after their first books had been published. Bishop remembered that they "just hit it off very well."[30] The bond between them embraced both life and art: They genuinely admired each other's work, and they quickly became devoted to each other. Although they were often geographically separated, the relationship's intensity was maintained through their correspondence.

This friendship offers a particularly good illustration of the complexity of the issue of romantic attraction between female and male friends. Elizabeth Bishop was predominantly a lesbian, but she had had several affairs with men before she met Robert Lowell. He was a heterosexual who had had numerous affairs and married three times. Early in their relationship, in 1948, Lowell hoped that they would marry, and many of their literary friends viewed them as a couple, although it is not clear that he ever actually proposed to her. Nine years later, he divulged his earlier feelings in a letter to Bishop, who now shared her life with Lota de Macedo Soares in Brazil: "I assumed that [it] would be just a matter of time before I proposed and I half believed that you would accept. . . . But asking you is *the* might have been for me, the one towering change, the other life that might have been had," he wrote. He assured her that although his romantic feelings for her had "boiled to the surface" during a recent visit, it would not happen again, "though of course I always feel a great blytheness [sic] and easiness with you . . . it's a great solace to me that you are with Lota, and I am sure it is the will of the heavens that all is as it is." Apparently it was Bishop's will as well. As she explained to another friend, "I love Cal [Lowell] more than anyone in the world, except Lota, but I never could have married him. He's so violent he'd destroy me."[31]

Their friendship resumed after Lowell's revelation of his earlier hopes. "You have no idea, Cal, how really grateful to you I am and how fortunate I feel myself in knowing you, having you for a friend," Bishop wrote from Brazil. "I am awfully happy with Lota . . . I don't seem to need or enjoy a lot of intellectual society—but I certainly need you," she continued.[32] The bonds between them were strong enough to survive a series of strains in the relationship during the 1960s and a serious rift in the early 1970s. "We (you and I) are together till life's end," Lowell told Bishop in 1972. When she assured him that she too hoped they would be friends "for the rest of our lives," she had no way of knowing that only five years later, Lowell would die in a New York taxi. Bishop paid eloquent tribute to their friendship of three decades in "North Haven," the only poem she ever addressed to Robert Lowell.[33]

Two final, related examples offer intriguing illustrations of the dimensions of cross-sex friendship after 1920. A unique set of circumstances initiated the development of a close friendship between Eleanor Roosevelt and the New York state trooper chosen by her husband to serve as her bodyguard. The wife of the future president was forty-four years old in 1929 when she met Corporal Earl Miller, who was twelve years her junior. The handsome trooper accompanied Mrs. Roosevelt in the performance of her duties as wife of the governor of New York, but his role quickly extended far beyond that of the individual responsible for her security. He coached her in tennis, taught her to dive and shoot, played the piano and sang with her, and championed her interests enthusiastically. The two soon became inseparable. Despite their geographic separation after Franklin D. Roosevelt's election to the presidency, their friendship endured for more than thirty years.

No written sources exist to reveal the precise nature of this relationship. Earl Miller's long, daily letters, spanning the years from 1929 to 1962, have disappeared, as have Eleanor Roosevelt's letters to him. Her only autobiographic references to her friend offer no insight into their relationship. But some sense of the quality of their interactions emerges obliquely, in photographs and home movies and through the observations of those around them. Some of her female friends disapproved of the level of familiarity between them. They objected to what they regarded as inappropriately affectionate gestures—Earl Miller's arm around Mrs. Roosevelt's waist or her shoulders, his hand on her knee or hers on his knee. James Roosevelt thought the relationship involved more than close friendship: "Mother may have had an affair with Earl Miller. . . . Their relationship deepened after father's death and ended only with mother's death," he wrote.

While it is impossible to capture the essence of the tie between Eleanor Roosevelt and Miller, particularly in the context of her concurrent friendship with Lorena Hickok, it is clear that the relationship was important to both of them. Earl Miller's loyalty, devotion, and support contrasted sharply with the perfunctory treatment Mrs. Roosevelt experienced from her husband and sons. As a bodyguard, Miller protected her publicly by providing for her physical security. As a friend, and perhaps also as something more, he protected her in other ways—by explicitly acknowledging and honoring her individuality and her talents, and ultimately by remaining silent about their relationship until the end of his life.[34]

For at least twelve years of the time that his wife enjoyed this supportive friendship, Franklin Roosevelt was involved in a close relationship with Margaret Suckley, a distant cousin whom he had first met in 1910. They saw one another casually during the intervening years, but after he invited her to attend his inauguration in March 1933, the friendship assumed a central role in both of their lives. While his involvements with Lucy Mercer, his wife's social secretary, and Marguerite LeHand, his own secretary, have been addressed frequently by historians and biographers, Roosevelt's relationship with this quiet, unassuming individual, known as Daisy, remained essentially a private matter until Suckley's death in 1991 at the age of nearly one hundred. When friends found a suitcase filled with diaries and letters under her bed, the story of her close companionship with the president was revealed for the first time.

Detailed diary entries and extensive correspondence, including thirty-eight handwritten letters from the president to Daisy Suckley as well as many of her letters to him, document a mutually sustaining relationship of affection and trust along with hints of romance. As in the case of Eleanor Roosevelt and Earl Miller, the romantic dimension of this friendship remains ambiguous. But the participants' own voices firmly document both the strength and the importance of their tie. Suckley's diaries refer to calls from the president; long drives in the countryside near the

Roosevelt home in Hyde Park, New York; visits for tea; invitations to accompany him on trips and to attend events at the White House; and small gifts that she treasured. Later entries chronicle her anxiety over his failing health and record occasions when she ate dinner with him in his room, read quietly while he rested, and even participated in his care.

Cryptic observations such as "The President is a MAN—mentally, physically, and spiritually—what more can I say?" invite speculation about the degree to which their early interactions involved romance as well as friendship. Although most observers apparently saw nothing particularly noteworthy about Daisy Suckley's presence in the president's circle, occasional comments suggest that the relationship elicited some curiosity. Suckley noted that she cared nothing about "petty gossips," but she thought it was important to avoid any appearance of impropriety that might provoke comment about either Franklin or Eleanor Roosevelt.[35]

Suckley's letters often reflect a domestic tone. She reported on her own activities; described the antics of her dog and of Fala, the terrier she had given the president; and responded to his detailed descriptions of trips and interactions with prominent figures such as Churchill and Stalin. Some of her letters contain small drawings and sketches; in one, she enclosed a four-leaf clover, which the president put in his pocket, "within 5 inches" of his heart. Early in the relationship, Suckley wrote several times about the nature of friendship—how it starts, how important it is, and how much friends say *"without* words." In turn, the president confided many personal thoughts in his letters and often expressed appreciation for her companionship and understanding.[36]

Daisy Suckley clearly cherished their friendship. She was content to spend time with the president and expected very little from him. "It is the greatest privilege to be of even the *slightest* help to F.D.R.," she confided to her diary. She believed that although Eleanor and Franklin Roosevelt loved each other, they could not relax together. "What I have been able to contribute was a complete lack of 'strain,' she recalled. "I was somebody nearby, so he wouldn't be alone—And we understood each other." Suckley was with the president when he suffered a fatal stroke, and she was devastated by his death: "I don't see how any loss could be worse than to lose the kind of a friend F.D.R. was," she lamented.

Aspects of their relationship will never be fully accessible to the historian, but from Daisy Suckley's point of view, there was no ambiguity. "I believe that my friendship with F.D.R. was one of those very rare relationships (outside of marriage), which is so simple, so completely clean and straightforward, that only a person who has experienced it can believe it and understand it," she asserted firmly in her diary. Like Earl Miller, who guarded his memories and never discussed his relationship with Eleanor Roosevelt, this modest, unpretentious woman *literally* hid her recollections of the man she called "a perfect friend" for the rest of her life.[37]

Probably no other woman described in the preceding examples was as self-effacing as Daisy Suckley in contemplating a cross-sex friendship—or as totally grateful for the privilege of spending time with a close male friend. Certainly no other woman encountered the Duke of Windsor, "completely insignificant looking but charming and quick," and his wife, "a completely unscrupulous woman, as is proved by her past life," or helped to entertain Mrs. Winston Churchill, in the course of such a friendship.[38] By any measure, a close relationship with the president of the United States represents a very unusual situation, as Daisy Suckley's bond with Franklin Roosevelt clearly illustrates.

To some degree, however, the same observation might apply to the friendship experiences of any woman, whether in the past or in contemporary society, since every individual is unusual in a sense. But the issue for the historian involves more than an explicit recognition of the connection between the idiosyncrasies of individual circumstances, personalities, commitments, and interests, and the nature of people's friendships. Hence it is imperative to consider what general conclusions the foregoing evidence suggests about the history of cross-sex friendships. How have friendships between women and men typically developed in the past? In what ways have such relationships resembled same-sex friendships? In what ways have they differed from women's friendships with one another? Does the evidence document the existence of platonic friendships in the past? How have historical factors influenced the nature of friendships between women and men? And finally, have such relationships changed over time?

The majority of middle-class American women in the past did not experience close friendships with men outside their families, but such relationships could develop in the first half of the twentieth century and earlier, even in the presence of restrictive social and cultural factors. Most female-male friendships evolved through shared creative and intellectual interests or social and political commitments. Thus career-oriented women, rather than those whose activities remained primarily domestic, were more likely to have male friends. Some of these relationships involved mentor-protégée associations, but others linked peers or colleagues, such as writers, painters, and academics.

While the sources do not always offer conclusive evidence of the presence or absence of romance between female and male friends, it is clear that the issue frequently surfaced in cross-sex friendships in which one or both participants had a heterosexual orientation. Sexual tension could take different forms. First, and perhaps most obviously, the dynamics of heterosexual flirtation could complicate the interactions between friends, as occurred with Gertrude Atherton and Ambrose Bierce. Elizabeth Nowell resisted Thomas Wolfe's efforts to introduce a romantic element into their friendship, and Hannah Arendt refused marriage proposals from two friends, Hans Morgenthau and W. H. Auden, pronouncing the prospect of marriage to the latter "worse than suicide."[39]

When personal preference or sexual orientation precluded one partner from reciprocating the romantic interest of another, a relationship might become strained and difficult. However, as the case of Elizabeth Bishop and Robert Lowell illustrates, such strain did not necessarily destroy a friendship. Furthermore, romantic attraction was not inevitable, as revealed by the relationships of Edith Wharton with Henry James and Ellen Gates Starr with Charles Wager.

Age could also influence the degree to which sexual tension complicated a friendship: For example, Hilda Doolittle and her considerably younger friend, Norman Pearson, did not confront romance in the context of their friendship. Nor did romantic concerns disrupt friendships when both participants were completely or primarily homosexual in orientation, as in the case of Gertrude Stein's relationships with Samuel Steward and Thornton Wilder.

At first glance, the clearest difference between heterosexual women's experiences of cross-sex and same-sex friendship derives from the general absence of complications due to romantic attraction in the latter category. Yet such complications could strain relationships between female romantic friends or self-identified lesbians in the same way as they caused difficulties for female and male friends. A less apparent, more nuanced, and possibly more fundamental difference emerges from the contrast between the essence of friendship as a voluntary, nonhierarchical affiliation between equals and the gendered structure of patriarchal society. Given the nature of gender socialization, the societal construction of women as other, and the attendant rules for female-male interaction, the possibility of equality between female and male friends becomes intrinsically questionable. While the shared status of middle-class American women incorporates the sort of equality that theoretically defines friendship, their subordinate status in relation to men, in both past and contemporary contexts, can add a problematic dimension to cross-sex friendship.

Communication between female and male friends has also been inhibited by the "different rhetoric"—different voices and interpersonal styles—that often distinguish women and men. Various contemporary researchers have examined this problem, which is related to patriarchal norms and gender socialization.[40] The historical evidence indicates that most female friendships in the past have involved shared confidences, mutuality, and empathic understanding, while friendships between women and men have sometimes encountered strong barriers to intimacy and self-disclosure, such as those that troubled Ralph Waldo Emerson in the context of his nineteenth-century relationship with Margaret Fuller. Nevertheless, other women and men, like female friends, have achieved a shared rhetoric, a meeting of minds, and a sense of spiritual elevation in their friendships: "Please never stop writing me letters—" Elizabeth Bishop entreated Robert Lowell after thirteen years of friendship; "they always manage to make me feel like my higher self."[41]

Two related major points remain to be addressed: the role of historical context and the phenomenon of change over time. First, it is evident that cross-sex friendship, like friendship between women, has been socially constructed and mediated by various influences, including emotional culture, gender expectations, prescriptive literature, and structural factors. Across the centuries, for the most part, such influences have discouraged the development of friendship between women and men. Eighteenth- and nineteenth-century views of women's nature, images of true womanhood and separate spheres, distinct gender roles and responsibilities, and the structural arrangements that corresponded to this ideology made cross-sex friendship an atypical experience for middle-class American women. The new twentieth-century stress on heterosexuality and a concomitant negative evaluation of close relationships between women did little to expand opportunities for cross-sex friendship. Although this ideology privileged interactions between women and men, it posited companionate marriage as the most appropriate setting for close friendship as well as for sexual relations. At the same time, however, ordinary young women and men actually encountered increased opportunities to interact informally in educational and work settings. For some, in the era of flaming youth, this translated into more sexual freedom and experimentation as well, although most middle-class women continued to espouse chastity at least until engagement, if not marriage.[42]

To some degree, increased exposure to one another fostered friendship between ordinary women and men. Unlike Ida Sophia Scudder at the turn of the century, an individual who was not able to return a male friend's romantic interest did not have to lament the loss of the friendship. Instead, she might resolve the situation differently: "Waxie and I after many misunderstandings have become very amicable; Best Platonic Freind [sic] same as always," one young woman reported happily to a female friend in 1921. Indeed, platonic friendship could be seen as a desirable resource for navigating the complexities of heterosexual social life. Yvonne Blue hoped that eventually she could "be friends" with a married man who was "in love" with her but was not her type of person. "There is something really wonderful about having a man friend. I used to tell him everything, and he would straighten out all my tangles for me, and the whole thing was swell," she told her diary in 1932. "One of the main reasons I am sorry it ever grew out of that stage is that I can no longer talk as freely with him as I used to."[43]

Not all young women shared these views, however. Beth Twiggar compared the possiblity of profound and energizing communication between a woman and a man with that between two women. "If only I could find a man with whom such communication were possible it would be perfect. But until I find one I am inclined to believe that it is possible only between two of the same sex," she observed pensively in 1940. "Then there is a basic, mutual understanding which, with a man and a woman, attraction and conflict make difficult." This opinion reflected her own experience of a "beautiful friendship" that was "seriously threatened on both sides— by a compelling pernicious Lust." After a visit that evolved from conversation into lovemaking, the young man "went away ruffled and frustrated, which is an effective beginning to the end of the friendship." Given the evidence of tension and conflict in this friendship, it is particularly interesting to note that a voluminous correspondence reveals that this woman and her friend resumed a friendly, affectionate relationship after many years had passed and both had married other people.[44]

The preceding three examples epitomize the nature of young women's cross-sex experiences in the first part of the twentieth century. They clearly reflect twentieth-century language conventions, the influence of more frequent and less formal interaction between the sexes, and the movement toward more sexual freedom implied in the images of the new woman and the flapper. They demonstrate, too, that expanded opportunities for cross-sex socialization did not automatically generate uncomplicated, harmonious friendships. This small subset of examples also recapitulates earlier themes in cross-sex friendship.

Like previous historical contexts, the more liberal social climate of the 1920s and beyond did not foster the development of close, lasting friendships between women and men. While the twentieth-century construction of the heterosexual imperative favored cross-sex rather than same-sex relationships, it stipulated marriage, not friendship, as the ultimate goal. Thus, in both the Victorian context of separate spheres and middle-class domesticity and the more modern setting that superseded it, adult cross-sex friendship remained an atypical occurrence, experienced primarily by some of the relatively small number of women whose commitments extended into the public realm. Most women in the past either did not have male friends or did not record their experiences of cross-sex friendship. For the few who did, the "sex part" did not necessarily destroy their relationships, but it frequently surfaced in some form and may have actually increased in intensity in the more permissive twentieth-century social climate of the 1920s.

As the century progressed, other social and cultural influences contributed to the restriction of cross-sex friendship. During the Depression and the years of World War II, domestic obligations and concerns consumed the energies of most women. In addition, the absence of the many young men serving in the armed forces limited young women's chances for both romance and cross-sex friendship. Finally, as public and private spaces were effectively resegregated with the rise of suburban life and the renewed domesticity of the postwar years, most middle-class women moved from dating to "going steady" to marriage—and ultimately, as part of a couple, to socializing with other couples. Moreover, aging exacerbated this situation, highlighting the shortage of available men for older widows who found themselves in need of male friendship.

For individuals subjected to the restrictive influence of the feminine mystique—the dominant emotionology of the 1950s that destroyed or crippled the self-images of countless middle-class women—female-male friendship must have seemed a remote possibility indeed. This ethos also limited the parameters of female friendship, particularly for young women, whose social lives were consumed by the search for an appropriate husband. But this situation would begin to change in succeeding decades, as the movement for women's liberation and subsequent events altered the landscape of sex and gender in American society. The concluding chapter will consider the degree to which women's experiences of friendship changed during the 1960s and thereafter in response to these developments.

7

Another Self?

The Fabric of Friendship after 1960

The twentieth-century climate of post-Freudian veneration of selfhood and individual enterprise has offered little impetus for a serious consideration of the role of interpersonal interactions, including friendship, in human development. Most theories of the self interpret development as an evolutionary process of separation and individuation through which an individual reaches increasingly autonomous psychological levels. Although these theories acknowledge the importance of relationships to individual development in the early years of life, they posit autonomy and separation as the hallmarks of maturity. In this context, the achievement of personal independence has taken precedence over the development of close relationships. The creation of an independent self as opposed to the cultivation of "another self" through friendship has represented the ultimate developmental goal. But this conceptualization of the self does not appear to fit women's experiences, which have more typically manifested a strong emphasis on affiliation rather than on disengagement.

Recent studies have reevaluated the place of relationships in the process of human development. Although most of this research has concentrated on the significance of family relationships and sexual partners, some work has also addressed the connections between friends. This scholarship suggests that friendship plays an important role as an integral component of individuals' relational lives, particularly for women.[1]

While it is difficult to capture the elusive, abstract quality of interpersonal relationships in a contemporary context, explaining human interactions within a matrix of past social and cultural influences is even more complicated. The development of a historical perspective on women's experiences of friendship encompasses the interaction of several variables, including emotional culture, gender and power issues, stages of life, structural factors, and the singular nature of individual relationships. Like any other element of past human experience, only some aspects of some friendships at a particular point in time are accessible to historical investigation. Although it is impossible to fully explain the chemistry between historical circumstances and the unique personalities and inclinations of individual women, however, clear parameters of change and continuity can be discerned in the friendship experiences of middle-class American women from 1900 to 1960.

The preceding chapters document the persistence of strong bonds between American women from the eighteenth century through the first two decades of the twentieth century. For adolescents, young adults, and mature married and single women, female friends provided vital emotional support as well as more concrete forms of comfort and assistance, often in lifelong relationships. Yet intimations of change are also apparent in the years preceding 1920. Some young women expressed ambivalence about intimacy between friends, and mature women found that other priorities could displace the primacy of female friendship in their lives. These tendencies developed further in the succeeding three decades. As dating and aspirations for marriage increasingly defined the goals of adolescents, college students, and young adults, female friendship was devalued in comparison to heterosexual social life. Women beyond the stage where these goals were relevant placed more importance on friendship, but other commitments encroached on their relationships as well. Just as the pursuit of "boys" became the center of young women's interactions with one another, the prerogatives of husbands infringed on married women's friendships to some degree.

Women's relationships in two additional categories also changed slightly. While romantic friends preserved earlier traditions more completely than was the case in other genres of female friendship after 1920, they became distinctly more discreet in their interactions in response to increasing cultural criticism of closeness between women. Finally, as in earlier historical periods, only a small subset of atypical women established friendships with men between 1900 and 1960, but more young women experienced such relationships after 1920.

These changes and continuities in the experience of female friendship reflect influential factors that structured American society and culture in the first half of the twentieth century. The revision of Victorian emotionology lessened the fervor of emotional expression and probably also diminished the intensity of the actual emotional experience of friendship. At the same time, the cultural emphasis on heterosexual social life and the concurrent censure of intimacy between women stigmatized female friendship and altered individuals' attitudes toward their relationships. Many women maintained strong friendships between 1920 and 1960, but the explicit cultural denigration of female relationships contrasted strongly with the nineteenth century's sentimentalization of friendship between women. It also differed from the earlier view that women were incapable of friendship. Finally, structural features of mature industrial society and an expanding consumer orientation also altered the nature of women's interactions.

Yet other gender-related influences counterbalanced these powerful forces for change. Most mature women remained subordinate to and economically dependent on men, as they had been in earlier periods. Linked by their shared status as wives with heavy domestic responsibilities and disillusioned by the contrast between the ideal of companionate marriage and the realities of married life, they continued to turn to one another for companionship and support. These circumstances highlight the relevance of age and life stage as determinants of friendship style, and they help explain why mature women's relationships did not change as extensively as those of younger individuals.

The foregoing evidence of both changes and strong continuities across the genres of female friendship confirms the historicity of women's experiences of friendship. This evidence also marks the years between 1900 and 1960 as a unique period in the history of middle-class American women's relationships with their friends. Like other social historical transformations, the evolution of interpersonal relationships is a gradual process that spans decades. In contrast to more sudden historical changes, as, for example, in the realm of politics and diplomacy, alterations in friendship styles emerge slowly. Hence, although a full examination of the dynamics of women's friendships during the second half of the twentieth century remains beyond the scope of this volume, it is relevant to ask whether the years after 1960 witnessed an extension of earlier trends or the dawn of another historical period in women's friendships. In the context of a new millennium, the question of how the last four decades have shaped female friendship has special resonance.

In 1960 the United States was on the verge of a series of cataclysmic changes. The civil rights movement, the counterculture, the antiwar movement, and the campaign for women's liberation would alter expectations and priorities in all segments of society, create strong intergenerational conflict, and construct new social and cultural alliances. Each of these developments affected women, but the feminist movement affected the history of female friendship most directly.

The rebirth of feminism in the late twentieth century explicitly encouraged a cultural reauthorization of close female relationships as part of its ideology of sisterhood. This ideology incorporated a distinctly twentieth-century political element, but at the same time it recalled the nineteenth-century model of sororal friendship. For numerous individuals touched by the feminist movement in some way, the concept of sisterhood mitigated the emotional isolation portrayed by Betty Friedan in *The Feminine Mystique* and provided vital support against societal and familial pressures. Women gained strength from the recognition and acknowledgment of common experiences, as in the context of the consciousness-raising groups that made sisterhood concrete for many. The pre-1960 image of female friendship as an inferior substitute for heterosexual relationships began to decline as more women perceived the time they spent with one another as valuable in itself. Yet not all middle-class women took part in feminist activities, and even for those who did, the idealization of sisterhood could create unrealistic expectations for friendship that were impossible to fulfill.[2] Furthermore, even where strong commitments to the ideology of sisterhood existed, individual personality traits and preferences could complicate the interactions of friends.

The dissemination of this ideology, then, did not necessarily alter key elements of the female friendship styles that had developed between 1920 and 1960. For example, the heterosexual imperative continued to regulate the relationships of adolescents and young women. One young woman who kept extensive diaries during the 1960s consistently recorded experiences that closely resembled those of her counterparts in the preceding decades. Her interactions with female friends focused primarily on heterosexual social life. Boys, popularity, and personal appearance clearly dominated her thoughts, as well as the conversations she had with friends. At thirteen, she speculated about which boys "liked" whom and which girls would be angry if boys danced with her.[3]

Maternal expectations about social life also worried her, as they had troubled some of her predecessors in the 1950s: "I feel the constant pressure of mom [*sic*] trying to find out why I'm not absolutely filled up to the brim with dates," she noted on one occasion. A few months later, she expressed a similar concern: "I know I'm not a cool thing in her eyes—but she should be used to it by now."[4] Yet other diary entries suggest continuities with the friendship styles of young women in earlier centuries. She eagerly anticipated letters and phone calls from a friend who had moved away and noted the latter's birthday in her diary. "I'm going out to Chicago either in July or during Eastertime. She's still the same sweet girl," she reported happily after one telephone conversation.

Nevertheless, as the following example illustrates, this individual's relationships, like those of adolescents between 1920 and 1960, unmistakably reflect the dominance of the heterosexual imperative rather than any nineteenth- or late twentieth-century manifestation of the ideology of sisterhood. "They are both whores—it's an established fact," she wrote disparagingly about two other girls. "They might just as well write—'Gwen gives' on the boys [*sic*] lavatory wall."[5] Two years later, she wondered whether she would be friends in college with two girls she knew at home and concluded pragmatically that she probably would, "for security reasons," even though she felt superior to them. As an undergraduate, she enjoyed conversations with female friends about identity issues and academic matters, but she continued to care more about dating than about friendship—and she recognized this: "I have very few true friends as I do not really cultivate that many friendships," she commented in the middle of her first year in college.[6]

Other forms of evidence corroborate the impressions conveyed by the diaries of this frank and articulate young woman. An ethnographic study of white and African-American college women at two Southern universities in the early 1980s concluded that the peer culture at both institutions stressed heterosexual relations. This emphasis shaped women's friendships in two specific ways. For the white students, women's affiliations focused mainly on the pursuit of romantic relationships with men, as they had in the 1920s. While they sought female company, their shared activities were directed first toward meeting men, and then toward helping one another cope with the ensuing romances. The African-American students also sought male romantic partners and deemphasized female friendship. However, they were less open with one another about their romances. Because they were also more concerned about protecting themselves from manipulation and gaining the respect of friends, they found it harder to develop trusting relationships with other women. Despite these differences, the peer culture in both universities stressed romantic relationships with men as the route to self-worth and prestige, and in response, both groups of women made female friendship secondary.[7]

These examples suggest that the influence of the heterosexual imperative persisted in the decades following 1960, even as the feminist movement reconfirmed the legitimacy of female friendship. They also highlight the difference between cultural prescriptions and actual experiences. For adolescents and young women after 1960, as for their earlier twentieth-century predecessors, the pursuit of young men apparently continued to define the major goal of social life. But even young women who had no direct contact with the feminist movement may have responded to its influence in other forms. For example, the informal dissemination of feminist theory through popular culture—and, more formally, in academic contexts such as courses in women's studies and women's history—undoubtedly altered the views of some individuals. Certainly as films, novels, and television series portrayed various images of female friends, both young women and more mature adults were exposed to a range of possibilities for female friendship. Yet while many such portrayals presented positive images, the mass media often emphasized what one author refers to as "the catfight" as a dominant motif.[8]

Other examples indicate that the ideology of sisterhood may have been more compelling for women as they moved beyond dating and the search for a husband. Like their predecessors, mature individuals after 1960 seem to have found strength in one another's support. Nan Bishop, Clare Bowman, and Sarah Hamilton met in the summer of 1966 and briefly shared an apartment. Ten years later, they rediscovered their friendship as each faced a disintegrating marriage and the challenge of single parenthood. Their three-way correspondence became a major source of support as they coped with these transitions. "I find I am constantly writing you letters out loud in my head," Clare Bowman told Sarah Hamilton on one occasion. "I am basking in the joy of our friendship," Hamilton wrote to Bowman and Nan Bishop a month later. Bishop articulated similar feelings: "How wonderful . . . to know there are two people who love me out there in the world, and how lucky I am to be able to do mundane things like dishes, while looking forward to writing to you, and getting letters in return." Their language incorporates casual, late twentieth-century idioms, and their discussions encompass topics that would not have appeared in eighteenth- and nineteenth-century letters. Thus Bishop told her friends, "I am sometimes, I fear, weird," and Hamilton expressed curiosity about lesbianism. Yet the centrality of their friendship in the lives of these three women clearly recalls earlier relationships.[9]

The post-1960 evidence also documents long-term, close friendships between women who met as children and have maintained their relationships. Marcia Lustgarten Hammer and Marilyn Blau Klainberg, born six days apart, lived across the hall from one another in an apartment building in the Bronx until they were fourteen years old. Their friendship survived Hammer's family's move to a larger apartment in another building, their assignment to different classes in junior high school, and the pitfalls of high-school social life. "There never was a time when boys came between us," Hammer remembers. Although their paths diverged in college and Klainberg married five years before her friend, they still considered themselves "best friends." Eventually their husbands played tennis together weekly, and their children thought of each other as cousins. When Marcia Hammer faced serious illness, Marilyn Klainberg's support was crucial: "I hope I never have to be as good a friend to her as she was to me at that time in my life," Hammer recalls. They celebrated their friendship along with their fiftieth birthdays at a gala "hundredth" birthday party, and they continue to talk to each other at least once a day.

"Marcia is my grounding, she hears me out and helps me find the right way for me," Klainberg says. "I could not imagine life without her." Although they live in different communities, have other friends, and occasionally get angry with one another, the bond between them remains special. "We are a mix of grownup and child when we are together. There is an unspoken history and it is often evident in our own shortcuts in the spoken word," she adds. Hammer also describes a kind of "shorthand" in their communication: "My daughters can tell when I'm on the phone with Marilyn," she claims. "I cannot imagine life without Marilyn and consider her, after my children, to be the greatest gift that God has given me."[10] (See figures 14, 15, and 16.)

This classic illustration of enduring female friendship is not unique in the late twentieth century. It appears that "boys" have not always taken precedence over friends of the same sex in the decades since 1960, as the experiences of Jill McCorkle and Jackie See demonstrate.[11] Even when romantic relationships with men have preoccupied adolescents and young adults, as they have matured, women have viewed female friendship as central to their lives. Thus, for example, fifteen women who grew

up together in Hastings, Nebraska, have held annual slumber party reunions since they gathered to celebrate turning 40 in 1988. The group
first came together as junior-high-school students. They kept in touch
after their high-school graduation in 1966 and enjoyed an impromptu
evening together at their tenth class reunion, but busy schedules and the
responsibilities of motherhood precluded frequent gatherings. They decided to mark the milestone represented by their fortieth birthdays with
the sort of party they had shared as teenagers, and after that event, the
women voted to have an annual slumber party "for the rest of our
lives."[12]

For many contemporary women, female friendship plays a similar or
an even more powerful role. Friends provide a safety valve that enables
them to accept the limits of their marriages and to preserve their individual identities. The support of friends has empowered some to defy a husband or to cope with an affair or a divorce. As the recent proliferation of
"book groups" suggests, increasing numbers of contemporary women
with both active careers and family responsibilities welcome organized
opportunities to enjoy the intellectual and emotional support of female
peers.[13]

Although the contemporary cultural climate seems to offer more support for close relationships between women than was evident during the
first half of the century, various influences still complicate these relationships. While the massive influx of women into the workplace since 1960
has created new opportunities for the development of female friendships,
it has also promoted competition as individuals pursue advancement and
success on the job. Issues of hierarchy and status in the workplace have
influenced women's friendships patterns too. A recent study suggests that
the explosive impact of the contemporary feminist movement has caused
a crisis in female friendship by destroying the unity created by the crusade
for women's rights. The study's authors, two female therapists, describe
a new privatization of experience, different from women's earlier isolation, that is suggested by their clients' expressed reluctance to discuss certain things even with close female friends.[14]

Other complicating factors can also inhibit friendship. For example,
although married women with heavy personal and professional responsibilities tend to maintain at least one or two close friendships, the com-
peting demands of their busy lives and the limitations of human energy
often leave little room for such relationships. Moreover, the movement of
women into the workplace has limited their availability during the day,

making them less accessible for friendship with those not employed out-side the home. Finally, overt disapproval by husbands can also cause dif-ficulties. "Last night I went to a meeting and left her sitting on the couch talking to a friend. And would you believe it, three hours later, they're still there talking? Yeah, yeah, I've seen it before, but it always sets me off," one disgruntled man complained.[15]

Other data also suggest problems in late twentieth-century women's friendships. For example, Mary Pipher's research on early female adoles-cence in contemporary society identified only one positive example of peer support among her young subjects. Pipher argues that other girls function as enforcers of the dominant culture rather than as allies for one another. This conclusion supports the idea that the bonds of female friendship formed by younger women differ from those of mature adults, although the latter can encounter obstacles as well.[16]

While friends frequently serve as a primary source of support for con-temporary single women, their friendships often change when the pres-ence of a man in the life of one participant makes her less available. This situation introduces a quality of temporariness into single women's friendships and highlights the potential for emotional distress.[17] Never-theless, as playwright Wendy Wasserstein points out, unmarried women consistently rely on one another: "Ask any single woman who's been to a we're-having-a-second-child baby shower how it was, and she'll tell you she immediately ran home to have a Scotch with an unmarried friend," she has observed candidly. Wasserstein has also analyzed the role of her own feelings of competitiveness and inadequacy in the demise of four close friendships over the years and the tentative renewal of one relation-ship. "Great friendships with women are some of life's most difficult and caring intimacies. If I work harder at them, I hope to have them forever," she concludes.[18]

Susan Lee, single at the age of thirty in 1975, described friends as "the ongoing relationships in my life." Although she had expected that a shared commitment to writing would preserve her friendship with a woman she met in graduate school, the relationship cooled when the lat-ter married and abandoned their mutual ambition. Lee's anger at her friend's passivity and the latter's corresponding feelings of betrayal effec-tively ended the friendship. For Lee, feminist consciousness meant that fe-male friendships could be valued more highly, but it also incorporated the assumption that women should take responsibility for their lives and not act powerless. Hence she could not accept her friend's willingness to allow her husband's needs to deflect her from her own goals. Eventually Lee concluded that "social and political dislocations" could end friendships.[19]

During the decades since 1960, several specific issues have affected the genre of romantic friendship. In the context of lesbian feminism and the quest for gay and lesbian rights, the reticence of earlier romantic friends gave way to a more open declaration of sexual preference on the part of many middle-class women who previously would not have chosen to identify themselves in that fashion. In this sense, the growing tendency for woman-committed women to "come out" transformed the tradition of romantic friendship into a new relationship. Because lesbians may experience rejection by family members and colleagues, friends can be even more important for them than for heterosexual women. Although only a small amount of literature touches on contemporary lesbian friendships, existing studies cite several different types of relationships in this category. Friendships between lesbians may involve an erotic or sexual dimension, but many do not. Lesbian lovers may also be considered friends, former lovers can become friends, and former friends can become lovers. Some asexual, partnered relationships also exist, a pattern that seems to resemble traditional romantic friendships most closely. Relationships between lesbians and heterosexual women can be difficult to maintain, because disclosing one's sexual orientation can undermine such a friendship. Even a friendship of some duration may end when the heterosexual partner becomes aware that her friend is a lesbian.[20]

In contrast to the paucity of literature on lesbian friendships, the literature on cross-sex friendship has proliferated since 1960. While the problem of sexual attraction and the related matter of spousal jealousy remain salient to the structure of such relationships, their number has increased significantly, beginning in adolescence. The highest occurrence of friendships between women and men has been among college students, with a significant decline after marriage. These findings differentiate contemporary women's experiences of cross-sex friendship from the nineteenth-century atmosphere of hostility and distance described by Carroll Smith-Rosenberg. They also suggest an extension of the pre-1960 trend toward more interaction between young women and men, undoubtedly due in part to the increased presence of women in the workplace.

As in past periods, social pressures and expectations and the absence of a cultural script for friendship between women and men enhance the potential for misunderstanding between the partners in such relationships. Yet cross-sex friendship, along with friendship in general, has been celebrated as a key emotional experience in contemporary society: As one popular periodical claimed in a special issue on the topic, friendship is the love of the nineties. Most data on cross-sex friendship document relationships between heterosexual friends, but some evidence indicates that close friendships between heterosexual women and homosexual men and between lesbians and gay men manifest gender-related complications similar to those between heterosexual women and men. Heterosexual women and gay men seem to experience more equality and fewer tensions in their friendships, although the presence of a new love interest in the life of one partner may create problems.[21]

The preceding discussion has offered selected examples based on a brief survey of primary and secondary sources that illuminate aspects of women's friendship experiences since 1960. While it is impossible to draw conclusions on this basis, such a survey can suggest hypotheses for additional investigation. The late twentieth-century valorization of sisterhood distinguishes the cultural representation of female friendship in the decades since 1960, but further research will be necessary to determine the impact of that representation and of other contemporary social and cultural influences on the nature of women's friendship experiences.

In 1776, Mercy Otis Warren celebrated "the balm of life, a kind and faithful friend." From the eighteenth century through the first two decades of the twentieth century, adolescents, young adults, and mature women essentially experienced their relationships with one another in this fashion. Female friends served as sources of comfort and reassurance for women of all ages, and for fewer individuals, male friends also played important roles. Much of the history of American women's friendship experiences, then, belies the Western cultural tradition of denigrating female capacities for friendship. To some extent, the four decades between 1920 and 1960 disrupted this pattern, as social and cultural influences altered friendship patterns, especially those of younger women. In the words of one young woman around 1920, "In my city some business women are hesitating to take apartments together for fear of the interpretation that may be put upon it."[22] The contrast between this matter-of-fact observation and Mercy Otis Warren's view of friendship epitomizes the significance of the first half of the twentieth century as a distinct period in the history of female friendship. It also highlights the historicity of friendship and its character as a socially constructed experience.

The degree to which the post-1960 period defines another discrete his-torical era in women's friendship experiences, as opposed to a nostalgic recapitulation of earlier friendship styles, remains to be assessed. But one final example testifies eloquently to the endurance of an element common to Aristotle's classic representation of male friendship and to many women's actual experiences of the relationship. On a June afternoon in 1994, Denise Meyer, a young woman from South Africa, sat in the audi-ence scanning the ranks of fellow Oxford students who were preparing to receive their degrees. Suddenly she experienced what she called a "weird" moment: She felt as if she were outside of herself, watching herself be about to graduate. Then she realized that she was looking at an Ameri-can friend with whom she felt a powerful connection. They had shared numerous intense discussions about identity issues—"growing up 'smart' and a 'girl,' and what that all means." They even resembled one another physically. (See figure 24.) Greeting her friend after the graduation cere-mony, Denise articulated the sensation she had just experienced in the form of a question: "Are you me?" she asked her friend.[23]

This unusual query captures the essence and intensity of one young woman's experience of female friendship in the untraditional, late twen-tieth-century context of a global society, where it is possible for middle-class young women from distant continents to meet and form friendships as students at a venerable institution that has been a bastion of Western, male intellectual tradition. It also echoes a major theme in the history of female friendship, suggesting that the image and perception of a friend as another self remain integral components of the experience of friendship, despite changing social and cultural contexts and influences.

Notes

Notes to the Introduction

1. Jill McCorkle, "Cathy, Now and Then"; Carolyn See, "Best Friend, My Wellspring in the Wilderness!"; both in Mickey Pearlman, ed., *Between Friends: Writing Women Celebrate Friendship* (Boston: Houghton Mifflin, 1994), 43, 73.

2. D. J. Enright and David Rawlinson, eds., *The Oxford Book of Friendship* (New York: Oxford University Press, 1991), 96; Alberta Contarello and Chiara Volpato, "Images of Friendship: Literary Depictions through the Ages," *Journal of Social and Personal Relationships* 8 (1991): 49–75; Harriette Andreadis, "The Sapphic-Platonics of Katherine Philips, 1632–1664," *Signs* 15, 1 (Autumn 1989); Janet Todd, *Women's Friendships in Literature* (New York: Columbia University Press, 1980); Tess Coslett, *Woman to Woman: Female Friendship in Victorian Fiction* (Atlantic Highlands, NJ: Humanities Press International, 1988).

3. *Lysis and Phaedrus, Ethica Eudemia* and *Nicomachean Ethics*, tr. H. Rackham, quoted in Enright and Rawlinson, eds., *The Oxford Book of Friendship*, 7; *On Old Age and on Friendship*, tr. Frank O. Copley (Ann Arbor, MI: University of Michigan Press, 1967); Francis Bacon, "On Friendship," quoted in Louise Bernikow, *Among Women* (New York: Harmony Books, 1980), 117; "Of Friendship," in *The Complete Essays of Montaigne*, ed. and tr. Donald M. Frame (Stanford, CA: Stanford University Press, 1958); Ralph Waldo Emerson, "Friendship," in *Emerson's Essays* (New York: Thomas Y. Crowell, 1951), 144, 148. For an interesting analysis of Western literature addressing love and friendship, see Allan Bloom, *Love and Friendship* (New York: Simon and Schuster, 1993).

4. Mary Hunt, *Fierce Tenderness: A Feminist Theology of Friendship* (New York: Crossroad, 1992), 29. For a comprehensive overview of research on

the defining characteristics of women's friendships, see Pat O'Connor, *Friendships between Women: A Critical Review* (New York and London: Guilford, 1992).

5.   Janice Raymond, *A Passion for Friends: Toward a Philosophy of Female Affection* (Boston: Beacon Press, 1986), 173–76.

6.   Nancy Woloch, *Women and the American Experience: A Concise History* (New York: McGraw-Hill, 1996), 43.

7.   Rebecca G. Adams, "Conceptual and Methodological Issues in Studying Friendships of Older Adults," and Graham Allan and Rebecca Adams, "Aging and the Structure of Friendship," in Rebecca G. Adams and Rosemary Blieszner, *Older Adult Friendship: Structure and Process* (Newbury Park, CA: Sage Publications 1989); Contarello and Volpato, "Images of Friendship."

8.   Graham Allan, *Friendship: Developing a Sociological Perspective* (Boulder, CO: Westview Press, 1989); and "Class Variation in Friendship Patterns," *British Journal of Sociology* 28, 3 (September 1977): 389–93. Allan and Rebecca Adams, "Aging and the Structure of Friendship," 45.

9.   Mark Snyder and Dave Smith, "Personality and Friendship: The Friendship Worlds of Self-Monitoring," in Valerian J. Derlega and Barbara A. Winstead, eds., *Friendship and Social Interaction* (New York: Springer-Verlag, 1986), 65–69; Steve Duck and Kris Pond, "Friends, Romans, Countrymen, Lend Me Your Retrospections: Rhetoric and Reality in Personal Relationships," and Clyde Hendrick, "Close Relationships," in Clyde Hendrick, ed., *Close Relationships* (Newbury Park, CA: Sage Publications, 1989), 1–16; 17–38.

10.   See, for example, Jean Baker Miller, *Toward a New Psychology of Women,* 2d ed. (Boston: Beacon Press, 1987); Carol Gilligan, *In a Different Voice: Psychological Theories and Women's Development* (Cambridge, MA: Harvard University Press, 1982); Ruthellen Josselson, *The Space between Us: Exploring the Dimensions of Human Relationships* (San Francisco: Jossey-Bass, 1992). See also the essays by Judith V. Jordan, Alexandra G. Kaplan, Jean Baker Miller, Irene P. Stiver, and Janet L. Surrey in *Women's Growth in Connection: Writings from the Stone Center* (New York: Guilford Press, 1991).

11.   Studies that address gender differences include Paul H. Wright, "Gender Differences in Adults' Same- and Cross-Gender Friendships," in Adams and Blieszner, *Older Adult Friendship,* 197–221; "Interpreting Research on Gender Differences in Friendship: A Case for Moderation and a Plea for Caution," *Journal of Social and Personal Relationships* 45 (1988): 367–73; "Men's Friendships, Women's Friendships, and the Alleged Inferiority of the Latter," *Sex Roles* 8, 1:1–20; Paul H. Wright and Mary Beth Scanlon, "Gender Role Orientations and Friendship: Some Attenuation, but Gender

Differences Abound," *Sex Roles* 24, 9–10 (May 1991): 551–66; Steve Duck and Paul H. Wright, "Reexamining Gender Differences in Same-Gender Friendships: A Close Look at Two Kinds of Data," *Sex Roles* 28, 11–12 (June 1993): 709–27; Sandra Gibbs Candy, Lillian E. Troll, and Sheldon G. Levy, "A Developmental Exploration of Friendship Functions in Women," *Psychology of Women Quarterly* 5, 3 (Summer 1995): 465–72; Drury Sherrod, "The Influence of Gender on Same-Sex Friendships," in Clyde Hendrick, ed., *Close Relationships,* 164–86; Drury Sherrod, "The Bonds of Men: Problems and Possibilities in Close Male Relationships," in Harry Brod, ed., *The Making of Masculinities: The New Men's Studies* (New York: Routledge, Chapman and Hall, 1987); Lillian Rubin, *Just Friends: The Role of Friendship in Our Lives* (New York: Harper and Row, 1985), 59–108; Joseph Pleck, "Man to Man: Is Brotherhood Possible," in Nona Glazer-Malbin, ed., *Old Family/New Family* (New York: D. Van Nostrand, 1975); Karen Walker, "Men, Women, and Friendship: What They Say, What They Do," *Gender and Society* 8, 2 (June 1994): 246–65.

12. Jane Flax, "The Conflict between Nurturance and Autonomy in Mother-Daughter Relationships and within Feminism," *Feminist Studies* 4, 2 (June 1978): 171–91; Eva Margolies, *The Best of Friends, the Worst of Enemies* (Garden City, NY: Dial Press, 1985), 7–9.

13. Raymond, *A Passion for Friends,* 185–86.

14. Margolies, *The Best of Friends, the Worst of Enemies*; O'Connor, *Friendships between Women.*

15. Carroll Smith-Rosenberg, "The Female World of Love and Ritual: Relations between Women in Nineteenth-Century America," in Smith-Rosenberg, ed., *Disorderly Conduct: Visions of Gender in Victorian America* (New York: Alfred A. Knopf, 1985), 53–76. See also Nancy F. Cott, *The Bonds of Womanhood: "Woman's Sphere" in New England, 1780–1835* (New Haven, CT: Yale University Press, 1977); Terri L. Premo, *Winter Friends: Women Growing Old in the New Republic, 1785–1835* (Urbana, IL: University of Illinois Press, 1990); and Marilyn Ferris Motz, *True Sisterhood: Michigan Women and Their Kin* (Albany, NY: State University of New York Press, 1983). Sarah Butler Wistar to Jeannie Field, February 29, 1864; Jeannie Field to Sarah Butler Wistar, January 4, 1863; and Sarah Butler Wistar to Jeannie Field, June 18, 1870; all quoted in Smith-Rosenberg, "The Female World of Love and Ritual," 55.

16. For an overview of the field of emotions history and a relevant bibliography, see Peter N. Stearns, "History of Emotions: The Issue of Change," in Michael Lewis and Jeannette M. Haviland, *Handbook of Emotions* (New York: Guilford Press, 1993), 17–28. See also Peter N. Stearns with Carol Z. Stearns, "Emotionology: Clarifying the History of Emotions and Emotional Standards," *American Historical Review* 90 (October 1985):

813–36; Peter N. Stearns, *American Cool: Constructing a Twentieth-Century Emotional Style* (New York: New York University Press, 1994); Peter N. Stearns and Deborah C. Stearns, "Historical Issues in Emotions Research: Causation and Timing," in *Social Perspectives on Emotion*, Vol. 2 (Greenwich, CT: JAI Press Inc., 1994), 239–66; Shula Sommers, "Understanding Emotions: Some Interdisciplinary Considerations," in Carol Z. Stearns and Peter N. Stearns, eds., *Emotion and Social Change: Toward a New Psychohistory* (New York: Holmes and Meier, 1988), 23–38; and Margaret S. Clark, "Historical Emotionology: From a Social Psychologist's Perspective," in Andrew E. Barnes and Peter N. Stearns, eds., *Social History and Issues in Human Consciousness: Some Interdisciplinary Connections* (New York: New York University Press, 1989), 262–69.

17.   For examples of recent research in emotions history, see the essays in Peter N. Stearns and Jan Lewis, eds., *An Emotional History of the United States* (New York: New York University Press, 1998). Other relevant studies include Jan Lewis, "Mother's Love: The Construction of an Emotion in Nineteenth-Century America," and Peter N. Stearns, "Suppressing Unpleasant Emotions: The Development of a Twentieth-Century Emotional Style," in Barnes and Stearns, eds., *Social History and Issues in Human Consciousness*, 209–29, 230–61; Carol Z. Stearns and Peter N. Stearns, *Anger: The Struggle for Emotional Control in America's History* (Chicago: University of Chicago Press, 1986); Carol Z. Stearns, "'Lord Help Me Walk Humbly': Anger and Sadness in England and America, 1570–1750," in Stearns and Stearns, eds., *Emotion and Social Change*, 39–68, 193–222; and Peter N. Stearns, *Jealousy: The Evolution of an Emotion in American History* (New York: New York University Press, 1989).

18.   Harriet Badeau to Rachel McClelland, n.d. 1903, Box 1, Folder 3, Rachel McClelland Sutton Correspondence, McClelland Family Papers, MSS #111, Pittsburgh Regional History Center.

19.   February 9, 1931, Box 1, Vol. 6, Yvonne Blue Skinner Diaries, Schlesinger Library, Radcliffe College.

20.   Peter N. Stearns, "History of Emotions," in Lewis and Haviland, eds., *Handbook of Emotions*, 17–28; "Gender and Emotion: A Twentieth-Century Transition," in David D. Franks, ed., *Social Perspectives on Emotion*, Vol. 1 (Greenwich, CT: JAI Press, Inc., 1992), 127–60.

21.   David Lowenthal, *The Past Is a Foreign Country* (New York: Cambridge University Press, 1986); Liz Stanley, "Feminism and Friendship," in *The Auto/Biographical I: The Theory and Practice of Feminist Auto/Biography* (New York and Manchester, England: Manchester University Press, 1992), 214–37.

22.   Josselson, *The Space between Us*, 26–28, 166, and note 5, 268; Lillian Rubin, *Between Friends*.

23. Karen Hansen, "'Our Eyes Behold Each Other': Masculinity and Intimate Friendship in Antebellum New England," in Peter M. Nardi, ed., *Men's Friendships* (Newbury Park, CA: Sage Publications, 1992), 52–53.

24. Linda Gordon, "On Difference," *Genders* 10 (Spring 1991): 91–111.

25. Raymond, *A Passion for Friends.*

26. Abigail J. Stewart, "Toward a Feminist Strategy for Studying Women's Lives," in Carol E. Franz and Abigail J. Stewart, eds., *Women Creating Lives: Identities, Resilience, and Resistance* (Boulder, CO: Westview Press, 1994), 11–35; Stanley, "Feminism and Friendship," 219; and Mieneke Bosch, "Women's Culture in Women's History: Historical Notion or Feminist Vision," in Maaike Meijer and Jetty Schaap, eds., *Historiography of Women's Cultural Traditions* (Providence, RI: Foris, 1987), 46. For examples of women's exercise of power in their own lives, see discussions of domestic feminism in Daniel Scott Smith, "Family Limitation, Sexual Control, and Domestic Feminism in Victorian America," in Mary S. Hartman and Lois Banner, eds., *Clio's Consciousness Raised* (New York: Harper and Row, 1974), 119–36; Nancy F. Cott, *The Bonds of Womanhood*; Mary Beth Norton, "The Paradox of 'Women's Sphere,'" in Carol R. Berkin and Mary Beth Norton, eds., *Women of America: A History* (Boston: Houghton Mifflin, 1979); Glenna Matthews, *"Just a Housewife": The Rise and Fall of Domesticity in America* (New York: Oxford University Press, 1987); and Carl Degler, *At Odds: Women and the Family in America from the Revolution to the Present* (New York: Oxford University Press, 1980), 247–78.

27. Raymond, *A Passion for Friends,* 4–5; Stanley, "Feminism and Friendship."

28. Smith-Rosenberg, "The Female World of Love and Ritual"; Cott, *The Bonds of Womanhood*; Mary Ryan, *Cradle of the Middle Class* (New York: Cambridge University Press, 1982); Nancy Hewitt, *Women's Activism and Social Change* (Ithaca, NY: Cornell University Press, 1984); Anne Firor Scott, *Natural Allies: Women's Associations in American History* (Urbana, IL: University of Illinois Press, 1991).

29. Estelle Freedman, "Separatism as Strategy: Female Institution Building and American Feminism, 1870–1930," *Feminist Studies* 15, 3 (Fall 1979): 512–29; Ellen DuBois, Mari Jo Buhle, Temma Kaplan, Gerda Lerner, and Carroll Smith-Rosenberg, "Politics and Culture in Women's History: A Symposium," *Feminist Studies* 6, 1 (Spring 1980): 63; Blanche Wiesen Cook, "Female Support Networks and Political Activism," *Chrysalis* 3 (1977); Leila J. Rupp, "Constructing Internationalism: The Case of Transnational Women's Organizations, 1888–1945," *American Historical Review* 99, 5 (December 1994): 1571–1600; Mieneke Bosch, ed. with Annemarie Kloosterman, *Politics and Friendship: Letters from the*

International Woman Suffrage Alliance, 1902–1942 (Columbus, OH: Ohio State University Press, 1990); Fia Dieteren, "Women's Networks: A Connection between Culture and Politics in Women's History," in Meijer and Schaap, eds., *Historiography of Women's Cultural Traditions*, 53–64.

Notes to Chapter 1

1. Charlotte Lennox, *Euphemia* (Dublin: P. Wogan, P. Byrne, et al., 1790), 170, quoted in Janet Todd, *Women's Friendships in Literature*, 310.
2. Mary Astell, quoted in Jessie Bernard, *The Female World* (New York: Free Press, 1981), 290–91.
3. Quoted in Carmen Renee Berry and Tamara Traeder, *Girlfriends: Enduring Ties* (Berkeley, CA: Wildcat Canyon Press, 1995), 126.
4. Cott, *The Bonds of Womanhood*; Smith-Rosenberg, "The Female World of Love and Ritual"; Motz, *True Sisterhood*; Norton, *Liberty's Daughters*; Premo, *Winter Friends*.
5. For a concise overview of women's lives in the seventeenth and eighteenth centuries, see Woloch, *Women and the American Experience*, 1–66.
6. Cott, *The Bonds of Womanhood*, 160–96. See also Mary Beth Norton's discussion of the community of women in seventeenth-century colonial society in *Founding Mothers and Fathers: Gendered Power and the Forming of American Society* (New York: Alfred A. Knopf, 1996), 203–39, and Judith Walzer Leavitt, "Under the Shadow of Maternity: American Women's Responses to Death and Debility Fears in Nineteenth-Century Childbirth," *Feminist Studies* 12 (1986): 129–54.
7. William R. Alger, *Friendships of Women*, 12th ed. (Boston: Roberts Brothers, 1890 [first published 1868]), 203.
8. From *Journal of Esther Edwards Burr, 1754–1757*, eds. Carol F. Karlsen and Laurie F. Crumpacker (New Haven, CT: Yale University Press, 1984): Letter No. 9, October 11, 1754; Letter No. 16, August 23, 1775; Letter No. 4, June 21, 1757; Letter No. 11, March 10, March 12, and March 20, 1755; Letter No. 3, April 11, 1757; Letter No. 19, November 29, 1755, and December 16, 1755.
9. Letter No. 9, October 4, 1754, and Letter No. 14, June 4, 1755, ibid.
10. Sarah Prince's Eulogy, ibid., 308.
11. See Jennine Hensley, ed., *The Works of Anne Bradstreet* (Cambridge, MA: Harvard University Press, 1967), and Laurel Thatcher Ulrich, *Good Wives: Image and Reality in the Lives of Women in Northern New England, 1650–1750* (New York: Random House, 1991), both cited by Carol F. Karlsen and Laurie F. Crumpacker in the Introduction to Burr's journal, note 75, p. 35.

12.   Susanna Anthony to Sarah Osborn and Martha Lauren to Elizabeth Brails-
      ford, both quoted in Woloch, *Women and the American Experience,* 43.

13.   Emily Dickinson to Abiah Root, May 7, 1845; May 16, 1848; and July 25,
      1854; all in *Letters of Emily Dickinson,* ed. Thomas H. Johnson (Cam-
      bridge, MA: Belknap Press of Harvard University Press, 1986), 12–15,
      297–99, reprinted in Angela G. Dorenkamp et al., *Images of Women in
      American Popular Culture,* 2d ed. (New York: Harcourt Brace, 1995),
      328–32.

14.   Ryan, *Cradle of the Middle Class,* 194–96; Lucy Orr to Polly, quoted in
      Woloch, *Women and the American Experience,* 43; Smith-Rosenberg,
      "The Female World of Love and Ritual."

15.   Ellen Rothman, *Hands and Hearts: A History of Courtship in America*
      (New York: Basic Books, 1984); Karen Lystra, *Searching the Heart:
      Women, Men and Romantic Love in Nineteenth-Century America* (New
      York: Oxford University Press, 1989).

16.   Karen Hansen, *A Very Social Time: Crafting Community in Antebellum
      New England* (Berkeley, CA: University of California Press, 1994), 52–53,
      65.

17.   Diary of Nannie Jackson, July 27, 1890, in *Vinegar Pie and Chicken Bread:
      A Woman's Diary of Life in the Rural South, 1890–1891,* ed. Margaret
      Jones Bosterli (Fayetteville, AR: University of Arkansas Press, 1982), 38,
      quoted in Leavitt, "Under the Shadow of Maternity," 203.

18.   Lee Virginia Chambers-Schiller, *Liberty, a Better Husband: Single Women
      in America, the Generations of 1780–1840* (New Haven, CT: Yale Univer-
      sity Press, 1984), 124–26, 148–56.

19.   Carol Lasser, "'Let Us Be Sisters Forever': The Sororal Model of Nine-
      teenth-Century Female Friendship," *Signs* 14 (Autumn 1988): 158–81. For
      an interesting discussion of friendship and community among single
      women in England, see Deborah Epstein Nord, "'Neither Pairs Nor Odd,'
      Female Community in Late Nineteenth-Century London," *Signs* 15, 41
      (1990): 733–54.

20.   Antoinette Brown to Lucy Stone, October 9, 1846, and n.d. 1850, in Carol
      Lasser and Marlene Merrill, eds., *Friends and Sisters: Letters between Lucy
      Stone and Antoinette Brown Blackwell, 1846–1893* (Urbana, IL: Univer-
      sity of Illinois Press, 1987), 15, 67.

21.   Antoinette Brown to Lucy Stone, September 22, 1847; Lucy Stone to An-
      toinette Brown, March 29, 1855, and January 20, 1856; all in ibid., 31,
      143, 146.

22.   *Woman's Journal,* February 10, 1894, quoted in Lasser, "'Let Us Be Sisters
      Forever,'" 178.

23.   Elizabeth Cady Stanton, *Eighty Years and More (1815–1897): Reminis-
      cences of Elizabeth Cady Stanton* (New York: Schocken Books, 1971),

155–85. Quoted material appears on 187, 165–66, and 184. See also letters between Stanton and Anthony in Ellen Carol DuBois, ed., *Elizabeth Cady Stanton, Susan B. Anthony: Correspondence, Writings, Speeches* (New York: Schocken Books, 1981), 53–69 and 277–300; see especially those from Anthony to Stanton, written sometime before October 26, 1902, 298–99.

24. Nancy Mowll Mathews, ed., *Cassatt and Her Circle: Selected Letters* (New York: Abbeville Press, 1984). The letter, dated July 5, 1915, appears on 324–25. See also Nancy Mowll Mathews, *Mary Cassatt: A Life* (New York: Villard Books, 1994).

25. Smith-Rosenberg, "The Female World of Love and Ritual." See, for example, letters from Emily Dickinson to Jane Humphrey dated May 12, 1842; April 3, 1850; April 1852; and October 16, 1855 in *The Letters of Emily Dickinson*, ed. Thomas H. Johnson (Cambridge, MA: Belknap Press, 1958), Vol. 1, Nos. 3, 35, 86, and 180, quoted in Mabel Collins Donnelly, *The American Victorian Woman: The Myth and the Reality* (New York: Greenwood Press, 1986), 25–26.

26. Nancy Sahli, "Smashing: Women's Relationships before the Fall," *Chrysalis* 8 (Summer 1979): 18–27; Christie Anne Farnham, *The Education of the Southern Belle* (New York: New York University Press, 1994).

27. Linda Otto Lipset, *Remember Me: Women and Their Friendship Quilts* (San Francisco: Quilt Digest Press, 1997); Hunt, *Fierce Tenderness*, 58–59; Mary Ann Longley Riggs to Lucretia Longley Cooley, July 1, 1850, quoted in Sara M. Evans, *Born for Liberty: A History of Women in America* (New York: Free Press, 1989), 97.

28. Peter N. Stearns, *American Cool*, 16–94; Lipsett, *Remember Me*; Alger, *Friendships of Women*, 364.

29. Smith-Rosenberg, "The Female World of Love and Ritual"; Ellen Rothman, *Hands and Hearts*; Lillian Faderman, *Surpassing the Love of Men: Romantic Friendship and Love Between Women from the Renaissance to the Present* (New York: William Morrow, 1981).

30. Anthony E. Rotundo, *American Manhood: Transformations in Masculinity from the Revolution to the Modern Era* (New York: Basic Books, 1993), and "Romantic Friendship: Male Intimacy and Middle Class Youth in the Northern United States, 1800–1900," *Journal of Social History* 23 (1989): 1–26. The subculture of Mormonism offers an interesting illustration of the historicity of relationships of this type. While Mormon cross-sex relationships displayed a unique pattern in the nineteenth century, the community mirrored national patterns in same-sex dynamics, supporting physical and emotional intimacy during that period. D. Michael Quinn, *Same-Sex Dynamics among Nineteenth-Century Americans: A Mormon Example* (Champaign, IL: University of Illinois Press, 1996).

31. Christie Anne Farnham, *The Education of the Southern Belle.*

32. See, for example, Lucy Stone to Antoinette Brown, June 9, 1850, in Lasser and Merrill, eds., *Friends and Sisters,* 73.

33. Farnham, *The Education of the Southern Belle.*

34. For examples of different viewpoints on this issue, see Faderman, *Surpassing the Love of Men;* Liz Stanley, "Feminism and Friendship," in *The Auto/Biographical I;* Leila J. Rupp, "'Imagine My Surprise': Women's Relationships in Mid-Twentieth-Century America," in Martin B. Duberman et al., eds., *Hidden from History: Reclaiming the Gay and Lesbian Past* (New York: New American Library, 1989); Blanche Wiesen Cook, "The Historical Denial of Lesbianism," *Radical History Review* 20 (1979): 60–65, and "Female Support Networks and Political Activism."

35. Sarah Orne Jewett to Annie Fields, n.d. 1886, Sarah Orne Jewett Collection, Houghton Library, quoted in Judith Roman, "A Closer Look at the Jewett-Fields Relationship," in Gwen L. Nagel, ed., *Critical Essays on Sarah Orne Jewett* (Boston: G. K. Hall, 1984), 119. See also Josephine Donovan, *Sarah Orne Jewett* (New York: Frederick Ungar, 1980), 12–18, and Faderman, *Surpassing the Love of Men,* 197–203.

36. Antoinette Brown Blackwell to Lucy Stone, June 1848, in Lasser and Merrill, eds., *Friends and Sisters,* 40.

37. Paula Blanchard, *Sarah Orne Jewett: Her Life and Work* (Reading, MA: Addison Wesley, 1994), 219.

38. For an interesting description of a romantic friendship between two African-American women, see Karen V. Hansen, "'No Kisses Is Like Youres': An Erotic Friendship Between Two African-American Women during the Mid-Nineteenth Century," *Gender and History* 7, 2 (August 1995): 153–82.

39. Judith Allen, "Evidence and Silence," in Carole Patman and Elizabeth Gross, eds., *Feminist Challenges* (Boston: Northeastern University Press, 1986); Evelyn Brooks Higginbotham, "Beyond the Sound of Silence: Afro-American Women's History," *Gender and History* 1, 1 (Spring 1989): 50–67; Nannerl Keohane, "Speaking from Silence: Women and the Science of Politics," *Soundings* 64, 4 (Winter 1981): 422–36; and John D. Wrathall, "Provenance as Text: Reading the Silences around Sexuality in Manuscript Collections," *Journal of American History* 79, 1 (June 1992): 165–78.

40. Stearns, *American Cool;* Stearns and Stearns, *Anger;* Edward Shorter, "Paralysis: The Rise and Fall of a 'Hysterical' Symptom," in Peter N. Stearns, ed., *Expanding the Past: A Reader in Social History* (New York: New York University Press, 1988), 215–48; Joan Jacobs Brumberg, *Fasting Girls: The Emergence of Anorexia Nervosa as a Modern Disease* (Cambridge, MA: Harvard University Press, 1988).

41. Stanton, *Eighty Years and More,* 166.
42. Antoinette Brown Blackwell to Lucy Stone, late February 1850, in Lasser and Merrill, eds., *Friends and Sisters,* 70.
43. Stearns, *American Cool,* 16–94; Shula Sommers, "Understanding Emotions"; and Margaret S. Clark, "Historical Emotionology."
44. Linda W. Rosenzweig, *The Anchor of My Life: Middle-Class American Mothers and Daughters, 1880–1920* (New York: New York University Press, 1993), 15–21.
45. Mary Cassatt to Joseph Durand-Ruel, March 1, 1924, in Mathews, *Cassatt and Her Circle,* 340.
46. Louisine Havemeyer to Joseph Durand-Ruel, June 16, 1926, in *Cassatt and Her Circle,* 342.
47. Chambers-Schiller, *Liberty, a Better Husband,* 148–55.
48. Ibid., 135, 155–56. Deborah Nord also touches on conflict between female friends in her discussion of female community in nineteenth-century London. See "'Neither Pairs Nor Odd.'"
49. Nancy Grey Osterud makes this point in *Bonds of Community,* 1–13. See Carroll Smith-Rosenberg, "The Female World of Love and Ritual," and Marilyn Ferris Motz, *True Sisterhood.*
50. Lystra, *Searching the Heart*; Rothman, *Hands and Hearts*; Jan Lewis, "The Republican Wife: Virtue and Seduction in the Early Republic," *William and Mary Quarterly* 44 (October 1987): 689–721; Lucia McMahon, "'While Our Souls Together Blend': Narrating a Romantic Readership in the Early Republic," in Stearns and Lewis, eds., *An Emotional History of the United States,* 66–90.
51. Alger, *Friendships of Women,* 130.
52. Esther Edwards Burr to Sarah Prince, April 12, 1757; October 9, 1754; April 19, 1756; Aaron Burr to Sarah Prince, October 23, 1756; all in *Journal of Esther Edwards Burr, 1754–1757,* 257, 52, 197, 233.
53. Glenna Matthews, *The Rise of Public Woman: Women's Power and Woman's Place in the United States, 1630–1970* (New York: Oxford University Press, 1992); Mary P. Ryan, *Women in Public: Between Banners and Ballots, 1825–1880* (Baltimore: Johns Hopkins University Press, 1990); Nancy Grey Osterud, "'She Helped Me Hay It as Good as a Man': Relations among Women and Men in an Agricultural Community," in Carol Groneman and Mary Beth Norton, eds., *"To Toil the Livelong Day": America's Women at Work, 1780–1980* (Ithaca, NY: Cornell University Press, 1987), 87–97, and *Bonds of Community,* 150–56, 186–91, 233, 245–48, 278–79; Karen Hansen, "'Our Eyes Behold Each Other,'" 49–50.
54. Mary Cassatt to Ambroise Vollard, n.d. 1903, quoted in Mathews, *Mary Cassatt: A Life,* 126; Edgar Degas to Mary Cassatt, Nancy Caldwell Sorel,

"Edgar Degas and Mary Cassatt," *Atlantic Monthly* (November 1993): 137.

55. Mathews, *Mary Cassatt: A Life,* 149, 312.
56. Emerson to Fuller, quoted in Dorothy Berkson, "'Born and Bred in Different Nations': Margaret Fuller and Ralph Waldo Emerson," in Shirley Marchalonis, ed., *Patrons and Protégées: Gender, Friendship, and Writing in Nineteenth-Century America* (New Brunswick, NJ: Rutgers University Press, 1988), 8.
57. Ibid., 22. Emerson's dour complaint sounds a familiar note to late twentieth-century readers of popular literature that addresses gender-based communication problems. See, for example, John Gray, *Men Are from Mars, Women Are from Venus* (New York: Harper Collins, 1993); Deborah Tannen, *You Just Don't Understand: Women and Men in Conversation* (New York: Ballantine Books, 1991); *That's Not What I Meant: How Conversational Style Makes or Breaks Relationships* (New York: Ballantine Books, 1987); and *Gender and Discourse* (New York: Oxford University Press, 1994).
58. Quoted in Berkson, "'Born and Bred in Different Nations,'" 24.
59. Louise Bernikow, *Among Women,* 127.
60. Recent research on women's relational development suggests that conflict functions as a means of elaborating the continuity of connection to significant others, a way to work out differences to preserve and strengthen a valued relationship. Although this work pertains specifically to the mother-daughter relationship, it may also have relevance for women's relationships with others who are important to them, such as close friends or "other selves." Hence conflict between Fuller and Emerson, Woolf and Mansfield may reflect the importance of these friendships to the participants. Alexandra G. Kaplan and Rona Klein, "The Relational Self in Late Adolescent Women," in Judith V. Jordan et al., *Women's Growth in Connection,* 122–31.
61. Dorothy Berkson suggests that the barrier between them reflected the sort of gender differences revealed in Carol Gilligan's research on women's psychological development. Emerson prized self-reliance and individualism, and Fuller valued intimacy and human relationships. She could understand his ideas, although she disagreed, but as he admitted, he remained "a stranger to [her] state of mind." In "'Born and Bred in Different Nations.'" For discussions of Fuller's more clearly romantic cross-sex friendships with George Davis and James Clarke, see Charles Capper, *Margaret Fuller, An American Romantic Life: The Private Years* (New York: Oxford University Press, 1992).
62. Mary G. De Jong, "Lines from a Partly Published Drama: The Romance of Frances Sargent Osgood and Edgar Allan Poe"; Joyce W. Warren,

"Subversions versus Celebration: The Aborted Friendship of Fanny Fern and Walt Whitman"; and Shirley Marchalonis, "A Model for Mentors? Lucy Larcom and John Greenleaf Whittier," all in Marchalonis, ed., *Patrons and Protégées*, 31–58, 59–93, 94–121. Although most of her friends were female, Sarah Orne Jewett enjoyed a close friendship with Whittier, who served as "literary aid and model, fellow moralist and spiritualist, country boy and surrogate father" for her.

63.   Thomas Bender, *Community and Social Change in America* (New Brunswick, NJ: Rutgers University Press, 1978), 62–120; John Higham, "The Reorientation of American Culture in the 1890s," in John Higham, *Writing American History: Essays in Modern Scholarship* (Bloomington, IN: Indiana University Press, 1970); and Peter Conn, *The Divided Mind: Ideology and Imagination in America, 1898–1917* (New York: Cambridge University Press, 1983), especially Chapter 1.

Notes to Chapter 2

1.   Mary Pratt Sears to Edith Paine, August 21, 1884, Book of Letters, 1864–1928, in Ella Lyman Cabot Papers, Schlesinger Library, Radcliffe College.

2.   Stearns, *American Cool,* 97–100.

3.   "The Eclipse of Friendship," *New York Evening Post,* reprinted in *Current Literature* 28 (June 1900): 342; "The Art of Friendship," *Littell's Living Age* 232 (February 8, 1902): 331–36; "Freshening of Life by New Friendship," *Pall Mall Gazette,* reprinted in *Current Literature* 29 (December 1900): 696; "The Larger Relationship," *Outlook* 64 (January 20, 1900): 158; "Passing of Friendship," *Atlantic Monthly* 95 (June 1905): 854–55; Reverend Lyman P. Powell, "The Literature of Friendship," *Good Housekeeping* 52 (February 1911): 223–25; "Reconstituted Friendship," *Living Age* 275 (December 7, 1912): 627–29.

4.   Margaret E. Sangster, "Talks on Friendship: Of Woman and Woman," *Harper's Bazaar,* 33 (November 10, 1900): 1784–85; Anne Bryan McCall, "Friendship in a Girl's Life," *Woman's Home Companion* 38 (January 1911): 27; Arthur C. Benson, "Essentials of Friendship," *Putnam's Monthly* 2 (September 1907): 673–80.

5.   E. Aria, "Concerning Companionship," *Living Age* 295 (October 6, 1917): 36–40; Mrs. L. H. Harris, *Independent* 56 (April 21, 1904): 906–908; Rafford Pyke, "What Women Like in Women," *Cosmopolitan* 34 (November 1902): 35–40; "My Grandmother, Myself and My Girlfriends," *Ladies Home Journal* 28 (October 1911): 15; Harriet Brunkhurst, "Danger of a Girl's 'Intimate' Friend," *Ladies Home Journal* 28 (May 15, 1911): 10; Albert Bigelow Paine, "Of Friendship among Women," *North American Re-*

view 183 (November 16, 1906): 1082–84, also in *Harper's Bazaar* 41 (February 1907): 192.

6. Virginia Blair, "Adventures in Girlhood: The Quest for Friends," *Good Housekeeping* 61 (November 1915): 610–14; Clara E. Laughlin, "Friends and Fun," *Ladies Home Journal* 28 (November 1911): 22; Caroline Wormeley Latimer, "When a Girl Is between 12 and 21," *Ladies Home Journal* 29 (February 1912): 38, 64; Rafford Pyke, "What Women Like in Women"; Judith Lloyde, "In and after Business Hours," *Ladies Home Journal* 22 (June 1905): 24; Albert Bigelow Paine, "Of Friendship among Women"; Harriet Brunkhurst, "Danger of a Girl's 'Intimate' Friend"; Anne Bryan McCall, "Our Ideals of Friendship," *Woman's Home Companion* 42 (September 1915): 22; and Aria, "Concerning Companionship."

7. Mary A. Jordan, "On College Friendships," *Harper's Bazaar* 35 (December 1901): 722–7.

8. Anne Bryan McCall, "Our Ideals of Friendship"; "My Friendships: What They Have Taught and Brought Me," *Harper's Bazaar* 46 (November 1912): 548.

9. "When We Were Social Gypsies," *Ladies Home Journal* 34 (February 1917): 16; Edward Howard Grigg, "Most Powerful Influence Known to Man," *Ladies Home Journal* 28 (March 1, 1911): 22; "The Impersonal Attitude," *Woman's Home Companion* 42 (September 1915): 22.

10. January 16 and 20, 1890, Diary, Series II, Box 1, Folder 41, Ida Sophia Scudder Papers, Schlesinger Library, Radcliffe College.

11. Letter to Ida Sophia Scudder, signature unclear, February 11, 1890, Series II, Box 2, Folder 58, ibid.

12. Sara L. Washburne to Ida Sophia Scudder, June 10, 1890; Nettie Chapman to Ida Sophia Scudder, June 11, 1890; both in Series II, Box 2, Folder 59, ibid.

13. Letter from May to Maida Herman and "Chum," August 20, 1907, Box 4, Folder 39, Maida Herman Solomon Papers, Schlesinger Library, Radcliffe College; January 20, 1890, Series II, Box 1, Folder 41, Scudder Papers.

14. February 9, March 19, April 9, 1915; January 11, 1916; September 19, October n.d., 1917; all from Diary of Marion Taylor, in Penelope Franklin, ed., *Private Pages: Diaries of American Women, 1830s–1970s* (New York: Ballantine Books, 1986), 6–8, 22–23, 34–35.

15. February n.d., 1919, Diary of Marion Taylor, ibid., 45–46.

16. "Chum" to Maida Herman, August 14, 1907; May to Maida Herman and "Chum," August 20, 1907, both in Box 4, Folder 39, Solomon Papers.

17. "Chum" to Maida Herman, August 14, 1907, Box 4, Folder 39, ibid.

18. Ethel to Maida Herman, February 16, 1911, Box 4, Folder 43, ibid.

19. Quoted in John C. Spurlock and Cynthia A. Magistro, *New and Improved:*

The Transformation of American Women's Emotional Culture (New York: New York University Press, 1998), 46.

20. Nancy Marshall to Rachel McClelland, January 1, 1904; Elsie to Rachel McClelland, May 11, 1904; both in Box 1, Folder 4, Rachel McClelland Sutton Correspondence, McClelland Family Papers, Pittsburgh Regional History Center.

21. Nancy Marshall to Rachel McClelland, May 20, 1908; February 1, 1909; August 22, 1909; all in Box 4, Folder 5, ibid.

22. Unsigned fragment, December 2, 1918, Box 2, Folder 3, ibid.

23. See, for example, letters of thanks to Rachel McClelland from Elsie, April 1, 1913, Box 2, Folder 1; from Gladys, December 14, 1921; and from Esther, December 30, 1921, and December 31, 1922; all in Box 2, Folder 4, ibid.

24. Josephine P. Peabody to Abbie Farwell Brown, Spring 1891; February 18, 1893; April 20, 1892; and November 4, 1892; all in Box 1, Josephine Preston Peabody's Letters to Abbie Farwell Brown, Houghton Library, Harvard University.

25. Degler, *At Odds,* 377.

26. Josephine P. Peabody to Abbie Farwell Brown, October 27, 1891, and penciled notation on envelope; February 1, 1894; April 26, 1897; all in Box 1, Peabody Letters to Brown.

27. Sahli, "Smashing: Women's Relationships before the Fall"; Helen Lefkowitz Horowitz, "Smith College and Changing Conceptions of Educated Women," in Ronald Story, ed., *Five Colleges, Five Histories* (Amherst, MA: Five Colleges, Inc., and Historic Deerfield, Inc., 1992), 79–102.

28. Lillian Faderman, *Odd Girls and Twilight Lovers: A History of Lesbian Life in Twentieth-Century America* (New York: Penguin Books, 1991): 37–61.

29. Martha Vicinus, "Distance and Desire: English Boarding School Friendships, 1870–1920," in Duberman et al., *Hidden from History,* 218.

30. Katharine Bement Davis, *Factors in the Sex Life of Twenty-Two Hundred Women* (New York: Harper and Brothers, 1929); Lynn D. Gordon, *Gender and Higher Education in the Progressive Era* (New Haven, CT: Yale University Press, 1990), 105–108.

31. Estelle B. Freedman, *Maternal Justice: Miriam Van Waters and the Female Reform Tradition* (Chicago: University of Chicago Press, 1996), 18, 25–27.

32. Patricia A. Palmieri, *In Adamless Eden: The Community of Women Faculty at Wellesley* (New Haven: Yale University Press, 1995), 203–204; Jane Cary to her mother, n.d. 1910, and typed comments, both in Folder 1910–11, Jane Cary Letters, Wellesley College.

33. Barbara Miller Solomon, *In the Company of Educated Women: A History*

of Women and Higher Education in America (New Haven, CT: Yale University Press, 1985), 102–103.

34. Ruth Sapin Hurwitz, "Coming of Age at Wellesley," *Menorah Journal* 38 (Fall 1950); Gordon, *Gender and Higher Education*, 69, 105–108.

35. Typed autobiography, Dorothy Reed Mendenhall Papers, Folder D, 1891–95, 10–11, 13–14, Sophia Smith Collection, Smith College.

36. Jane Cary to her family, September 2, 1913, in folder dated September 1913–February 1914; April 13, 1914, in folder dated February 1914–July 1914; January 8, 1911, in folder dated 1910–11; January 20, 1912, and January 28, 1912, in folder dated 1912–13; and typed comments in folder dated 1910–11; all in Cary Letters.

37. See letters from Ethel [no last name] to Marion Butler, Maida Herman, and Adelaide [no last name], July 15, 16, and 29, 1910; September 16, 1910; September 22, 1910; and October 9, 1910; all in Series I, Box 4, Folder 42, Solomon Papers.

38. Jane Cary to her mother, April 6, 1911, in folder dated 1910–11; May 10 and 17, 1913, in folder dated 1912–13; all in Cary Letters.

39. Fan [no last name] to Dearest Kids, n.d., and Fan to Maida Herman, n.d., Box 4, Folder 48; "Your Chum" to Maida Herman, March 17, 1911, Box 4, Folder 43; all in Solomon Papers.

40. Aimee [no last name] to Maida Herman, n.d., Box 4, Folder 48, ibid.

41. May [no last name] to Maida Herman, n.d., and Ethel [no last name] to Maida Herman, n.d., both in Box 4, Folder 47, ibid.

42. May [no last name] to Maida Herman, n.d., Box 4, Folder 47, ibid.

43. Jane Cary to her mother, March 8, 1914, in folder dated September 1913–February 1914, Cary Letters.

44. Josephine P. Peabody to Abbie Farwell Brown, July 2, 1899; August 17, 1899; and May 7, 1906; all in Box 2, Peabody Letters to Brown.

45. Josephine P. Peabody to Abbie Farwell Brown, June 29, 1906, Box 2, ibid.

46. See, for example, Josephine P. Peabody to Abbie Farwell Brown, June 29, 1906; January 1, 1907; March 29, 1910; and December 30, 1913; all in Box 2, ibid.

47. Annie Lyman Sears to Frances Rousmaniere, September 26, 1904; January 30, 1905; June 7, 1905; August 27, 1905; December 15, 1905; August 19, 1906; May 19, 1907; all in Certain Letters of Annie Lyman Sears, Box 8, Vol. 176, Ella Lyman Cabot Papers.

48. October 1, 1903; November 8, 1907; ibid.

49. October 10, 1908, ibid.

50. March 25, 1910; May 23, 1910; ibid.

51. Christmas 1914; December 26, 1914; May 23, 1915; December 7, 1915; February 13, 1916; November 14, 1914; all in Box 8, Vol. 176, ibid.

52. January 1, 1912; May 15, 1913; both in Box 2, Folder 1, Sutton Corre-

spondence. January 6, 1921; December 30, 1921; and December 31, 1922; all in Box 2, Folder 4, ibid.

53. Winifred to Rachel McClelland, September 26, 1911; and Elsie to Rachel McClelland, April 1, 1913; both in Box 2, Folder 1, ibid.

54. See below, Chapter 5.

55. Alice Duryee to Elizabeth McGrew Kimball, May 25, 1904, and October 15, 1904, in folder marked May 25, 1904–October 15, 1904; January 29, 1905, and September 25, 1905, in folder marked January 29, 1905–November 19, 1905; all in Kimball Faculty Letters, Smith College Archives.

56. Alice Duryee to Elizabeth McGrew Kimball, April 28, 1906; January 25, 1907; June 4, 1908; July 9, 1909; December 17, 1909; October 10, 1909; December 17, 1909; and December 20, 1909; all in Folder 1908–1916, ibid.

57. Alice Duryee to Elizabeth McGrew Kimball, November 13, 1910; *New York Times,* February 1, 1911, and February 2, 1911; Susan D. Fahmy to Elizabeth McGrew Kimball, n.d. 1911 and March 11, 1911; all in ibid.

58. Typed autobiography, Box 3, Folder E, p. 48, Mendenhall Papers.

59. Diary of Azalia Emma Peet, September 21 and December 14, 1913; June 19, 1916; all in Franklin, ed., *Private Pages,* 242, 245, 267.

60. Diary of Azalia Emma Peet, January 17, 1915; March 13, 1915; April 15, 1915; September 17, 1915; April 8, 1915; February 8, 1915; July 1, 1915; all in ibid., 256, 258, 262, 256–57, 259.

61. Georgia O'Keeffe to Anita Pollitzer, August 25, 1915; Pollitzer to O'Keeffe, September n.d., 1915; O'Keeffe to Pollitzer, September n.d., 1915; Pollitzer to O'Keeffe, October n.d., 1915; O'Keeffe to Pollitzer, October n.d., 1915; all in *Lovingly, Georgia: The Complete Correspondence of Georgia O'Keeffe and Anita Pollitzer,* ed. Clive Giboire (New York: Simon and Schuster, 1990), 14, 18, 32–33, 39–42.

62. Georgia O'Keeffe to Anita Pollitzer, October n.d., 1915; O'Keeffe to Pollitzer, October n.d., 1915; Pollitzer to O'Keeffe, October n.d., 1915; January 1, 1916; and January 4, 1916; all in ibid., 48, 52–53, 56, 116, 118.

63. Georgia O'Keeffe to Anita Pollitzer, July n.d., 1916, and September n.d., 1916; Pollitzer to O'Keeffe, February 10, 1923; all in ibid., 164, 201, 268.

64. The complexities that characterized their relationship as mature and aging women are discussed below in Chapter 5.

65. Helen Tufts Bailie, Personal Journal, n.d. 1895; January 31, 1896; September 25, 1896; October 7, 1896; January 9, 1897; October 6, 1897; November 13, 1897; all in Helen Matilda Tufts Bailie Papers, Sophia Smith Collection.

66. Helen Tufts Bailie, June 2, 1898; June 7, 1898; October 22, 1898; August 28, 1900; January 7, 1901; January 17, 1901; January 22, 1901; February 27, 1901; May 11, 1901; June 7, 1901; March 19, 1906; all in ibid.

67. Ibid.
68. Lisa M. Fine, "Between Two Worlds: Business Women in a Chicago Boarding House, 1900–1930," *Journal of Social History* 19, 3 (Spring 1986): 511–19.
69. Higham, "The Reorientation of American Culture in the 1890s"; Conn, *The Divided Mind*, especially Chapter 1.
70. For overviews of the changes in women's lives, see Degler, *At Odds*; Margaret G. Wilson, *The American Woman in Transition: 1870–1920* (New York: Greenwood Press, 1979); Mary P. Ryan, *Womanhood in America* (New York: New Viewpoints, 1975); Peter G. Filene, *Him/Her/Self: Sex Roles in Modern America*, 2d. ed. (Baltimore: Johns Hopkins University Press, 1986), Chapter 1; and Sara M. Evans, *Born for Liberty: A History of Women in America* (New York: Free Press, 1989), Chapters 6 and 7.
71. Carroll Smith-Rosenberg, "The New Woman as Androgyne: Social Disorder and Gender Crisis, 1870–1936," in *Disorderly Conduct: Visions of Gender in Victorian America* (New York: A. A. Knopf, 1985), 245–96; Carolyn Forrey, "The New Woman Revisited," *Women's Studies* 2, 1 (1974); and Filene, *Him/Her/Self*, Chapter 1.
72. Filene, *Him/Her/Self*, 29.

Notes to Chapter 3

1. April 20, April 29, September 14, and October 11, 1931, Box 1, Vol. 6, Yvonne Blue Skinner Diaries, Schlesinger Library, Radcliffe College.
2. December 11, 1931, Box 1, Vol. 6, ibid.
3. Stearns, *American Cool*, 139–92.
4. Stearns, ibid., 229–63.
5. See, for example, Robert Bridges, "Affection," *Forum* 69 (June 1923): 1649–50; Walter B. Pitkin, "Add Friends, Multiply Opportunity," *Rotarian* 53 (October 1938): 34–36; "Wanted: Friendship Spreaders," *Scholastic* 33 (September 17, 1938): 2; Ruth Fedder, *A Girl Grows Up*, 2d ed. (New York: McGraw-Hill, 1948), 83–87, 98–109, and *You, the Person You Want to Be* (New York: Whittlesey House, 1957), 123–40; and Jean Schick Grossman, *Do You Know Your Daughter?* (New York and London: Appleton-Century, 1944), 45. On the new culture, see Warren Susman, *Culture as History: The Transformation of American Society in the Twentieth Century* (New York: Pantheon Books, 1984). For an interesting discussion of the connections between the culture of consumption and women's emotions, see Spurlock and Magistro, *New and Improved*.
6. "How I Lost My Friends," *Woman's Home Companion* 55 (June 1928): 4+; Frances Parkinson Keyes, "Letter on Friendship," *Good Housekeeping*

79 (December 1924): 51; Zona Gale, "Do Women Really Like One Another?" *Pictorial Review* 27 (October 1925): 25+.

7. Agnes Burke, "Friendship," *Ladies Home Journal* 52 (June 1935): 70;
Della T. Lutes, "Losing Friends and Being Influenced," *Forum* 98 (Novem-
ber 1937): 262–66; Dorothy Walworth, "Don't Let Them Tell It to You:
Troubles of a Confidante," *Good Housekeeping* 116 (March 1943): 431;
Zulma Steele, "Is Your Best Friend Good Enough for You?" *Good House-
keeping* 118 (January 1944): 27+; Henrietta Ripperger, "Will Any Buddy
Do?" *Good Housekeeping* 111 (September 1940): 10.

8. "What a Woman of Forty Thinks about Men," *Harper's Monthly Maga-
zine* 143 (October 1921): 610–13; William Lynn Phelps, "Five Famous
Friendships," *Good Housekeeping* 117 (June 1943): 40; Bettina Loomis,
"Bride's Best Friend," *Good Housekeeping,* 138 (February 1954): 115.

9. In *Rotarian:* John Nelson, "Let's Mobilize Friendship," 46 (February
1935): 22–25+; E. Dimnet, "Let's Speak of Friendship," 49 (December
1936): 8–11; Walter B. Pitkin, "Add Friends, Multiply Opportunity," 53
(October 1938): 34–36; Charles Hanson Towne, "New Friends," 63 (July
1943): 23; H. W. Scandlin, "Friendship," 67 (November 1945): 50; Grove
Patterson, "What Friendship Means to Me," 72 (June 1948): 18–22; O. A.
Battista, "Friends Can Show You How to Live," 79 (July 1951): 42–43;
Fred DeArmond, "What Friends Mean to Me," 81 (December 1952): 8–9;
Rube Goldberg, "I Always Make It a Rule: Friendships in Business," 81
(September 1952): 10–12; Allen Raymond, "May Friends Go with You,"
88 (March 1956): 34–36. John Appleton, "St. Francis and Others," *Com-
monweal* 12 (October 8, 1930): 580–81; Oswald Garrison Villard, "Issues
and Men: Politics and Friendship," *Nation* 142 (February 19, 1936): 211.

10. Evans, *Born for Liberty,* 175–96; Rosalind Rosenberg, *Divided Lives:
America Women in the Twentieth Century* (New York: Hill and Wang,
1992), 93; Linda Gordon, *Woman's Body, Woman's Right: A Social His-
tory of Birth Control in America* (New York: Grossman, 1976), 193–94.
Child-rearing literature also stressed the centrality of heterosexual rela-
tionships. See, for example, Bernard Glueck, "The Family Drama," and
Ernest R. Groves, "Loosening Family Ties," both in Dorothy Canfield
Fisher and Sidonie M. Gruenberg, eds., *Our Children: A Handbook for
Parents* (New York: Viking Press, 1932), 169–81, 257–65. See also
Christina Simmons, "Companionate Marriage and the Lesbian Threat,"
Frontiers 4 (1979). While many historians argue that close relationships be-
tween women were not pathologized until the twentieth century, a recent
study offers an interesting revisionist perspective on this issue. See Mary-
lynne Diggs, "Romantic Friends or a 'Different Race of Creatures'? The
Representation of Lesbian Pathology in Nineteenth-Century America,"
Feminist Studies 21, 2 (Summer 1995): 317–40.

11. Rosenberg, *Divided Lives*, 92; John Modell, *Into One's Own: From Youth to Adulthood in the United States, 1920–1975* (Berkeley, CA: University of California Press, 1989), especially Chapter 3; Spurlock and Magistro, *New and Improved*, Chapter 2; Beth Bailey, *Front Porch to Back Seat* (Baltimore: Johns Hopkins University Press, 1988); Paula S. Fass, *The Damned and the Beautiful: American Youth in the 1920s* (New York: Oxford University Press, 1977); Robert S. Lynd and Helen Merrell Lynd, *Middletown: A Study in American Culture* (New York: Harcourt Brace Jovanovich, 1929), 133, 135–36, 143, 162–63, 522–23.

12. Fass, *The Damned and the Beautiful*, 139–67, 191–221; Lynd and Lynd, *Middletown*, 135, 162–63, 176; Horowitz, "Smith College and Changing Conceptions of Educated Women"; Sheila M. Rothman, *Woman's Proper Place: A History of Changing Ideals and Practices, 1870 to the Present* (New York: Basic Books, 1978), 181–84. It is interesting to note that among African-American women, sororities have fulfilled broader functions than the structuring of social life. See, for example, Susan L. Smith, "Sharecroppers and Sorority Women: The Alpha Kappa Alpha Mississippi Health Project," in Susan L. Smith, *Sick and Tired of Being Sick and Tired: Black Women's Health Activism in America, 1890–1950* (Philadelphia: University of Pennsylvania Press, 1995).

13. June 20, 1919; June 22, 1919; both in Box 3, Folder 1, Dorothy Smith Dushkin Papers, Sophia Smith Collection.

14. May 14, June 15, and October 7, 1924, Vol. 2; March 30, March 31, April 3, and May 25, 1925, Vol. 3; December 22 and April 18, 1926, Vol. 6; all in Box 1, Yvonne Blue Skinner Diaries.

15. May 23, July 25, July 26, and October 11, 1923, Vol. 1; July 17, 1926, Vol. 6; all in ibid.

16. September 23 and December 18, 1926, Vol. 6; Addenda, Folder 3; all in ibid.

17. Peter N. Stearns, *Fat History: Bodies and Beauty in the Modern West* (New York: New York University Press, 1997), 71–97.

18. April 23, June 21, and August 12, 1927, Vol. 6, Box 1, Yvonne Blue Skinner Diaries.

19. For an interesting discussion of consumerism and envy in childhood, see Peter N. Stearns, "Consumerism and Childhood: New Targets for American Emotions," in Stearns and Lewis, eds., *An Emotional History of the United States*, 396–413.

20. April 20 or 21, 1929, Vol. 2, Book 16; January 22, 1929, Vol. 1, Book 13; April 23, 1929, Vol. 2, Book 16; all in Series II, Beth Twiggar Goff Papers, Schlesinger Library, Radcliffe College.

21. May 28, 1928, Series I, Vol. 5; March 16, 1929, Series II, Vol. 3, Book 15; all in ibid.

22. March 3, 1928, Vol. 1; March 20 and 21, 1928, Vol. 2; all in Series I, ibid. N.d. 1929, Vol. 7, Book 19, Series II; March 15, 1928, Vol. 2, Series I; all in ibid.

23. In *New and Improved,* John Spurlock and Cynthia Magistro argue that despite their expressions of interest in the opposite sex, high-school girls actually preferred female friends to male friends during the period 1915 to 1935. If this hypothesis is correct, it appears that young women sublimated their actual feelings in response to the cultural pressure for popularity with the opposite sex.

24. June 29, 1928, Vol. 6, Series I; June 24, 1929, Vol. 6, Book 18, Series II; all in Beth Twiggar Goff Papers.

25. December 16, February 10, January 8, and January 9, 1929, Edythe Weiner First Diary, Schlesinger Library, Radcliffe College.

26. Joan Jacobs Brumberg, "Coming of Age in the 1920s: The Diaries of Yvonne Blue and Helen Laprovitz," in Susan Ware, ed., *New Viewpoints in Women's History: Working Papers from the Schlesinger Library 50th Anniversary Conference, March 4–5, 1994* (Cambridge, MA: Schlesinger Library, 1994), 215–21.

27. See correspondence from 1937 and 1938, Folder 1, Box 5, Alan Summersby Emmet Papers, Schlesinger Library, Radcliffe College.

28. February 18, April 13, April n.d., April 29, June 12, June 13, September 8, and May 17, 1933, Helen Snyder Diary, in author's possession. This friendship, which endured for over seventy years, is discussed further in Chapter 5.

29. April 7 and 14, May 27, June 13 and 22, and July 4, 1933, ibid.

30. See, for example, Diaries for 1931 and 1932, Carton 1, Adele Siegel Rosenfield Papers, Schlesinger Library, Radcliffe College.

31. January 24, 1945, paper fragment with Adele Mongan Fasick Diary, Schlesinger Library, Radcliffe College.

32. February 16 and 17, 1945, ibid.

33. June 1, April 16, June 23, March 26, June 8, and April 9, 1945, ibid.

34. May 30, 1945, ibid.

35. August 5, 1953, June Calender Diaries, Schlesinger Library, Radcliffe College. See also entries dated February 27 and July 7, 1953, and January 25, 1954.

36. Annie Dillard, *An American Childhood* (New York: Harper and Row, 1987), 86–93, 186–88, 195, 215.

37. Wini Breines, *Young, White, and Miserable: Growing Up Female in the Fifties* (Boston: Beacon Press, 1992), 110–12; November 2, 1959, Ruth Teischman [pseudonym] Diary, Schlesinger Library, Radcliffe College. The original diary is closed until January 1, 2043, but a copy with names removed is available for research.

38. Brumberg, "Coming of Age in the 1920s."
39. Breines, *Young, White, and Miserable,* 111–13.
40. Solomon, *In the Company of Educated Women,* 157–62, 186–98; Susan M. Hartmann, *The Home Front and Beyond: American Women in the 1940s* (Boston: Twayne, 1982), 101–102. The image of "flaming youth" derives from a bestselling novel about the flapper age. See Warner Fabian, *Flaming Youth* (New York: Boni Liveright, 1923). The advertisement is quoted in Rosenberg, *Divided Lives,* 147.
41. Virginia Durr, *Outside the Magic Circle: The Autobiography of Virginia Foster Durr,* ed. Hollinger F. Barnard (Birmingham, AL: University of Alabama Press, 1985), 51–52.
42. Margaret Mead, *Blackberry Winter: My Earlier Years* (New York: Morrow, 1972), 102–109.
43. Ibid., 104, 109. Interestingly, although she married three times, Margaret Mead's most intense and significant adult relationship appears to have been her long, intimate friendship with Ruth Benedict, which is discussed below in Chapter 6.
44. E. Gertrude Palmer to her parents, n.d., Box 5, Folder 74, Elsie Miller Palmer Papers, Schlesinger Library, Radcliffe College.
45. Jane Shugg to her family, September 25, 1936, and January 26, 1939, Unprocessed collection, Wellesley College Archives.
46. Jane Shugg to her family, January 18, 1940, Unprocessed collection, ibid.
47. October 26, 1933; January 4 and July 22, 1934; April 28, 1935; February 6, 1936; all in Helen Snyder Diary.
48. August 18, 1934; July 4 and 31, 1936; January 2, 1937; all in ibid.
49. October 2, 1934; January 16, February 14, October 14 and 15, 1935; all in ibid.
50. Durr, *Outside the Magic Circle,* 59; Jane Shugg, Unprocessed collection; Yvonne Blue Skinner Diaries; Ethel Chase, "Some Concrete Problems Facing the Dean," Sixteenth Yearbook, National Association of Deans of Women (1929), 109, quoted in Rothman, *Woman's Proper Place,* 182.
51. Durr, *Outside the Magic Circle,* 59. It is especially interesting that Virginia Foster Durr and her husband later participated actively in the civil rights movement.
52. November 27, 19, and October 22, 1930; February 1, October 24, and June 11, 1931; all in Box 1, Vol. 6, Yvonne Blue Skinner Diaries.
53. Jane Shugg to her family, October 9 and 13, 1936; September 27, 1937; April 23, 1939; Unprocessed collection.
54. *Blackberry Winter,* 105.
55. February 14, 1934, Helen Snyder Diary.
56. October 5, 1926, Box 1, Vol. 6, Yvonne Blue Skinner Diaries.
57. Val to Yvonne Blue, September 13, October n.d., October 2, December 4,

202 Notes to Chapter 3

1930, Addendum, Box 1, Folder 6, 1930, ibid.; November 19, 1931, Addendum, Box 1, Folder 7, 1931, ibid.

58. Diary of Martha Lavell, September 26, 1926; October 3, 1927; January 8, 1928; May 4, 1928; July 12, 1930; August 16, 1929; May 1, 1931; all in Franklin, ed., *Private Pages*, 191, 192–93, 197, 202, 212, 207, 219–20.

59. October 26, 1930, Vol. 6, Box 1; Val to Yvonne Blue, November 19, 1931, Folder 7, Box 1, Addendum; Maryellen to Yvonne, September 24, 1932, Folder 8, Box 2, Addendum; all in Yvonne Blue Skinner Diaries. See also letters from Val dated January 16, 1929; December 4, 1930; and June 5, 1931.

60. November 27, 1930, November 30, 1930; Vol. 6, Box 1, ibid.

61. November 19, 1930; June 11, 1931; both in Vol. 6, Box 1, ibid.

62. N.d. 29, 1949; n.d. 25, 1949; n.d. 18, 1949, and n.d. 22, 1950; all in Box 3, Notebook 1949–50, Mary Sill Peck Papers, Wellesley College Archives.

63. October 6, 1940, and February 2, 1941, Folder dated September–December 1940, Freshman Year, Jean Nearing Papers, Wellesley College Archives.

64. May 17, August 30, September 30, 1942, Folder dated August 1942–May 1943, ibid. September 5, 1943; March 16, 1944; August 29, 1943; Folder dated September 1943–January 1944, Senior Year, ibid.

65. October 26, 1941, Folder dated April–June 1941, Freshman Year, and September–November 1941, Sophomore Year; August 30, 1942, Folder dated August 1942–May 1943, Junior Year; all in ibid. Jane Cary's Wellesley friendships are discussed above in Chapter 3.

66. See, for example, letters dated October 19, 1941, and May 12 and September 30, 1943, Folders dated Freshman Year, April–June 1941, and Sophomore Year, September–November 1941; and September 1943–January 1944, Senior Year, ibid.

67. August 31 and December 6, 11, and 18, 1931, Box 1, Vol. 6, Yvonne Blue Skinner Diaries.

68. Phoebe Jacobus to Yvonne Blue, January 19, 1931, Folder 7, Box 1 Addendum, 1931, ibid.

69. Eleanor Olcott to Eleanor Coit, n.d., marked before 1924, Folder 40; Alice Burbank to Eleanor Coit, June 9, n.d., and April 26, n.d., Folder 34; Marjorie Paret to Eleanor Coit, October 29, 1920, and December 19, 1920, Folder 41; all in Box 1, Eleanor Coit Papers, Sophia Smith Collection, Smith College.

70. January 11, February 9, June 16, and November 1, 1925; June 25, 1924; January 6, 1927; June 30, 1932; all in Diary of Gladys Bell Penrod, Indiana County Historical and Genealogical Society, Indiana, Pennsylvania. I am grateful to Cynthia Magistro for sharing the Gladys Bell Diary with me.

71. Josephine Crisfield Connerat to Dorothy Smith, August 22, 1926, Folder 11, Dushkin Papers. February 27, 1927; May 24, 1928; May 3, 1929; May 28, 1930; all in Folder 10, Box 2, Dushkin Papers. Dorothy Smith enjoyed

a similar friendship with another college classmate, Jessie Lloyd. See, for example, Lloyd's letter, dated July 16, 1929, Folder 18, also in Box 2.

72. October 13, 1935, Book 34, Beth Twiggar Goff Papers. January 14, 1936; n.d.; and March 1, 1936; all in Book 35, Beth Twiggar Goff Papers.

73. October 10 and October 24, 1931; November 20, 1932; all in Folder 2, Series I, Box 1, Harriet Louise Hardy Papers, Schlesinger Library, Radcliffe College. December 31, 1932, Folder 3, ibid. See also entries dated January 22 and March 4, 1933, Folder 3, and March 5, 1938, Folder 6.

74. September 30, 1954, and September 27, 1953, Box 3, Notebook 1953–55, Mary Sill Peck Papers.

75. Quoted in Susman, *Culture as History*, 105.

Notes to Chapter 4

1. April 28, 1937, Book 36, Beth Twiggar Goff Papers.

2. Lillian Hellman, *An Unfinished Woman: A Memoir* (Boston: Little Brown, 1969), 29–30. Recent discussion about the nature of Eleanor Roosevelt's friendships clearly illustrates the potential pitfalls for the historian; see the contrasting interpretations offered in Doris Faber, *The Life of Lorena Hickok: E. R.'s Friend* (New York: William Morrow, 1980), and Blanche Wiesen Cook, *Eleanor Roosevelt: Volume I, 1884–1933* (New York: Penguin Books, 1992). The relationship between Roosevelt and Hickok is discussed below in Chapter 6. See also Leila J. Rupp, "'Imagine My Surprise,'" and Carroll Smith-Rosenberg, "The New Woman as Androgyne," in *Disorderly Conduct*, 245–96.

3. Estelle Freedman, "Female Institution Building, 1870–1930," *Feminist Studies* 5, 3 (Fall 1979): 512–29; Blanche Wiesen Cook, "Female Support Networks and Political Activism."

4. Mary Pratt Sears to Julia Lyman, August 12, 1911, 303, and Ella Lyman Cabot, Introduction, vii, in Mary Pratt Sears Book of Letters; Louise Amory to Ella Lyman Cabot, n.d. [1931–34?], Box 4, Folder 100; both in Ella Lyman Cabot Papers.

5. "Frances Crane Lillie: A Memoir by Mary Prentice Lillie Barrows," Box 10, Vol. 2, and letters from Lillie to Ellen Gates Starr, Box 10, Folders 94–101, all in Ellen Gates Starr Papers, Sophia Smith Collection, Smith College.

6. Anna Lee Allan Tracy to Mary Helen Humphrey, February 23, 1927, Box 2, Folder 2; December 30, 1914, and June 14, 1917, Box 2, Folder 1; all in Anna Lee Allan Tracy Papers, Schlesinger Library, Radcliffe College.

7. Barbara to Mary Helen Humphrey, August 23, 1947, Box 2, Folder 4, ibid.

8. Margaret Sanger to Juliet Rublee, n.d., c. 1923, and August 6, 1925; Sanger to Dorothy Brush, January 14, 1947; Rublee to Sanger, September 11,

1925; Brush to Sanger, March 24, 1949; all quoted in Ellen Chesler, *Woman of Valor: Margaret Sanger and the Birth Control Movement in America* (New York: Simon and Schuster, 1992), 233, 250, 262, 399, 235, 406.

9. Patricia R. Everett, ed., *A History of Having a Great Many Times Not Continued to Be Friends* (Albuquerque: University of New Mexico Press, 1996). Dodge's recollection of their meeting is quoted in Everett's Introduction, 1.

10. Mabel Dodge to Gertrude Stein, c. April 1911; c. December 1913; May 8, 1914; February 6, 1918; Gertrude Stein to Mabel Dodge, December 28, 1925; Dodge to Stein, January 11, 1926; all in ibid., 29, 210, 228, 248, 255, and Introduction, 5.

11. Their relationship followed a pattern similar to that of many other friendships Stein formed, particularly after she and Toklas became partners. Ibid., Introduction, 2.

12. Alice Shoemaker to Eleanor G. Coit, February 26, 1935, Box 1, Folder 44, and Amy Bruce to Eleanor G. Coit, March 31, 1935, Box 1, Folder 33, both in Coit Papers. It is interesting to note that Amy Bruce eventually became Coit's long-term companion. See also letters from other friends, Folders 30–32 and 47–50, Box 1.

13. Jeannette Rankin to Flora Belle Surles, February 21, 1938; February 7, March 3, June 22, 1944; January 2, n.d.; and March 21, 1946; all in Flora Belle Surles Papers, Schlesinger Library, Radcliffe College; Jeannette Rankin to Harriet Yarrow, September 25, 1943; May 21, 1953; both in Harriet Yarrow Papers, Schlesinger Library, Radcliffe College.

14. Sarah Norcliffe Cleghorn to Elizabeth Kent, October 22, October 27, November 20, 1936; February 27, 1937; all in Folder 1; sonnets dated in pencil 1938, Folder 2; all in Sarah Norcliffe Cleghorn Papers, Schlesinger Library, Radcliffe College.

15. Degler, *At Odds*, 150–51; Susan J. Matt, "Frocks, Finery, and Feelings: Rural and Urban Women's Envy, 1890–1930," and Stearns, "Consumerism and Childhood," in Stearns and Lewis, eds., *An Emotional History of the United States*, 377–95, 396–413; Richard W. Fox and T. J. Jackson Lears, eds., *The Culture of Consumption: Critical Essays on American History, 1880–1980* (New York: Pantheon Books, 1983); Mary Louise Roberts, "Gender, Consumption, and Commodity Culture," *American Historical Review* 103, 3 (June 1998): 817–44; Susman, *Culture as History;* Lynd and Lynd, *Middletown,* 272–81; Rothman, *Woman's Proper Place,* 64–74; Theodora Penny Martin, *The Sound of Our Own Voices: Women's Study Clubs, 1860–1910* (Boston: Beacon Press, 1987), 128–33.

16. Spurlock and Magistro, *New and Improved;* John C. Spurlock, "The Prob-

lem of Modern Married Love for Middle-Class Women," in Stearns and Lewis, eds., *An Emotional History of the United States*, 319–32.

17. Elsie Frances Hagemann Noetzel to her daughter, December 12, 1995, in author's possession.

18. *In Red Hats, Beads, and Bags: 1908 Graduates Sharing Their Lives through Letters,* compiled by Dolores Avelleyra Murphy (Morrison, CO: Cassiopeia Press, 1990). The quotations appear on 276–77 and 291–92.

19. Round-Robin Letters, Class of 1943, Wellesley College, in Wellesley College Archives. Quotations are from Mary Falconer Bell's letters of July 19, 1946, and September 1, 1978.

20. William Plummer and Sandra Gurvis, "After 58 Years, a Round-Robin Letter Keeps on Delivering," *People Weekly* 32, 2 (January 16, 1989): 99–100.

21. Gladys to Rachel McClelland Sutton, August 4, 1924; Polly to Sutton, January 11, 1925, both in Box 2, Folder 5, Sutton Correspondence. Esther Morgan McCullough to Sutton, n.d. 1931, Box 3, Folder 1; Winifred to Sutton, May 19, 1942; McCullough to Sutton, December 8, 1943, and May 17, 1943; all in Box 4, Folder 2, ibid.

22. Esther Morgan McCullough to Rachel McClelland Sutton, September 6 and December 3, 1939; June 9, 1938; all in Box 3, Folder 6, ibid. Winifred to Rachel McClelland Sutton, January 18, 1945, Box 4, Folder 2; Louise to Rachel McClelland Sutton, July 31, 1930, Box 3, Folder 3; both in ibid.

23. Susan Schindette and Barbara Wegher, "Six Texas Pals, Class of '44, Still Share Lunch, Life and Laughter," *People Weekly* 30, 8 (August 22, 1988): 52–54.

24. *In Red Hats, Beads, and Bags*, 73.

25. June 12, 1955, Box 3, Folder 4, Dushkin Papers.

26. Janet Oppenheimer Landis to author, February 22, 1993; January n.d., 1994. See references to "Jan" in quotations from the diary of Helen Snyder in Chapters 3 and 4.

27. Jeannette to Rachel McClelland Sutton, June 26, 1944, Box 4, Folder 2, Sutton Correspondence.

28. Esther Morgan McCullough to Rachel McClelland Sutton, n.d., Box 2, Folder 5, ibid.

29. Louise De Schweinitz Interview Transcripts, February 18 and February 25, 1977, p. 93, Medical College of Pennsylvania Oral History Project, Schlesinger Library, Radcliffe College.

30. May 10, 1933, and November 23, 1934, Box 3, Folder 4, Dushkin Papers.

31. Patricia Frazer Lamb to Kathryn Joyce Holwein, September 8, 1956, and Kathryn Joyce Holwein to Patricia Frazer Lamb, November 4, 1959, both in *Touchstones: Letters between Two Women, 1953–1964,* ed. Patricia Frazer Lamb (Boston: G. K. Hall, 1986), 84, 182. For an interesting discussion of the importance of friendship to women troubled by the discrep-

ancy between their own experiences and cultural prescriptions regarding marriage, see Spurlock and Magistro, *New and Improved,* Chapter 4.

32. Dorothy Thompson to Rose Wilder Lane, July 15, 1921, and September 24, 1921; Rose Wilder Lane to Dorothy Thompson, n.d.; all in *Dorothy Thompson and Rose Wilder Lane: Forty Years of Friendship, Letters, 1921–1960,* ed. William Holtz (Columbia, MO: University of Missouri Press, 1991), 12, 29, 39.

33. Rose Wilder Lane to Dorothy Thompson, October 26, 1927, and March 12, 1929, ibid., 62, 105.

34. Rose Wilder Lane to Dorothy Thompson, June 1 and June 6, 1939; Dorothy Thompson to Rose Wilder Lane, June 6, 1939; all in ibid., 157, 159, 162–63.

35. Rose Wilder Lane to Dorothy Thompson, September 25, 1960; Dorothy Thompson to Rose Wilder Lane, n.d.; Rose Wilder Lane to Dorothy Thompson, November 18, 1960; Dorothy Thompson to Rose Wilder Lane, December 8, 1960; all in ibid., 187, 188–89, 192–93, 196–97.

36. Rose Wilder Lane to Dorothy Thompson, May 20, 1939; Dorothy Thompson to Rose Wilder Lane, May 31, 1939; both in ibid., 153–55.

37. Georgia O'Keeffe to Anita Pollitzer, August 5, 1937, in *Lovingly Georgia,* 280. Pollitzer's memoir, "That's Georgia," appeared in the November 4, 1950, issue of the *Saturday Review.* For discussion of the proposed biography, see O'Keeffe's letters of January 11, 1956; February 4, 1956; and February 28, 1968; all in *Lovingly Georgia,* 303, 307, 320ff.

38. Stearns, *American Cool,* 240. For a discussion of conflict and anger between nineteenth-century friends, see above, Chapter 2.

39. Ellen C. Sabin to Lucia Russell Briggs, August 8, 1923, and Lucia Russell Briggs, speech to Milwaukee-Downer College students, 1949, in Virginia A. Palmer, ed., "'Faithfully Yours, Ellen C. Sabin': Correspondence between Ellen C. Sabin and Lucia R. Briggs from January 1921 to August 1921," *Wisconsin Magazine of History* 67 (Autumn 1983): 40–41.

40. Susan Ware, *Beyond Suffrage: Women in the New Deal* (Cambridge, MA: Harvard University Press, 1981), 3–17.

41. Rose Schneiderman to Eleanor Roosevelt and Eleanor Roosevelt to Molly Dewson, quoted in Frances M. Seeber, "Eleanor Roosevelt and Women in the New Deal: A Network of Friends," *Presidential Studies Quarterly* 20, 4 (Fall 1990): 713, 709. After Dewson retired and left Washington, she tried to keep in touch with Roosevelt, but the intimacy of their earlier friendship ended. See Susan Ware, *Partner and I: Molly Dewson, Feminism, and New Deal Politics* (New Haven: Yale University Press, 1987), 247. On Roosevelt's friendships with Esther Lape, Elizabeth Read, Nancy Cook, Marion Dickerson, and Caroline O'Day, see Blanche Wiesen Cook, *Eleanor Roosevelt, Volume One, 1884–1933* (New York: Penguin Books,

1992), 296–98, 319–28, 383–86. Roosevelt's relationship with Lorena Hickok and Molly Dewson's partnership with Polly Porter are discussed below in Chapter 6.

42. Ware, *Partner and I,* 144; Ware, *Beyond Suffrage,* 13. It is interesting to note that although Mary McLeod Bethune also held an important federal job as head of the Office of Minority Affairs in the National Youth Administration from 1936–1944, she was not a part of the New Deal network. Susan Ware argues that the other women in the network had worked together earlier and viewed themselves as personal friends, while Bethune was seen, and saw herself, as representing the interests of African Americans rather than of women. Ware suggests that even those who were not close friends had strong feelings about one another as professional friends. *Beyond Suffrage,* 12–13.

43. Freedman, *Maternal Justice,* 66, 77, 102.

44. Rose Schneiderman to Mary Elizabeth Dreier, December 17, 1929, and other letters from 1929, 1933, and 1937–50, all in Series I, Box 5, Folder 66, Mary Elizabeth Dreier Papers, Schlesinger Library, Radcliffe College; letters from Elizabeth Christman to Dreier, Folders 64 and 65, Box 5, ibid.

45. Leila J. Rupp, "The Woman's Community in the National Woman's Party, 1945 to the 1960s," *Signs* 10, 4 (Summer 1985): 715–40. Personal connections and political commitment were also intertwined in the context of international women's organizations. See Leila J. Rupp, *Worlds of Women* (Princeton, NJ: Princeton University Press, 1998).

46. See, for example, the correspondence between Alice Hamilton and Harriet Louise Hardy, Series II, Box 3, Folders 44, 45, and 46, Harriet Louise Hardy Papers, Schlesinger Library, Radcliffe College; see also Maxine Bennet, Interview Transcript, May 13, 1977, and Doris Bartuska, Interview Transcript, April 4 and 5, 1977, both in Medical College of Pennsylvania Oral History Project.

47. Esther Clark, Interview Transcript, December 19, 1977, 35–36, ibid.

48. Harriet Dustan, Interview Transcript, April 4 and 5, 1977, 52, ibid.

49. Nina Starr Braunwald, Interview Transcript, September 24, 1977, 51, ibid.

50. See correspondence in Carol Brightman, ed., *Between Friends: The Correspondence of Hannah Arendt and Mary McCarthy, 1949–1975* (New York: Harcourt Brace, 1995). The quotation appears on 392.

51. Ayn Rand to Isabel Paterson, October 10, 1943, and May 17, 1948, in *Letters of Ayn Rand,* ed. Michael S. Berliner (New York: Dutton, 1995), 173–74, 215–17. See also Rand's letters of July 4 and 26, 1945; February 28, 1948; and April 3 and 11, 1948; all in ibid., 185, 197, 202, 205–206. For evidence of the decline of the friendship, see the impersonal, businesslike tone of Rand's letters of July 14, August 11, September 8, and October 6, 1950, 217–18.

52. Ellen Glasgow to Marjorie Kinnan Rawlings, July 24, 1941, and April 20, 1942; Caroline Gordon to Katherine Anne Porter, n.d.; all quoted in Rosemary M. Magee, ed., *Friendship and Sympathy: Communities of Southern Women Writers* (Jackson, MI: University of Mississippi Press, 1992), xv–xvi.

53. Eudora Welty, "My Introduction to Katherine Anne Porter," in ibid., 121, 127, 129–32, also in *Georgia Review* (Spring/Summer 1990): 13–27; David Laskin, *A Common Life: Four Generations of American Literary Friendship and Influence* (New York: Simon and Schuster, 1994), 195–273. Laskin suggests that the relationship became "a friendship more on paper than in fact," 271.

54. Elizabeth Bishop, "Efforts of Affection: A Memoir of Marianne Moore," in *Elizabeth Bishop, the Collected Prose,* ed. Robert Giroux (New York: Farrar Straus Giroux, 1984), 124, 137, 145.

55. See, for example, Elizabeth Bishop to Marianne Moore, April 6, 1936; May 21, 1936; June 11, 1936; August 9, 1937; September 7, 1937; and November 24, 1937; all in Elizabeth Bishop, *One Art: Letters Selected and Edited by Robert Giroux* (New York: Farrar Straus Giroux, 1994), 40–43, 60–65.

56. Bishop, "Efforts of Affection," 155, 146.

57. David Kalstone, *Becoming a Poet: Elizabeth Bishop with Marianne Moore and Robert Lowell,* ed. Robert Hemenway (New York: Farrar Straus Giroux, 1989), 100; Bishop, "Efforts of Affection," 141.

58. Kalstone, *Becoming a Poet,* 99–106. Kalstone alludes to the quasi-familial nature of the relationship between Bishop and Moore on 39. For a detailed analysis of this aspect of the friendship, see Joanne Feit Diehl, *Elizabeth Bishop and Marianne Moore: The Psychodynamics of Creativity* (Princeton, NJ: Princeton University Press, 1993). Diehl sees complex links between their personal relationship and their literary interactions. Using object relations theory to examine Bishop's interactions with her "literary mother," she argues that Moore functioned as a controlling, maternal-surrogate figure for Bishop, who expressed but did not necessarily acknowledge ambivalent feelings toward Moore.

59. Sally Wood, Prologue, 14–15; Caroline Gordon to Sally Wood, September 9, 1926, 27; Fall, n.d., 1926, 30; August 21, 1931, 86; January n.d., 1931, 69; Fall, n.d., 1928, 38; June 15, 1935, 190; April 4 and 25, 1932, 105; February 5, 1926, 19; and September 9, 1926, 27; all in *The Southern Mandarins: Letters of Caroline Gordon to Sally Wood, 1924–1937,* ed. Sally Wood (Baton Rouge: Louisiana State University Press, 1984). The allusion to "scribbling women" refers to Nathaniel Hawthorne's mid-nineteenth-century complaint about the popularity of works by female authors: "Besides, America is now wholly given over to a d____d mob of scribbling

women, and I should have no chance of success while the public taste is oc-
cupied with their trash—and should be ashamed of myself if I did succeed."
Nathaniel Hawthorne to William Ticknor, January 19, 1855, quoted in
Lucy Freibert, *Hidden Hands* (New Brunswick, NJ: Rutgers University
Press, 1985), 356.

60. Margaret Sherwood to Elizabeth Kendall, December 2, 1945, Elizabeth K.
Kendall Papers; Martha Hale Shackford to Jeannette Marks, August 20,
1953, autograph letter signed; both in Wellesley College Archives, quoted
in Palmieri, *In Adamless Eden*, 257.

61. Sarah Cleghorn to Elizabeth Kent, April 16, 1945, Folder 1, Cleghorn Papers. Alice Shoemaker to Eleanor G. Coit, November 13, 1957, Folder 48;
January 22, 1962, Folder 44; both in Box 1, Coit Papers.

62. Rose Abramson to Mary Elizabeth Dreier, March 21, 1956, Box 6, Folder
89, Dreier Papers.

63. Janet Brown to Mary Elizabeth Dreier, September 24, n.d.; January 19,
1954; October 6, 1947; May 9, 1953; February 19, 1952; and July 25,
1935; Mary Elizabeth Dreier to Janet Brown, typed copy, November 11,
1962; all in Box 6, Folder 97, ibid.

64. Janet Brown to Mary Elizabeth Dreier, March 16, 1955, Box 6, Folder 97,
ibid.

65. Judith Schwarz, *Radical Feminists of Heterodoxy: Greenwich Village,
1912–1940* (Lebanon, NH: New Victoria Publishers, 1982).

Notes to Chapter 5

1. Janet Flanner, *Darlinghissima: Letters to a Friend*, ed. Natalia Danesi Murray (New York: Harcourt Brace Jovanovich, 1985), xvi, xiii.

2. Introduction, xiii, ibid.; Flanner to Murray, December 31, 1958, and Murray, editorial comment, ibid., 235, 236.

3. Murray, editorial comment, ibid., 265.

4. Murray, editorial comment, ibid., 264; Carroll Smith-Rosenberg, "The Female World of Love and Ritual"; Faderman, *Surpassing the Love of Men*.

5. Marylynne Diggs, "Romantic Friends or a 'Different Race of Creatures'?
The Representation of Lesbian Pathology in Nineteenth-Century Amer-
ica," *Feminist Studies* 21, 2 (Summer 1995): 317–40; George Chauncey, Jr.,
"From Sexual Inversion to Homosexuality: The Changing Medical Con-
ceptualization of Female 'Deviance,'" in Kathy Peiss and Christina Sim-
mons, eds., with Robert Padgug, *Passion and Power: Sexuality in History*
(Philadelphia: Temple University Press, 1989), 87–117; Lillian Faderman,
"The Morbidification of Love between Women by Nineteenth-Century
Sexologists," *Journal of Homosexuality* 4, 1 (Fall 1978): 73–90; Lisa
Moore, "'Something More Tender Still than Friendship': Romantic Friend-

ship in Early Nineteenth-Century England," *Feminist Studies* 18, 3 (Fall 1992): 499–520; Alger, *The Friendships of Women*, 27.

6. See the discussion in Chapter 3.

7. Smith-Rosenberg, "The New Woman as Androgyne," 272; Sahli, "Smashing"; Elizabeth Edwards, "Homoerotic Friendship and College Principals, 1880–1960," *Women's History Review* 4, 2 (1995): 149–63.

8. Faderman, *Surpassing the Love of Men*, 174–76; Helen Howe, *The Gentle Americans, 1864–1960: Biography of a Breed* (New York: Harper and Row, 1965), 84. Despite this practical advice, Howe apparently recognized and respected the nature of the bond between Jewett and Fields. According to his daughter, he thought of their "marriage" as a "union—there is no truer word for it," *The Gentle Americans*, 83. As recently as the 1970s, an American Historical Association committee had to persuade the administration of Mount Holyoke College to keep the Jeannette Marks-Mary Woolley papers open to researchers after Anna Mary Wells discovered the romantic nature of their relationship.

9. Introduction, Flanner, *Darlinghissima*, xvi–xvii.

10. Faderman, *Odd Girls and Twilight Lovers*, 72–81.

11. Blanche Wiesen Cook, "The Historical Denial of Lesbianism," *Radical History Review* 20 (1979): 60–65; Martha Vicinus, "'They Wonder to Which Sex I Belong': The Historical Roots of the Modern Lesbian Identity," *Feminist Studies* 18, 3 (Fall 1992): 467–97; Moore, "'Something More Tender Still than Friendship'"; Rupp, "'Imagine My Surprise'; Liz Stanley, "Romantic Friendship? Some Issues in Researching Lesbian History and Biography," *Women's History Review* 1, 2 (1992): 193–216.

12. Vicinus, "'They Wonder to Which Sex I Belong.'"

13. Prior to her relationship with Mary Rozet Smith, Jane Addams had an intense friendship with Ellen Gates Starr, whom she met in college. Faderman, *Odd Girls*, 24–28. For a recent analysis of the women's community of Hull House, see Eleanor J. Stebner, *The Women of Hull House: A Study in Spirituality, Vocation, and Friendship* (Albany, NY: State University of New York Press, 1997).

14. Trisha Franzen, *Spinsters and Lesbians: Independent Womanhood in the United States* (New York: New York University Press, 1996), 107–32; Barbara R. Finn, "Anna Howard Shaw and Women's Work," *Frontiers* 4, 3 (1979), 21–25; Vida Dutton Scudder, *On Journey* (New York: E. P. Dutton, 1937); Nan Bauer Maglin, "Vida to Florence: 'Comrade and Companion,'" *Frontiers* 4, 3 (1979): 13–20; Palmieri, *In Adamless Eden*, 133–42 ; Judith Schwartz, "Yellow Clover: Katharine Lee Bates and Katharine Coman," *Frontiers* 4, 1 (Spring 1979): 59–67.

15. Ludella M. Peck to Mary Frances Willard, September 28, 1890; August 2,

1893; and March 7, 1905; all in Smith College Archives, Faculty Letters #42.

16. Anna Mary Wells, *Miss Marks and Miss Woolley* (Boston: Houghton Mifflin, 1978); Faderman, *Surpassing the Love of Men,* 229–30.

17. Louise Marion Bosworth, Diary of 1943, Carton 3, Louise Marion Bosworth Papers, Schlesinger Library, Radcliffe College. Ethel Sturtevant to Louise Marion Bosworth, June 14, 1904, and July 11, 1904, Folder 106; April 3, 1904, and July 20, 1904, Folder 101; September 14, 1904, Folder 103; all in Carton 2, ibid.

18. Louise Marion Bosworth, Diary of 1943, Carton 3, ibid.

19. Carroll Smith-Rosenberg, "Discourses of Sexuality and Subjectivity: The New Woman, 1870–1936," in Duberman et al., *Hidden from History,* 280; Margaret Gibson, "The Masculine Degenerate: American Doctors' Portrayals of the Lesbian Intellect, 1880–1949," *Journal of Women's History* 9, 4 (Winter 1998): 78–103.

20. Hilary Lapsley, "Ruth Benedict and Margaret Mead: Portrait of an Extraordinary Friendship," in Jacqueline S. Weinstock and Esther D. Rothblum, eds., *Lesbian Friendships: For Ourselves and Others* (New York: New York University Press, 1996), 80–97; Margaret Mead, *Blackberry Winter,* 125. Mead's reticence about her relationship with Ruth Benedict was consistent with the anxiety she and her college friends had experienced when they first learned about homosexual relationships among women. See above, Chapter 4.

21. Louise Bernikow, *Among Women* (New York: Harper Colophon Books, 1981), 156–92.

22. Molly Dewson to Maud Wood Park, March 12, 1920, quoted in Susan Ware, *Partner and I,* 60. See the discussion of friendship among New Deal women and also Mrs. Roosevelt's friendship with Molly Dewson in Chapter 5.

23. Ibid., especially Chapter 4; Polly Porter to Marion Hall, 1963, quoted on 61, ibid.

24. Mary Elisabeth Dreier to Miss Curtis, January 31, 1952, Box 6, Folder 85, Dreier Papers; Frances Kellor to Mary Elisabeth Dreier, n.d., and August 5, 1905; both in Box 5, Folder 77, ibid.

25. Frances Kellor to Mary Elisabeth Dreier, n.d., 1925, Box 5, Folder 78, and Frances Kellor to Mary Elisabeth Dreier, February 16, 1951, Box 6, Folder 82, ibid. Mary Elisabeth Dreier to Miss Holbrook, November 23, 1960, and Mary Elisabeth Dreier to Mrs. Alice Weiler, May 6, 1961, both in Box 6, Folder 86, ibid.

26. Frieda Segelke Miller to Pauline Newman, n.d. [probably 1949], Box 3, Folder 40; Pauline Newman to Frieda Segelke Miller, March 3, n.d. [prob-

ably 1944], Box 1, Folder 8; both in Series I, Frieda Segelke Miller Papers, Schlesinger Library, Radcliffe College.

27. See, for example, letters dated August 14, 1948; August 27, 1948; September 9, 1948; August 7, 1949; and December 2, 1957; all in Box 3, Folder 40, Series I, ibid. Pauline Newman to Frieda Segelke Miller, n.d., Box 1, Folder 11, Series I, ibid. On the tensions in the relationship, see Franzen, *Spinsters and Lesbians,* 121, 127–28. Franzen speculates that the difference in their class backgrounds contributed to the development of financial conflict between Miller and Newman.

28. Frances Doyle to Pauline Newman, July 28, 1973, Box 3, Folder 50, Series I, Pauline Newman Papers, Schlesinger Library, Radcliffe College. See also other condolence letters and lists in this folder.

29. See, for example, letters from Leonora O'Reilly to Pauline Newman, Box 5, Folder 80, Series I, ibid.

30. Leila J. Rupp, "'Imagine My Surprise,'" 395–410, and "The Women's Community in the National Woman's Party, 1945 to the 1960s," *Signs* 10, 4 (Summer 1985): 715–40.

31. September 20, 1928, and September 9, 1930, Vol. 5; n.d. [probably 1931 or 1932], and letter from Frances Perry to Winnifred Wygal, March 15, 1932, Vol. 8; all in Box 1, Winnifred Wygal Diaries, Schlesinger Library, Radcliffe College.

32. September 13, 1932, and December 29, 1931, Vol. 8; September 23, 1930, and October 12, 1930, Vol. 6; all in Box 1, ibid.

33. September 13, 1932, and October 3, 1932, Vol. 8; December 31, 1942, Vol. 15; all in Box 1, ibid.

34. Elizabeth Bishop to U. T. and Joseph Summers, September 23 and 28, 1967, in Bishop, *One Art,* 467–70. See also letters to Ilse and Kit Barker, September 28, 1967; Maria Osser, October 2, 1967; Ashley Brown, October 3, 1967; and Dr. Anny Baumann, October 11, 1967; all in ibid., 470–75.

35. On Deming's relationship with Vida Ginsberg, see letters in Folders 235–36, Box 13; Folders 240, 243, 250, and 253, Box 14; and Ginsberg's autobiographical statement, Folder 252, Box 14; all in Series II, Barbara Deming Papers, Schlesinger Library, Radcliffe College. On Deming's relationship with Annie Poor and her friendship with Poor's mother, Bessie Breuer Poor, see letters in Folders 519 and 521–24, Box 26, Series II, ibid.

36. Geraldine Thompson to Miriam Van Waters, April 2, 1936, Folder 267, Box 7, Anna Spicer Gladding and Miriam Van Waters Papers, Schlesinger Library, Radcliffe College. See also Thompson's letters of February 21, 1936, and March 17, 1936, Folder 267, and November 4, 1930, Folder 262, all in Box 7, ibid.

37. Freedman, *Maternal Justice,* 168–69, 171–75; Geraldine Thompson to

Miriam Van Waters, November 12 and 13, 1930, Folder 263, Box 7, Gladding and Van Waters Papers.

38. Freedman, *Maternal Justice,* 247, 280, 291–312, 315, 325–28, 342; Estelle B. Freedman, "'The Burning of Letters Continues': Elusive Identities and the Historical Construction of Sexuality," *Journal of Women's History* 9, 4 (Winter 1998): 181–200. The quotation from Van Waters's journal appears on 181.

39. December 28, 1932, Dorothy Thompson Diary, quoted in Peter Kurth, *American Cassandra: The Life of Dorothy Thompson* (Boston: Little, Brown, 1990), 178–79.

40. Ibid., 190, 192, 216. While Thompson's letters to Rose Wilder Lane contain no mention of her relationship with Christa Winsloe, it is possible that, like her heterosexual romances, this involvement also accounts for her negligence as a correspondent. See above, Chapter 5.

41. Ibid., 190, 217. See also James Vincent Sheean's discussion of the relationship between Thompson and Winsloe in *Dorothy and Red* (Boston: Houghton Mifflin, 1963), Chapter 9, and excerpts from Thompson's diary in Jonathan Katz, *Gay American History: Lesbians and Gay Men, A Documentary History* (New York: Meridian, 1992), 556–62. It is interesting, though not surprising, to note that Thompson's extensive correspondence with Rose Wilder Lane contains no mention of her romantic friendship experiences. See above, Chapter 5.

42. Quoted in Cook, *Eleanor Roosevelt, Volume One,* 479, 496, 497.

43. Ibid., 15. Over 300 of the remaining letters between Roosevelt and Hickok appear in Rodger Streitmatter, ed., *Empty Without You: The Intimate Letters of Eleanor Roosevelt and Lorena Hickok* (New York: Free Press, 1998).

44. Blanche Wiesen Cook, "The Historical Denial of Lesbianism," *Radical History Review* 20 (1979): 60–65; Faber, *The Life of Lorena Hickok*; Marjorie H. Dobkin, ed., *The Making of a Feminist: Early Journals and Letters of M. Carey Thomas* (Kent, OH: Kent State University Press, 1980); Streitmatter, ed., *Empty Without You,* xiv–xvi.

45. Rachel Carson to Dorothy Freeman, December 15, 1952, and February 13, 1954, in *Always, Rachel: The Letters of Rachel Carson and Dorothy Freeman, 1952–1964,* ed. Martha Freeman (Boston: Beacon Press, 1995), 3, 23.

46. Rachel Carson to Dorothy Freeman, February 6, 1954; Dorothy Freeman to Rachel Carson, February 29, 1964, 8:30 a.m.; both in ibid., 20, 529–30.

47. Rachel Carson to Dorothy Freeman, February 6, 1954; Dorothy Freeman to Rachel Carson, January 31, 1955; both in ibid., 19–22, 91.

48. Rachel Carson to Dorothy Freeman, April 12 and April 19, 1955, both in ibid., 106–107, 108–109.

49. Dorothy Freeman to Rachel Carson, February 27 and February 29, 1964, both in ibid., 528, 531.
50. Rachel Carson to Dorothy Freeman, February 5, 1964; January 24, 1963; April 30, 1963; all in ibid., 525, 542, 543.
51. On the transition in heterosexual relationships, see Peter Stearns's discussion of the evolution of romantic love in *American Cool*, 171–81.

Notes to Chapter 6

1. Mary Pratt Sears, n.d., To _____ [*sic*], Book of Letters, 250, Cabot Papers.
2. This issue provides the main theme in the film *When Harry Met Sally*.
3. Ida Sophia Scudder to her mother, n.d. See also another undated letter and one written on May 1, 1899, on the same topic, all in Box 2, Folder 77, Ida Sophia Scudder Papers, Schlesinger Library, Radcliffe College.
4. William Garland, "Friendship between the Sexes," *Westminster Review,* 153 (March 1900): 30–32; L. Keith Stribbard, "Friendship between the Sexes," *Westminster Review,* 154 (November 1900): 583–85; Rafford Pyke, "Platonic Friendship," *Cosmopolitan* 35 (May 1903): 45–48; Aria, "Concerning Companionship"; E. S. Roscoe, "A Seventeenth-Century Friendship: John Evelyn and Margaret Godolphin," *Contemporary Review* 139 (January 1931): 78–84; Katharine Ferguson, "A Girl's Friendship with Boys—A Talk to Girls by Katharine Ferguson," *Women's Home Companion* 40 (February 1913): 34; Elizabeth King Manner, "The Friendship of Boy and Girl," *Harper's Weekly* 58 (December 20, 1913): 13–15.
5. Floyd Dell, "New Morals for Old: Can Men and Women Be Friends?" *Nation* 118 (May 28, 1924): 605–606.
6. G. M. White, "Why I Like Women," *Ladies Home Journal* 67 (November 1950): 61+.
7. Emily Leider, "Your Picture Hangs in My Salon: The Letters of Gertrude Atherton to Ambrose Bierce," *California History* 60, 4 (Winter 1981–1982): 332–49. The quotations appear on 334 and 344.
8. Ibid., 340, 348. See also Emily Leider, *California's Daughter: Gertrude Atherton and Her Times* (Stanford, CA: Stanford University Press, 1991).
9. See Ellen Gates Starr to Charles Wager, letters written in 1917, Box 8, Folder 76, and August 19, 1921, Folder 79, Starr Papers.
10. See the discussion of Starr's intense romantic relationship with Jane Addams in Allen F. Davis, *American Heroine: The Life and Legend of Jane Addams* (New York: Oxford University Press, 1973).
11. Ellen Gates Starr to Charles Wager, October 17, 1906, Folder 74; April 16, 1912, Folder 75; February 12, 1917, and several letters written in April 1917, Folder 76; November 13, 1917, Folder 77; October 4, 1938, Folder 83; all in Box 8, Starr Papers.

12. Edith Wharton, *A Backward Glance* (New York: D. Appleton-Century, 1934), 169, 173. According to R.W.B. Lewis, "it was a basic fact that she drew more substance from the company of men than of women, and the more so if the men in question could give her their undivided attention." *Edith Wharton: A Biography* (New York: Harper and Row, 1975), 57.

13. David Laskin, "Henry James and Edith Wharton," in *A Common Life: Four Generations of American Literary Friendship and Influence* (New York: Simon and Schuster, 1994), 101–88; Wharton, *A Backward Glance*, 173.

14. Edith Wharton to Gaillard Lapsley, quoted in Laskin, 185.

15. Wharton, *A Backward Glance*, 225–26, 244, 364–65, 92–95. Wharton's reminiscences also include references to her friendships with Theodore Roosevelt, Bernard Berenson, Paul Bourget, Eugene Lee-Hamilton, Edward Burlingame, Charles Eliot Norton, Robert Minturn, and Clyde Fitch.

16. Ibid., 107, 115–19; Lewis, *Edith Wharton*, 343–44. The quotations from Wharton's diary and her letter to Lapsley appear in Lewis on 478; Lewis suggests that Wharton's infatuation with Berry distressed Bernard Berenson, who seems to have been jealous of her affection for their mutual friend, 294.

17. Ella Lyman Cabot's voluminous correspondence with her friends is contained in folders organized alphabetically, Series III, Boxes 4–8, Ella Lyman Cabot Papers. For one example of Cabot's relationships with male friends, see her letters to Philip Brown, August 6, n.d.; January 20, 1915; January 24, 1915; all in Box 4, Folder 108, and to Helen and Philip Brown, January 13, n.d.; ibid.

18. For example, Mabel Dodge enjoyed close, apparently nonsexual relationships with the writer Hutchings Hapgood, the noted poet Edwin Arlington Robinson, and the *New York Times* critic Carl Van Vechten, as well as romantic adventures with other male friends. Winifred L. Frazer, *Mabel Dodge Luhan* (Boston: Twayne, 1984), 39–45. See also Mabel Dodge Luhan, *Movers and Shakers* (Albuquerque, NM: University of New Mexico Press, 1987) and Lois Rudnick, *Mabel Dodge Luhan: New Woman, New Worlds* (Albuquerque, NM: University of New Mexico Press, 1984). For other examples of apparently platonic friendships, see letters to Dorothy Smith Dushkin from Ross Lee Finney, Folder 11, Dushkin Papers, and Virginia Foster Durr's correspondence with Corliss Lamont, Bill Martin, Curtis MacDougall, and Otto Nathan, Folders 178–83, 189–93, and 217–22, all in Carton 3, Virginia Foster Durr Papers, Schlesinger Library, Radcliffe College.

19. Freedman, *Maternal Justice;* Hans Weiss to Miriam Van Waters, August 11, 1934, Box 8, Folder 280, Gladding and Van Waters Papers. See additional letters from Weiss to Van Waters in Folders 271–80. Van Waters's interpre-

tation of her relationship with Geraldine Thompson and her reaction to charges that homosexuality was permitted in the Framingham Women's Reformatory under her administration, described in Chapter 6, indicate that she experienced significant conflict over issues of sexual preference, primarily at the unconscious level. Thus, in addition to career concerns, her decision not to marry Hans Weiss probably reflects the same confusion and turmoil. See also Freedman, "'The Burning of Letters Continues.'"

20. Ada Louise Comstock to Wallace Notestein, April 10, 1912, Folder 8; August 16, 1935, Folder 11; and June 8, 1943, Folder 29; all in Carton 1, Ada Comstock Papers, Schlesinger Library, Radcliffe College. Carton 1 contains additional extensive correspondence documenting the nature and progress of their relationship from 1909 to 1943.

21. Kahlil Gibran to Josephine Preston Peabody, February 17, 1903, Folder 3; March 22, 1903, Folder 4; and May 30, 1906, Folder 8; all in Josephine Preston Peabody Papers, Houghton Library, Harvard University.

22. May 15, 1903; August 10, 1903; and January 18, 1904; all in Notes on Talks with Kahlil Gibran, ibid. For an interesting example of another relationship in which mysterious emotional ties figured importantly, in a different cultural setting, see the friendship of Maud Gonne and William Butler Yeats. Margaret Ward, *Maud Gonne: A Life* (London: Pandora, 1990).

23. These friendships are described in Howe, *The Gentle Americans*, 185–233. The quotation appears on 383.

24. December 15, 16, and 21, 1924, Gladys Bell Diary. November 6, 1931, Box 1, Vol. 6, and October 19, 1932, Folder 8, Box 2, Addendum, Yvonne Blue Skinner Diaries. September 15, 1959, June Calender Diary.

25. Elisabeth Young-Bruehl, *Hannah Arendt: For Love of the World* (New Haven, CT: Yale University Press,1982), xii–xvi.

26. *Dear Sammy: Letters from Gertrude Stein and Alice B. Toklas,* ed. Samuel M. Steward (Boston: Houghton Mifflin, 1977); *The Letters of Gertrude Stein and Thornton Wilder,* ed. Edward M. Burns and Ella E. Dydo with William Rice (New Haven, CT: Yale University Press, 1996). For examples of Stein's friendships with other men, see *The Flowers of Friendship: Letters Written to Gertrude Stein,* ed. Donald Gallup (New York: Alfred A. Knopf, 1953), and *The Letters of Gertrude Stein and Carl Van Vechten: 1913–1946,* 2 vols. (New York: Columbia University Press, 1986).

27. *Between History and Poetry: The Letters of H. D. and Norman Holmes Pearson,* ed. Donna Krolik Hollenberg (Iowa City, IA: University of Iowa Press, 1997).

28. *Beyond Love and Loyalty: The Letters of Thomas Wolfe and Elizabeth Nowell,* ed. Richard S. Kennedy (Chapel Hill, NC: University of North Carolina Press, 1983).

29. Margaret M. Caffrey, *Ruth Benedict: Stranger in This Land* (Austin, TX: University of Texas Press, 1989), 198–99. Benedict's relationship with Sapir cooled in the 1930s, after he had a brief affair with Margaret Mead, her closest friend. She was also offended by his publication of two articles that contained negative statements about homosexuality. See also letters from Sapir to Benedict in Mead, *Anthropologist at Work*, and Judith Modell's discussion of their relationship in *Ruth Benedict, Patterns of a Life* (Philadelphia: University of Pennsylvania Free Press, 1983).

30. Quoted in Laskin, *A Common Life,* 302.

31. Robert Lowell to Elizabeth Bishop, August 15, 1957, in Bishop, *One Art,* 345–46; Laskin, *A Common Life,* 310.

32. Quoted in Kalstone, *Becoming a Poet* 222–23.

33. Robert Lowell to Elizabeth Bishop, n.d. 1972; Elizabeth Bishop to Robert Lowell, October 26, 1972; both quoted in Laskin, *A Common Life,* 382–83. Laskin describes the last meetings between Bishop and Lowell on 388–89 and analyzes "North Haven" on 394–97.

34. Cook, *Eleanor Roosevelt, Volume One,* 429–47. The quotation appears on 435.

35. Diary of Margaret Suckley, August 7, 1933; Margaret Suckley to Franklin D. Roosevelt, August 17, 1935; both in *Closest Companion: The Unknown Story of the Intimate Friendship between Franklin Roosevelt and Margaret Suckley,* ed. Geoffrey C. Ward (Boston: Houghton Mifflin, 1995), 5, 30.

36. Franklin Roosevelt to Margaret Suckley, November 18, 1936, ibid., 92. Margaret Suckley to Franklin Roosevelt, September 16, 1935; May 1, 1936; September 22, 1935; Franklin Roosevelt to Margaret Suckley, September 23, 1935; all in ibid., 33, 81, 35, 37.

37. Diary of Margaret Suckley, March 5, 1945; April 12, 1945; April 15, 1945; May 21, 1945; all in ibid., 398, 420, 422, 424.

38. Diary of Margaret Suckley, September 11, 1944; August 31, 1943; September 2, 3, 4, and 5, 1943; all in ibid., 327, 231–35.

39. Introduction, *Beyond Love and Loyalty*; Young-Bruehl, *Hannah Arendt,* xii–xvi, 191–92. The quotation, from an undated letter in the Library of Congress, appears on 192. Young-Bruehl also discusses Arendt's friendship with her former teacher, Karl Jaspers, whom she visited on her first trip to Europe after World War II, and her relationship and love affair with Martin Heidegger, who had also been her teacher.

40. See, for example, Gilligan, *In a Different Voice;* Tannen, *That's Not What I Meant, You Just Don't Understand,* and *Gender and Discourse*; Gray, *Men Are from Mars, Women Are from Venus*; and the essays in Jordan et al., *Women's Growth in Connection.*

41. Elizabeth Bishop to Robert Lowell, July 27, 1960, in Bishop, *One Art,* 386.

42.   Spurlock, "The Problem of Married Love for Middle-Class Women," in Stearns and Lewis, eds., *An Emotional History of the United States,* 319–32.

43.   Esther to Rachel McClelland Sutton, December 30, 1921, Box 2, Folder 4, Sutton Correspondence; Yvonne Blue Diaries, November 25, 1932, Box 1, Vol. 6.

44.   September 30, 1940; November 15, 1940; and January 9, 1941; all in Beth Twiggar Goff Papers. The correspondence that documents the relationship's resumption encompasses the period between 1986 and 1992.

Notes to Chapter 7

1.   Miller, *Toward a New Psychology of Women,* 2d ed.; Gilligan, *In a Different Voice*; Josselson, *The Space between Us.* See also the essays by Judith V. Jordan, Alexandra G. Kaplan, Jean Baker Miller, Irene P. Stiver, and Janet L. Surrey in Jordan et al., *Women's Growth in Connection.*

2.   Anne M. Seiden and Pauline B. Bart, "Woman to Woman: Is Sisterhood Powerful?" in Glazer-Malbin, ed., *Old Family/New Family,* 189–228.

3.   See diary entries from April 10 to August 28, 1965, Vol. 2, Box 2, Diaries of Jennifer Stevens [pseudonym], unprocessed collection, Schlesinger Library, Radcliffe College.

4.   December 20, 1966, Vol. 5, and February 5, 1967, Vol. 6, Box 2, ibid.

5.   October 24, 1966, Vol. 4; December 25, 1966, Vol. 5; January 24, 1967, Vol. 6, all in Box 2, ibid.

6.   September 14, 1969, Vol. 10, Box 2; November 2 and 4 and December 25, 1969, Vol. 11, Box 1; all in ibid.

7.   Dorothy C. Holland and Margaret A. Eisenhart, *Educated in Romance: Women, Achievement, and College Culture* (Chicago: University of Chicago Press, 1990).

8.   Lynne C. Spangler, "A Historical Overview of Female Friendships on Prime-Time Television," *Journal of Popular Culture* 22 (Spring 1989): 13–24. Other relevant examples include the film *Thelma and Louise* and Iris Rainer Dart, *Beaches* (New York: Bantam, 1985). On negative portrayals in the mass media, see Susan Douglas, *Where the Girls Are: Growing Up Female with the Mass Media* (New York: Random House, 1995), 291.

9.   May 7, 1977; June 8, 1977; May 1, 23, 29, 1977; all in Nan Bishop, Sarah Hamilton, and Clare Bowman, *Nan, Sarah, and Clare: Letters between Friends* (New York: Avon Books, 1980), 204, 272, 196–97, 248, 255.

10.   Personal communications with author, May 18, 1998, and May 29, 1998.

11.   See above, Chapter 1.

12. "Pajama Games," *People* (July 13, 1998): 92–94; Sue Wilson, personal communication to author.

13. See, for example, Jill McCorkle, "Cathy, Now and Then," and Carolyn See, "Best Friend, My Wellspring in the Wilderness!" in Pearlman, ed., *Between Friends*, 28–43; 56–73, and Berry and Traeder, *Girlfriends*. On the proliferation of book groups, see Rollene Waterman Saal, "Looking at Books: Reading Groups—The Literary Salons of the Nineties," *Wellesley* (Fall 1995): 17–19. These organizations represent an interesting contemporary translation of two earlier types of group activities—female gatherings where domestic tasks such as quilting and sewing mingled with conversation, and nineteenth-century single women's reading clubs. On nineteenth-century reading clubs, see Chambers-Schiller, *Liberty, a Better Husband,* 124–26.

14. Luise Eichenbaum and Susie Orbach, *Between Women: Love, Envy, and Competition in Women's Friendships* (New York: Viking Penguin, 1988), 26–32; O'Connor, *Friendships between Women,* 162.

15. O'Connor, *Friendships between Women,* 82; Eva Margolies, *The Best of Friends, the Worst of Enemies: Women's Hidden Power over Women* (Garden City, NY: Dial Press, 1985), 89–99, 170; Rubin, *Just Friends,* 65–66, 109–48. The quotation is from Rubin, 138.

16. Mary Pipher, *Reviving Ophelia: Saving the Lives of Adolescent Girls* (New York: Ballantine, 1994).

17. Margolies, *The Best of Friends,* 52–58; 77.

18. Wendy Wasserstein, "The Ties That Wound," in Pearlman, ed., *Between Friends,* 110, 113.

19. Susan Lee, "Friendship, Feminism and Betrayal," in Angela C. Dorenkamp et al., *Images of Women in American Popular Culture,* 2d ed. (Fort Worth, TX: Harcourt Brace, 1995), 361–66, reprinted from *Village Voice,* 9 June 1975: 11–12.

20. Jacqueline S. Weinstock and Esther D. Rothblum, "What We Can Be Together"; Jeanne L. Stanley, "The Lesbian's Experience of Friendship"; and Cherie G. O'Boyle and Marie D. Thomas, "Friendships between Lesbian and Heterosexual Women"; all in Weinstock and Rothblum, eds., *Lesbian Friendships: For Ourselves and Each Other* (New York: New York University Press, 1996), 3–37, 39–59; 240–48; Kathleen A. Brehony, "Coming to Consciousness: Some Reflections on the Boston Marriage," and Lillian Faderman, "Nineteenth-Century Boston Marriage as a Possible Lesson for Today," both in Esther D. Rothblum and Kathleen A. Brehony, eds., *Boston Marriages: Romantic but Asexual Relationships among Contemporary Lesbians* (Amherst, MA: University of Massachusetts Press, 1993).

21. Kathy Werking, *We're Just Good Friends: Women and Men in Nonromantic Relationships* (New York: Guilford, 1997); Rubin, *Just Friends,* 149–74; Lee West et al., "Crossing the Barriers to Friendships between Men and Women," in Julia T. Wood, ed., *Gendered Relationships* (Mountain View, CA: Mayfield, 1996), 111–27; Scott O. Swain, "Men's Friendships with Women: Intimacy, Sexual Boundaries, and the Informant Role," in Peter M. Nardi, ed., *Men's Friendships* (Newbury Park, CA: Sage, 1992), 153–71; Robert R. Bell, *Worlds of Friendship* (Beverly Hills, CA: Sage, 1981) and "Friendships of Women and of Men," *Psychology of Women Quarterly* 5, 3 (Spring 1995): 402–17; Phyllis Rose, "Shall We Dance? Confessions of a Fag Hag," in Pearlman, ed., *Between Friends,* 204–13; Joan Nestle and Robert Preston, eds., *Sister and Brother: Lesbians and Gay Men Write About Their Lives Together* (San Francisco: Harper, 1994). For the equation of friendship with love, see *Interview* (February 1995). For discussions of other aspects of cross-sex friendship in the late twentieth century, see Constantina Safilios-Rothschild, "Toward a Social Psychology of Relationships," *Psychology of Women Quarterly* 5, 3 (Spring 1981): 377–84; Susan McWilliams and Judith A. Howard, "Solidarity and Hierarchy in Cross-Sex Friendships," *Journal of Social Issues* 49, 3 (Fall 1993): 191–202; Paul H. Wright, "Gender Differences in Adults' Same- and Cross-Gender Friendships," in Adams and Blieszner, eds., *Older Adult Friendship,* 197–221; and Caroline J. Simon, "Can Women and Men Be Friends?" *Christian Century* (February 19, 1997): 188–94.

22. Berry and Traeder, *Girlfriends,* 54; Rosenberg, *Divided Lives,* 93.

23. Personal communication to author, September 7, 1998.

Index

Conflict between friends, 10, 30–33, 89–90, 93, 103, 113–16, 120–21, 126, 137, 138–39, 160
Converse, Florence, 132
Cook, Blanche Wiesen, 130, 144
Cott, Nancy, 18
Craik, Dinah Mulock, 15
Crisfield, Josephine, 93
Cross-sex friendship: 33–38, 149–68, 170, 178–79; distinguished from female friendship, 149, 164–65; romantic attraction in, 149–50, 153–57, 159–60, 162, 164–67; social construction of, 149–50, 165
Crushes, 45, 47, 48, 50, 74, 75

Degas, Edgar, 35–36
Deming, Barbara, 140
Development of the self, 4, 169
Dewson, Molly, 116–17, 135–36
Dickinson, Emily, 20–21, 128
Dillard, Annie, 79–80
Dodge, Mabel, 103–104
Domesticity, 13–14, 18, 35, 99
Doolittle, Hilda [known as H. D.], 159, 164
Dreier, Mary Elisabeth, 117, 123, 136
Durr, Virginia Foster, 81–82, 85
Duryee, Alice, 57–58
Dushkin, Dorothy Smith, 72, 93, 111

Emerson, Ralph Waldo, 2, 36–38, 165
Emmet, Jane, 77
Emotional culture, 6, 7, 8, 27, 31, 33, 40, 43, 67, 70, 115–16, 147, 150, 171
Emotions history, 7, 9–10, 13
Evidence, 10, 11, 30

Female friendship: in the nineteenth century, 15–38; in the early twentieth century, 39–65; between 1920 and 1960, 66–96, 97–124; after 1960, 169–80; and biography, 13; in colonial America, 16–17; distinctiveness of, 3–6; in educational institutions, 17, 28, 44, 47, 48, 71–72; as an emotional outlet, 20; importance to women, 3, 16, 21, 25, 55, 56, 58, 62, 88, 94, 97, 175; patriarchal representations of, 2–3, 6, 14, 179; between professional women, 116–22; and

religious affiliation, 17; in rural settings, 22; and single women, 22, 33, 62, 101, 104–105; in the South, 28; and women's history, 12–14; in the workplace, 92, 176–77
Feminine mystique, 113, 152, 167, 172
Feminism, 168, 172, 174
Fern, Fanny, 37
Fields, Annie, 28–30, 126, 129
Flanner, Janet, 125–27, 129
Flax, Jane, 5
Friendship: definition of, 1–4; importance in western culture, 2–3; and life stage, 5; and mother-daughter relationships, 5; and relational development, 4, 5
Friendship quilts, 26, 27
Fuller, Margaret, 36–38

Gender, 171
Gibran, Kahlil, 157–58
Ginsberg, Vida, 140
Glasgow, Ellen, 119
Gonne, Maude, 216n. 22
Gordon, Caroline, 119, 121–22

Hamilton, Sarah, 174
Hammer, Marcia Lustgarten, 175
Hansen, Karen, 21, 22
Hardy, Harriet, 94
Havemeyer, Louisine Elder, 25, 31–32
Hazard, Caroline, 132
Hellman, Lillian, 98
Herman, Maida, 46–47, 52
Heterodoxy, 123–24
Heterosexual relationships: cultural emphasis on, 66, 70, 84, 88, 172, 174; impact on female friendship, 75–76, 80, 82–84, 100, 124, 172, 174–75; love letters, 67; maternal pressure regarding, 79, 80, 173
Hickok, Lorena, 13, 143–45
High school friendships, 109–10
Historicity of friendship, 7–8
Holley, Sallie, 32
Holwein, Kathryn Joyce, 113
Howe, Mark Antony De Wolfe, 129, 158
Human relationships, nature of, 10
Humphrey, Mary Helen, 100–102, 104
Husbands and female friendship, 22, 111, 112, 177

About the Author

Linda W. Rosenzweig is Professor of History at Chatham College. She is the author of *The Anchor of My Life: Middle-Class American Mothers and Daughters, 1880–1920,* and the mother of two grown daughters. She and her husband live in Pittsburgh, Pennsylvania, and Wellfleet, Massachusetts.